Builders, Housewives and the Construction of Modern Athens

Ioanna Theocharopoulou
Foreword by Kenneth Frampton

ONASSIS
FOUNDATION

Builders working in
polykatoikìa construction,
Athens, ca early 1950s.

Preface

Afroditi Panagiotakou
Director of Culture, Onassis Foundation

The people. Athens. The city centre. Art. Disruption. Igniting debates about crucial non-givens through culture and education is in the Onassis Foundation's DNA. We are not pedantic yet we wonder. We focus on the constant search for the Athenian reality and we believe in the relationship between the local and the global. We collaborate with those who share our concerns, fuelled by the same curiosity for whatever lies outside and within ourselves.

Athens is our playground and our battlefield, an undefinable, tumultuous place that lives the fate of the absolute in-between. Between East and West. Between North and South. Beyond beauty and ugliness.

Nothing happens in Athens without an apartment block being present. Every living generation of Athenians has mingled past, present and future near the entrance to one of these structures of co-existence, toleration, social stratification. The polykatoikia of Athens grew out of a need and became a permanent condition of life, a common space, a mistake, an ongoing inner conflict that will never end. It became a reality we assimilate and experience rather than analyse.

Builders, housewives, ourselves; bodies of now and of all times; apartment blocks and the Parthenon; stories and history – together, they make the city of Athens a functional anarchy worth living in.

Foreword

Kenneth Frampton

When I first encountered the Athenian *polykatoikìa* on my way back to London from Tel Aviv in 1959, I was impressed by the extraordinary continuity and sense of urbanity emanating from this seemingly endless aggregation of five- to seven-story apartment buildings, ingeniously integrated with the existing urban fabric. I would not have an occasion to express my enthusiasm in this regard until 1987, when, in the introduction to the Greek translation of my book, *Modern Architecture: A Critical History*, I highlighted the *polykatoikìa* as a uniquely modern manifestation of urban growth, stemming from the spontaneous evolution of the society, rather than from planned intervention. At that time, I still had no idea that this phenomenon was known by a Greek term, which in English translates blandly into "multiple dwellings", and it would be another decade before I understood the phenomenon more fully through the thesis of the author, which not only emphasized its unusual form, but also the equally unusual circumstances of its origin.

Essential to this last was the so-called *antiparochè*, "part-exchange", tradition, by which a freehold owner of a typical nineteenth-century Athenian neoclassical house was able, once the house had been demolished, to donate the land in exchange for a certain number of units in a mid-rise apartment block to be built on the same site. This was invariably built by a small-time builder, employing itinerant rural craftsmen; that is to say, paradoxically, the same migrant population who, once they had established themselves in the city, would become the clientele purchasing the apartments. Thus the *polykatoikìes* were the result of a continuous symbiotic process in which, between 1950 and 1970, close to half a million people fleeing rural poverty would establish themselves in the metropolis. As the author suggests, this was a classless transformation in which an aspiring population entered the lower middle class by virtue of a uniquely urbanizing operation.

As it happens, all of this will be bound up within a new concept of womanhood predicated as much on newfound service amenities, such as a labor-saving modern kitchen, a mandatory bathroom, and a petit bourgeois entry hall, as on the prerequisite living spaces, bedrooms, etc. This fashionable feminist identity was proselytized by the media as a viable mass consumerist alternative to the restrictive poverty of the countryside. All of this, as the author shows, was inescapably bound up with overcoming not only the repressive shade of Ottoman occupation, but also the erstwhile nemesis of the Greek Civil War which befell the country after the end of the Second World War.

There are multiple connections here which, as Theocharopoulou shows, link back not only to the International Style exhibition staged at the Museum of Modern Art, New York, in 1932, but also to the Greek exclusion from this exhibition;

which would lead to a counter-exhibition of modern Greek architecture, staged in Athens by local architects on the occasion of the International Congress of Modern Architecture (CIAM), held there in 1933. The received syntax of the *polykatoikìa*, that is to say the vocabulary of a white cubic architecture with pierced windows and projecting balconies, was patently derived from the received modernity of the time. Thus, as Theocharopoulou makes clear, the unofficial language of the *polykatoikìa*, largely designed by non-architects and engineers, emerged as a kind of *laïque* culture, built for the people, of the people, by the people. In this regard, the *polykatoikìa* yielded a remarkably unified urban texture, comparable to another Mediterranean/white city of virtually the same moment in time, namely the city of Tel Aviv, the primary difference between the two being that the Athenian fabric was much denser.

1959 was also the year in which I would first encounter the layered stone landscape of Philopappou Hill, immediately adjacent to the Athenian Acropolis, as designed and laid in place by the Greek architect Dimitris Pikionis. It is this popular milling ground that remains, even now, in my mind's eye as a quasi-folkloric link between the high architecture of Periclean Athens and the demotic character of *polykatoikìa*, built in the ever-changing and expanding city below.

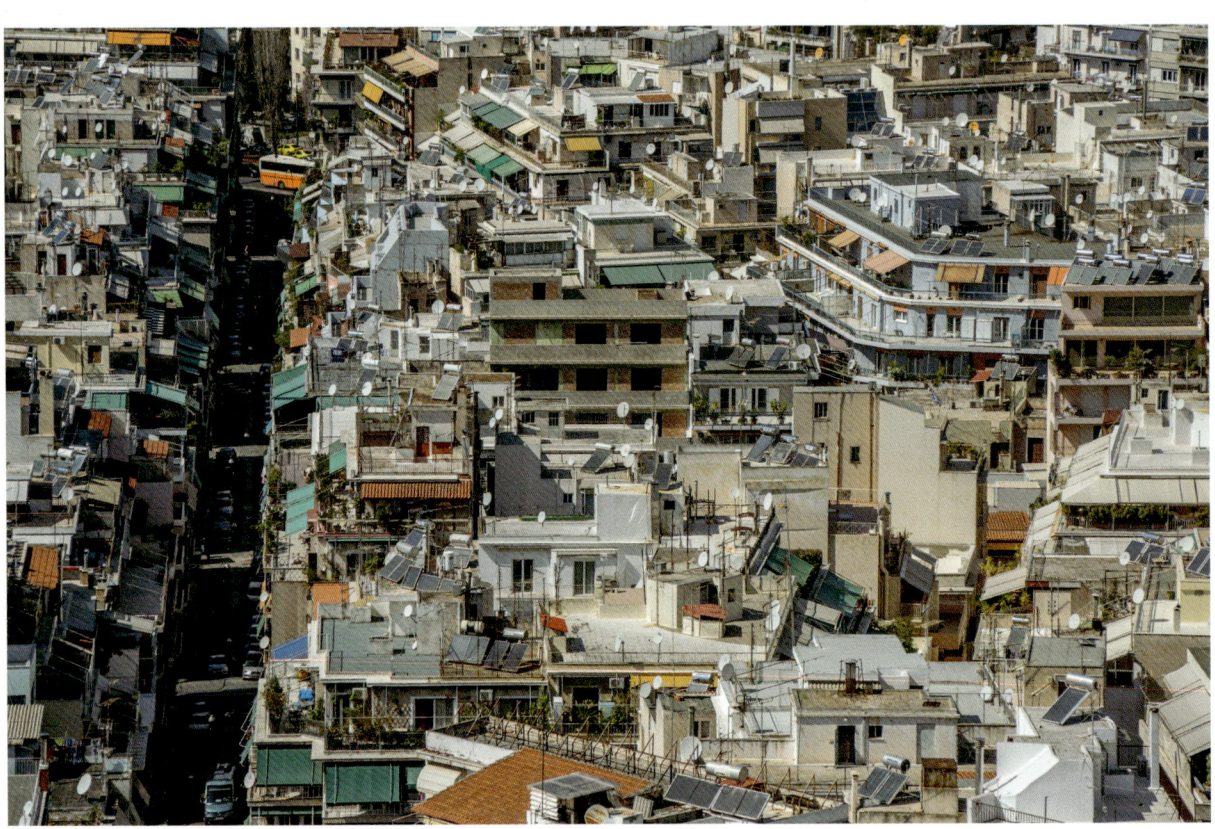

Athens, 2016.

Inside and Out

The City, the State and Domestic Life

To this day almost all descriptions of Athens have at their core a contrast between the grandeur of the Acropolis and the banality of the post-Second World War city. As we see in the image opposite, Athens today consists of a vast, mostly unplanned, nondescript (and polluted) expanse that stands in stark contrast to the cultural magnificence of its famous classical monuments. This book presents a different reading of the city, suggesting that, even if far from perfect, there is something rich and positive to discover in modern Athens that may also help us to understand and analyze other rapidly growing cities around the world.

Cities are never tidy. A vast majority of them, particularly in newly industrializing countries, are designed without architects or other urban professionals. Like some of these global cities today, Athens grew as a patchwork of improvisations and adaptations—ad hoc, individualistic and pragmatic. This does not make it—or other such global cities—uninteresting. In fact, architectural and urban historians have long held up the paradigmatic European cities—London, Paris, Rome, Milan, Berlin—as examples of city-making.

Athens fits none of these models. Athens' urban space did not grow in similar ways to that of other European cities. For a start, Greece suffered occupation for almost 400 years by the Ottoman Turks (1453–1821). As a province of the Ottoman Empire, Athens was a relatively important settlement of about 10,000 people up until the Greek War of Independence. At that point however, following fierce fighting, especially with the siege of the Acropolis by the forces of the Turkish officer Kütahı just before the end of the war (1826–1830), the city was destroyed, suffering great damage to its people and monuments.

Not having developed along historical paths familiar in European cities, Athens has often been identified as missing something important in terms of its larger European architectural "family". But what if we try to understand it in its own terms? And how can we do that? In this book I have tried to develop a methodology to identify and explore in depth the city's other, perhaps less familiar, histories: a set of processes specific to this context. I use these as explanatory-critical "sites", or as my lenses for interpretation. The processes I look at are social (internal migration), financial (the "part-exchange" system, *antiparochè*) and administrative (building codes and amendments). In themselves they are not newly explored here. But they are read and synthesized in new ways, proposing that this nondescript expanse is bound up with issues of identity and modernization and the particular forms these took in modern Greece.

The book offers conceptual tools with which to make sense of the particularities of Athenian development, based upon an analysis of political and cultural events and discourses about them, as well as an exploration of a set of behaviors, traditions and

Bernard Rudofsky, "The Classical Vernacular", Apanomerià, Santorini, from *Architecture Without Architects*.

attitudes towards architecture and building rooted in Greek history and social life. The development of postwar Athens in particular, this book suggests, was a direct consequence of a set of behaviors embedded and pervasive in Greek cultural life that might be called "informal" in contrast to the more organized, "rational", northwestern European approaches to architecture and urban development.

Paradoxically, one of the most stable characteristics of Greek cultural and political life from the nineteenth to the late twentieth centuries, if not up to the present, has been a strangely conflicted behavior towards urbanism shared by those in power, as well as by intellectuals and ordinary citizens. Far from being casual or "randomly" produced (this is a term used by critics and historians) the erratic and inconsistent attitude towards planning, and the lack thereof, obsesses Greeks (as any casual look in daily newspapers will attest).[1] This sense of ambivalence and tension has parallels with other cultural expressions such as language, which formed the background to the intellectual debates about building (with the question of the appropriate language for architecture and urbanism added to this mix).

This attitude came about in large part as a consequence of historical events. Since the nineteenth century and the founding of the Greek State in 1833, there has been a great deal of conflict and uncertainty over who is "Greek" (the *autochthon* or *heterochthon* Greeks?) as well as what is "Greek"—in architecture, language, music and the arts. This tension became particularly problematic during times when Greek identity was still in formation: in the period following Independence when new city plans were produced almost every year but none were fully implemented; in the 1920s following the failed war with Turkey; and at the end of the Axis occupation (1945) and during the Greek Civil War (1946–1949).

"Athens: The Planning Monster. Gigantic Proportions and Lack of Coherence", *Vradyni*, 1957.

The negative gaze and attitude of disapproving comparisons between the modern city, its irregular, unregulated, informal ways and its universally admired ancient past has a long lineage. It began in the late eighteenth century with the very first English and French scholars who braved the dangers of the still-occupied Greek territories in order to catch a glimpse of the ancient temples. Later on, the European philhellenes of the nineteenth century shared their predecessors' passion for uncovering ruins.[2] These Europeans engaged in a complex identification of themselves vis-à-vis these ruins: that is, to some extent they discovered their own modernity as they searched for Greece's ancient past.

In the twentieth century, many extraordinary foreign architects visited Athens. Amongst the most well documented was the 1933 CIAM IV meeting that took place aboard the *SS Patris II* traveling from Marseilles to Athens, carrying some of the most important figures of the modern movement in architecture (Le Corbusier, Josep Lluís Sert, Cornelis van Eesteren, László Moholy-Nagy, Giuseppe Terragni, the historian Sigfried Giedion, the artist Fernand Léger and many others). This time again, the Europeans admired the temples. They did not talk of their impressions of the modern city but they did take time to visit and admire examples of local modern architecture, particularly the school building program then in progress.

In addition, during this visit the CIAM members discovered and marveled at the indigenous architecture of the Aegean islands. Thus began an appreciation of Aegean architecture that influenced both Greek and international architects and became another point of negative comparison with the modern city. In the 1960s another cosmopolitan traveler, Bernard Rudofsky, revisited the Aegean and featured his black-and-white photographs in the widely known MoMA exhibition in New York Architecture

Without Architects, published as a book in 1964. Rudofsky praised Aegean domestic architecture and argued that it should be an example for contemporary architects. His admiration for Aegean architecture, a kind of pre-industrial spontaneous or self-built landscape, prompted a new reappraisal of such buildings amongst American and European architects. Yet Rudofsky, too, neglected to see Athens and its spontaneous informal building culture in similar terms, assuming that the "vernacular" can only be found in isolated rural areas. This book re-examines this assumption and tries to problematize the term "vernacular" vis-à-vis the Greek context.

At least since the 1950s, Greek critics and historians have either completely ignored the informal aspects of the city, or assessed twentieth-century Athenian urbanism in the most negative terms: the city itself was charged with being a "concrete jungle", "chaotic" or even becoming an "urban monster" entering into a state of "architectural and aesthetic anarchy". As one newspaper headline expressively announced in relation to the development of postwar Athens: "The Misfortune of Athens: Total Architectural Irresponsibility, Botched, Improvised Design. The Rule of Administrators, Committees and the Example of Kolokotroni Square. The Neglect of Important Sites."[3]

Yet it is still not immediately obvious how to go about exploring informal urbanism as an architectural historian, in any context, except to keep an open mind. It is a simplification to think that because there is no "planning" or organization in the expected European sense, there must be "chaos"—as if one condition precludes the other. What if there is something else? What other conditions, processes, histories give each such city its unique shape?

In Athens, post-Second World War development took the form of relatively small-scale multistory apartment blocks generically called *polykatoikìa*. The term *polykatoikìa* is derived from *poly* (multiple) and *oikia* (dwelling). This would prove to be the most ubiquitous building type of the postwar period. The criticism of the time often described *polykatoikìa* apartments as "sad", "terrible", "low-ceiling boxes that make one feel as if one was living in a drawer". Indeed the image of the *polykatoikìa* literally devouring the city's classical glory, including the Parthenon itself as we see in the cartoons on page 15, is a telling expression of the strong emotions people harbor towards the *polykatoikìa*.[4]

The rapid construction of *polykatoikìa* housing served the pressing need for shelter for the vast numbers of people who moved into the cities and particularly Athens after the end of the Second World War and the Greek Civil War. Mostly constructed by private initiative rather than organized State effort, and without financing from banks or other lending institutions, the successful production of the *polykatoikìa* might at first seem unlikely especially when compared with other European cities. The accelerated construction of the *polykatoikìa* took place alongside a large-scale destruction of the prewar city. Images of developers' bulldozers devouring nineteenth-century neoclassical buildings from the early part of the twentieth century, and the continual noise of digging and dust and tearing things down were a striking part of life in Athens even up to the mid-1970s. At times, especially during the rushed construction of the early postwar period, it was rumored that when developers came upon ancient remains by digging for foundations for *polykatoikìa* buildings, they would literally pour concrete over the top as quickly as possible before archaeologists could get the chance to see the remains and thus slow down or even stall the new construction indefinitely.[5]

Leo von Klenze, *Reconstruction of the Acropolis and Areus Pagus in Athens*, 1846, Neue Pinakothek, Munich. Von Klenze was a renowned architect who served as the court architect of Ludwig I of Bavaria. He was invited by King Otto, second son of Ludwig I, to design a new urban plan following the dissent met by the first urban plan by Kleanthis and Schaubert. Von Klenze was also an accomplished painter who used his paintings as studies for his architectural projects. He also participated in early archaeological excavations in Athens, and submitted plans for the restoration of the Acropolis.

The phenomenon of demolition is related to modernization processes and is a common feature in all cities everywhere. In Greece, the onset of architectural modernization, which began with Independence from the Ottoman Empire and the founding of the Greek State in the first part of the nineteenth century, was vastly different from that experienced in other countries—particularly northern European countries. In most accounts, up to the 1830s Athens appeared like a village rather than a city, composed of stone and timber houses with high walls for privacy and protection from the Ottoman rulers. There were hardly any public, civic or religious buildings since open public life was not allowed for Ottoman subjects. As their rule ended, Athenians tore down existing domestic buildings and began constructing neoclassical houses, introduced to Greece by the first king, the Bavarian Prince Otto of Wittelsbach, second son of Ludwig I.

Widely perceived as symbolizing the country's own classical past, neoclassicism was quickly adopted and became the most commonly used architectural expression both for domestic and public architecture. At the same time, Otto's advisors and archaeologists began a process of "cleansing" in Athens. Classical temples and monuments were restored and new ones patiently excavated, whereas memories of the Ottoman occupation were hastily buried, along with many other structures, including of Byzantine and medieval heritage.

The processes of destruction and rebuilding to a large extent managed to erase the evidence of different layers of time of Athenian history, thus increasing the sense of a chasm between the "civilization" of the classical city and the "anarchy" of the modern one. Since there are very few remaining buildings from the centuries between the classical times and the twentieth century—except for a few remaining Byzantine churches—the sense of disparity between the apparent perfection of the classical city and the evident problems of the modern one, is even greater. Even now, when travelers choose to see contemporary Athens they invariably disparage what they find by holding up an idealized image of the ancients to the impoverished present. As one writer declared in a book written just before the Athens Olympics in 2004:

> From the Acropolis, it looks as if a giant—in a moment of boredom, or perhaps disgust—threw his *toy houses* in the air. Where they landed, modern Athens was formed. Now the toys, in revenge for their neglect, seem to be multiplying, filling every nook of the Athenian basin and slowly climbing the mountains to the north, east, and west. [...] Only what's left standing of the Parthenon and the Aegean to the south have escaped the giant's sloppy hand. I turn to the ancient temple, honey-colored in the dull sun, and back to the glistening sea to the south, seeking something to counter the architectural frenzy below.[6]

Echoing the established opposition between the ancient heritage (the Parthenon), indigenous building (the Aegean) and modern Athens, George Sarrinikolaou, an American journalist of Greek origin, reiterated the very same negative characterizations as countless other travelers before him. As he suggested, above all, Athens is indeed characterized by the widespread construction of *polykatoikìa* multifamily dwellings—or "toy houses" in his terms.

One of the particularities of *polykatoikìa* development is that it *looks* modern. The basic model of each *polykatoikìa* is composed of a reinforced concrete frame with brick or other masonry infill; it is almost always white; it has unadorned facades, large window openings, flat roofs and even at times pilotis for cars. But unlike the didactic models of modern architecture with rational planning, aesthetic rigor and a utopian social vision, much of *polykatoikìa* housing was built in an informal, unplanned way. According to estimates, only about 5–15 percent was produced with any involvement by architects.

But does this make *polykatoikìa* housing a kind of vernacular architecture? The terms "popular building" and "popular architecture" are the closest equivalents to the Latin-derived *vernacular* used in studies of western European, northern European and US contexts, which is less relevant to Greece. For whereas the term *laiki* (popular) comes from the Greek *laòs* meaning "people", the term *vernacular* comes from the Latin *verna*, meaning "soil, earth", and connotes strong relations to the land and agricultural economies, much more typical of pre-modern Europe. Other scholars translate the term *popular* as "folk architecture". However "folk" has other, particularly northern European, connotations that are also not applicable to the Greek context. The issue of the untranslatability of certain key terms (such as this one singled out in this book) highlights the very different experiences of Greek architects and other intellectuals in this period compared to their colleagues in western and northern Europe.

In studying closely the particularly local conditions of Greek urban life, this book tries not so much to give a more positive account of events that took place but to provide a new set of tools and a new way in which to explore these events. It argues that we must understand urbanism as a mode of life, an expression of culture, the result of historical events and their interpretations, as well as their incorporation in everyday life. For the fact that informal building activity prevails is important and merits more scholarly research and analysis.

Left: A huge bulldozer relentlessly devouring nineteenth-century neoclassical domestic architecture to make way for *polykatoikìa* buildings, Athens, 1973. In the original cartoon by Kostas Mitropoulos the buildings were larger than the bulldozer. Here I have distorted the image to reflect how I remember this cartoon growing up: ominous and threatening.

Right: Cartoon by Kostas Mitropoulos showing an imaginary endless snake made up of *polykatoikìa* buildings strangling the Acropolis, ready to inflict its deadly bite onto the Parthenon, 1973.

In providing other ways in which to perceive this informal activity, this book contextualizes it within a historical perspective and suggests that it was an important expression of Greek culture and everyday life. It thus inserts informal urbanism and the postwar *polykatoikìa* into a cultural problematic in which this informal development enabled a rapid modernization and urbanization that provided not only affordable shelter but also opportunities for relatively small-scale builders, developers and other non-professional, truly informal groups, such as housewives.

This reappraisal of the *polykatoikìa* and the informal development it represents helps us in turn to contextualize the activities and theories of prominent architects and planners (Aris Konstantinidis, Constantinos Doxiadis) that, as elsewhere, failed to accommodate the vitality of everyday life. The problems this de facto urban development poses for architects are the background to a whole set of local cultural issues, including the role of design in the formation of national identity and the relationship between modern architecture and the supposedly universal processes, both "vernacular" and "international".

Especially in its initial stages, the book found inspiration in a small number of writers who found ways to express positive criticism towards Athenian urban development. One such text is a short article from 1978, where Greek architect Anastasia Tzakou, one of the few women with published projects and texts from the postwar period, fleetingly touched upon the idea of unplanned or "anonymous" development as it is also often called, forming the origins of a new "popular civilization". Tzakou wrote:

> One feels some comfort in the thought that this [postwar *polykatoikìa* housing] will be the future anonymous architecture in comparison with other European urban centers. Historians of architecture will find these urban forms, which came about without formal [*episimo*] urban planning, interesting.[7]

Tzakou's assessment hinted at another dimension of this development that needs attention, that is a kind of ethnography of architecture. This book tries to respond to, and expand upon, Tzakou's comment, by developing a methodology to explore informal urbanism as one part of larger social, cultural and economic phenomena.

A view of Lycabettus Hill, ca 1950. Below, a typical street in the upper-middle-class area of Kolonaki with neoclassical and early nineteenth-century domestic buildings, just starting to be developed with new *polykatoikìa*.

Interestingly, it was a foreign anthropologist who made the first thoroughly positive critique of Athenian urbanism in an article called "Positive Aspects of Greek Urbanization: The Case of Athens by 1980", published in *Ekistics* in 1986. The author, American anthropologist Peter S Allen, was the first scholar to point out that, despite its apparently chaotic character, unlike other rapidly modernized cities Athens experienced no persistent shanty towns, no soaring crime, nor the high unemployment usually associated with this kind of urban growth.[8] As will be discussed in chapter 5, Allen's explanation for this success was rooted in the very specific social and cultural factors of Greek migration.

One year later, in his introduction to the Greek translation of *Modern Architecture: A Critical History*, 1987, Kenneth Frampton was perhaps the first foreign architect to write positively of contemporary Athens. Frampton wrote that Athens is "a modern city par excellence" and praised its

> particularly civilized *'unconscious'* level of urban culture [that represents] the autonomous expression of a whole culture rather than the work of a single architect [and is] perhaps the only such example in the world.[9]

Later on, Italian architect Franco Purini, while repeating the often-cited epithet of "visual anarchy" to describe Athens, also expressed interest in the unfamiliar ways in which Greek cities negotiate their ancient history, writing that in Athens, unlike in Rome, "the persistence of antiquity has not undergone the process of tasteful distancing [as in Italy, and that] the ancient is an enigmatic view of the new [...]".[10]

In the 1990s, Lebanese architect and scholar Hashim Sarkis pointed out more positive aspects to Athenian urbanization in his article in *Isopolis,* provocatively titled "On the Beauty of Athens".[11] Urging us not to judge Athens only in relation to "European standards of beauty—whatever they might be—that tend to block any creative thinking about the physical environment in Athens", Sarkis argued that contemporary Athens "does possess a character that is particular to its own history, culture and conditions".

Around the same time, Kostas Moraitis, a Greek architect and critic, wrote an intriguing piece that was influential in framing my own questions. In concluding an article on larger questions of modernity, Moraitis pointed out the fascinating fact that even though Athens was primarily built without architects, it actually *looks* modern. Moraitis noted that this "vulgar" modernism constituted a popular "expressive field", even a "popular language". He proposed that the assortment of "popular modernists" who created it, that is "ex-farmers who had become builders, ex-builders who became developers, ex-merchants with some money who wanted to invest in real estate", managed to create a remarkable thing: "to transform international modernism into a popular Greek tradition."[12]

Greek architects and planners Dina Vaiou, Maria Mantouvalou and Maria Mavridou have also been critical about the "monotonously negative conversation" about Greek cities in the last half of the twentieth century. They discussed the fact that Athenian development has widely been seen as simply "a 'deviation' from a theoretically 'correct' model" and noted that it is unfortunate that all criticism "has been codified with the terms 'cement city', 'smog' etc". Not discounting these as real problems, they nevertheless urged us to see that there has been a real "lack or absence in this discussion" that would take account of local conditions and especially the influence of the Civil War.[13] This book sets out to address these comments by recognizing the role of diverse actors in the creation of cities—a story suppressed by "the expert visions" of architects and planners. Tracing interactions between informal groups—such as "vulgar" local builders—and international modernism, during a period of war, occupation, civil war and its aftermath, this book resists total explanations, trying instead to challenge how we understand urban space within specific cultural and historical parameters.

1   I refer to the term *afthaireto* (random, unplanned). This term is generically used to denote all kinds of informal buildings, both pre- and post-Second World War, both shacks and more solid structures, built with no planning permit at all, very often by people working at night, as well as parts of buildings that were deviously added without permit to existing older structures. In addition this term is routinely used with negative connotations in relation to urbanism (*authaireti poleodomia)*.

2   A philhellene was "a friend of the Greeks"; a term coined during the struggle for Independence from the Ottoman Empire. It is still in use today.

3   This article too comes from *Vradyni* newspaper, 9 March 1957. In this case the headline is particularly graphic. The article ends with the following sentence: "One wonders whether all those 'experts' do their best to make this urban monster uglier. And there is no one in sight to stop this urban anarchy, someone to put order to this chaos, who will stop this march to the worse." Kanellopoulos Archive, Hellenic Literary and Historical Archives.

4   The quotes on domesticity in a *polykatoikìa* apartment are from a special issue of the journal *Architektonika Themata/ Architecture in Greece*, vol 12, 1978: "*I exelixi tis polykatoikìas stin Athina meta ton polemo*" ("The development of the *polykatoikìa* in post-Second World War Athens"). This volume was edited by Dimitris Philippidis who cited these typical quotes about the *polykatoikìa*.

5   The fact that there must be some truth to these rumors becomes even more apparent since the recent excavations for the installation of subway lines and for the preparations for the 2004 Olympic Games, when large segments of the ancient city were uncovered at times only a few meters below the surface of the modern one, as was the case in Syntagma Square, an area developed during the nineteenth century around the first king's palace, which yielded a wealth of finds right under the surface of this busy city center (now permanently exhibited in the Syntagma metro station).

6   Sarrinikolaou, George, *Facing Athens: Encounters With the Modern City*, New York: North Point Press, 2004.

7   This is the only such critical article by Anastasia Tzakou, whose design work occupies an important place in Greek architectural history of the post-Second World War period. Tzakou studied with Dimitris Pikionis in Athens, worked with Doxiadis Associates in the Middle East in the early 1950s, lived in France for a long time,

then returned to Greece, taught (briefly) at the National Polytechnic School (School of Architecture) in Athens, and had a long career in the public sector. This article was "written from the point of view of Greek architects", and published in *Architektonika Themata/ Architecture in Greece,* ed Dimitris Philippidis, vol 12, 1978, pp 131–132.

8   Allen, Peter S, "Positive Aspects of Greek Urbanization: The Case of Athens by 1980", *Ekistics*, vol 53, no 318/319, 1986, pp 187–194.

9   Frampton, Kenneth, *Modern Architecture: A Critical History*, London: Thames & Hudson, 1987, p 14.

10 Purini, Franco, "Greek Discontinuities", *The Contemporary (Greek) City*, Yannis Simeoforidis and Yannis Aesopos eds, Athens: Metapolis Press, 2001, p 243.

11 Sarkis, Hashim, "On the Beauty of Athens", *Isopolis: Addressing Scales of Urban Life in Modern Athens,* Peter G Rowe and Hashim Sarkis eds, Cambridge, MA: Harvard Graduate School of Design, 1997.

12 Moraitis, Kostas, "*To Mellon tou neoterikou aitimatos. Ofeiloume na eimaste diarkws modernoi?*" ("The future of the question of modernity. Do we have to always be modern?") in *Architektonika Themata/ Architecture in Greece*, vol 30, 1996.

13 Vaiou, Dina, Maria Mantouvalou and Maria Mavridou, "Planning in Greece 1949–1974", Second Conference of the Greek Society for Urban History and Planning, *Postwar Greek Planning Between Theory and Chance*, Volos: University of Thessaly Press, 2000, p 36.

Panoramic view of
Athens showing the
Old Royal Palace and
Mount Lycabettus, taken
between 1850 and 1880.

Chapter 1: Urbanism and Domesticity

Identity, Language and Architecture

> Memory and history, far from being synonymous, appear now to be in fundamental opposition. Memory is life, borne by living societies founded in its name. It remains in permanent evolution, open to the dialectic of remembering and forgetting, unconscious of its successive deformations, vulnerable to manipulation and appropriation, susceptible to being long dormant and periodically revived. History, on the other hand, is the reconstruction, always problematic and incomplete, of what is no longer.[1]

Modern Athens grew and developed rapidly from the neoclassicism of the nineteenth century to the modernism of the first half of the twentieth century and onto the *polykatoikìa* of the postwar period. The city provides us with a built record of a whole sequence of cultural developments and conflicts exemplifying the interplay between received history and the spontaneous manifestation of collective memory. Pierre Nora's seminal and perceptive differentiation between the processes of memory and history might help us understand how modern Greek society collectively constructed the emerging sense of its own past while electing to forget or overtly erase certain events from national consciousness as it entered simultaneously into the larger project of modernizing Greek culture; a process of "erasure" that was both top-down, by the State, and bottom-up, by popular initiatives.

In fact, during the first half of the nineteenth century questions of history and memory started to be urgently relevant to the project of constructing a national identity and culture for modern Greece. After almost four centuries of Ottoman rule, the War of Independence that began in 1821 led to the formation of a republic and later, with the help of the European Great Powers, to the creation of a Hellenic kingdom.[2] This mediation initiated a long period of so-called "peaceful interference" of European nations in Greek political life. The 1832 Convention of London that involved Russia, Great Britain and France—but notably not Greece—confirmed hereditary sovereignty upon the 17-year-old Prince Otto of Wittelsbach (1815–1867), second son of Ludwig I of Bavaria, who arrived in 1833 in the city of Nafplion to be crowned the first King of the Hellenes. He would serve until 1862.

Alongside some 4,000 troops, Otto's entourage included Bavarian and other European architects and engineers who introduced neoclassicism, a European architectural idiom, to Greece.[3] The rediscovery of classical Greek architecture and the birth of neoclassicism in Europe coincided with greater accessibility of classical sites during the mid- to late eighteenth century. When liberated, Athens was chosen as the capital in 1834, neoclassical buildings, both public and private, replaced what had previously existed, and neoclassicism quickly became the official architectural language of the new Greek State.

Historic center street grid, ca 2000. We can still discern the original Kleanthis and Schaubert isosceles triangle of wide avenues surrounding the Plaka area at the center of this diagram. On the lower left the Acropolis Hill, on the right the Zappeion Exhibition Hall and Public Gardens, and at the top Omonoia Square.

The proximity to actual ancient monuments and sites that were then being discovered and studied for the first time contributed to neoclassicism's wide acceptance, both for public works and domestic buildings. In fact many foreign and Greek architects working in Greece during Otto's reign, such as Theophil and Christian Hansen from Denmark and Leo von Klenze from Munich, were also involved in archaeological excavations. Von Klenze, the author of one of Athens' first urban plans (1834), was involved in the process of "cleansing" classical monuments of buildings and constructions from other historical periods, whether Byzantine or Ottoman or anything in between. At that point, the desire to rediscover Greece's classical past took precedence over all other moments of Greek history.[4]

As urban historians of the nineteenth century have repeatedly noted, architecture and urban planning were crucial in the construction of a modern Greek identity. According to Vilma Chastaoglou,

> the modern city was regarded by those who ruled as a founding element of a new society, a tool that would facilitate the homogenization of the population coming from different backgrounds, a laboratory that would create and disseminate new social and national values and would transform the villagers to urban citizens of the new State".[5]

Forging a common language for this new society was no easy task. Newly liberated citizens came from a wide-ranging geographical background. During the early decades of the nineteenth century, Athens' population was made up not only of *autochthon,* indigenous Greeks, but also non-Greek speaking *autochthon* populations (speaking Albanian, Vlach, and other languages of ethnic minorities). There were Bavarians who had come to Greece with Otto, other western Europeans, such as Italians, who worked in construction, French military engineers and a significant number of *heterochthonous*, or diaspora Greeks, from a wide geographical area—ranging from modern-day Bulgaria, Romania and the coast of the Black Sea on the Russian side, to western Europe and of course modern-day Turkey.

Plan of Athens during
Ottoman times by Louis-
François-Sébastien Fauvel.

Stamatios Kleanthis and
Eduard Schaubert, Athens
plan showing the new
straight wide avenues
forming an isosceles
triangle "hugging" the
Acropolis, 1833.

Karl Baedeker, *Greece, Handbook for Travellers*, second revised edition, Leipzig: Karl Baedeker, 1894, showing the expansion of the grid to the north of the Acropolis area and the historic center.

Athens' first urban plan was drafted in 1832 following a careful topographical study by the Greek Stamatios Kleanthis and his friend and colleague, the Silesian-born Eduard Schaubert, even before Athens was the capital city and Otto was crowned King. The fact that these two architects had met at the Berlin Bauakademie where they studied under Karl Friedrich Schinkel is evidenced by the formal qualities of the plan for Athens they proposed. Conceived within the European tradition of great urban schemes, with wide boulevards and large gardens and public squares, the new urban plan had to re-imagine Athens as a contemporary city in close dialogue with its glorious classical history, and move away from the painful memories of Ottoman occupation. For instance, unlike what was there before, the new city center was to have wide and straight streets, unlike the "crooked", "Turkish" ones, as they were regarded in the press at the time.

Perhaps one of the most salient qualities of the Kleanthis and Schaubert plan was the clear, persuasive conceptual response to the pressing question of how to address the relationship between the present and the classical past. The shape of the plan demarcated an isosceles triangle, with its wide and straight sides defined by main avenues oriented toward Pireaus (the port), the Panathenaic Stadium and the Acropolis Hill. Historian Leonidas Kallivretakis has noted that "the Royal Palace

The Academy and
the National Library
by Theophil Hansen,
1885–1892.

Plans from Kostas Biris, *Ai
Athinai apo ton 19o–20o
aiona* (*Athens: From the
19th to the 20th Centuries*),
1966, showing the
Academy (left), and the
National Library (right).

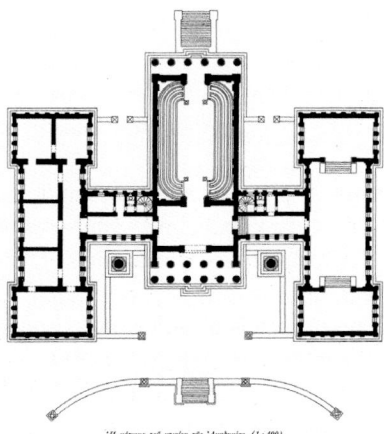

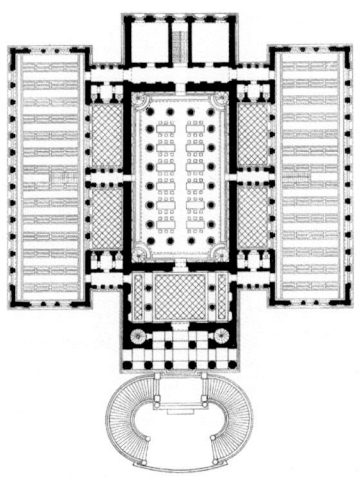

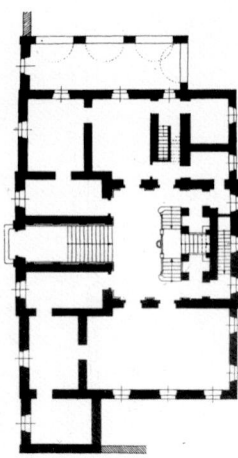

Wealthy Athenian house from 1837, designed by Stamatios Kleanthis. This house initially belonged to an individual (Amvrosios Rallis) but was soon converted into the British Embassy at Athens. From Kostas Biris, *Ai Athinai apo ton 19o–20o aiona* (*Athens: From the 19th to the 20th Centuries*), 1966.

was expected to stand at the peak of the triangle: a symbolic merger of the geometric apex and the apex of state power".[6] As the architects wrote in their memorandum, the orientation of the triangle was carefully thought through; its sides

> meet in such a manner that allows viewing simultaneously the comely Lycabettus, the Panathenaic Stadium, the rich-in-proud-memories Acropolis, and the military and commercial ships of Piraeus, from the balcony of the Royal Palace.[7]

Even though the Kleanthis and Schaubert plan was widely accepted, the State had almost no funds for expropriations. When Athenians actually saw the plan demarcated on the ground, there was uproar, and a wave of protests from property owners. The king felt he had to invite another architect to produce a new plan. In June 1834, the distinguished Bavarian Leo von Klenze, who had worked for Otto's father Ludwig I in Munich, arrived in Athens. Von Klenze's plan, approved in September 1834, kept the concept of Kleanthis and Schaubert's scheme in place, but reduced the extent and scale of its ambition, so as to pacify complaints. But the path to planning was never without resistance.

In one of several more revisions of Kleanthis and Schaubert's plan during the nineteenth century, the triangular concept was shifted in slight, yet meaningful ways. It was decided that the Old Royal Palace (today the seat of the Hellenic Parliament), should be positioned between the Acropolis and Lycabettus hills rather than on Omonoia Square, as originally envisioned in 1834, and not on top of the Acropolis itself, as Schinkel had suggested—an idea apparently rejected by Ludwig I of Bavaria himself. As a result, a large section of the "picturesque" Old City was preserved while new road networks were elaborated "in part as spokes with hubs at circular plazas, and in part as horizontals and verticals in the direction of the main axes, always with absolute regularity".[8]

Almost none of the public buildings were positioned where initially planned, but instead were placed on whatever public land was available. Athens' first public buildings were distinctly neoclassical, influenced by the wide acceptance of

Athens, middle-class neoclassical house from the late nineteenth or early twentieth century, with bakery on the ground floor and living quarters above. Photographed by Dimitris Papadimos, ca 1950s.

neoclassicism in northern Europe—after all, Bavaria under Otto's father Ludwig I's rule was a major center of neoclassical architecture. Important realized buildings from the first period after liberation were the University of Athens, 1839–1864, by Danish architect Christian Hansen; the Academy of Athens, 1859–1887, and the National Library, 1885–1892, by his brother Theophil Hansen; the National Polytechnic School, 1868, and the Arsakeio School for Girls, 1846–1852, by Italian-educated Greek Lyssandros Kaftanzoglou; the Old Royal Palace (now the Hellenic Parliament) by the German Friedrich von Gärtner, 1836–1843; and the Gennadius Library, 1854, that first housed the French School at Athens, 1845–1856.

A street grid of regular city blocks with straight lines and relatively narrow streets was implemented with difficulty in the 1830s around the center. By the late 1860s military engineers working for the Ministry of the Interior extended the grid beyond the University and the Academy, and on one side of Lycabettus Hill. They revised the earlier plan and enlarged it, creating new gridded areas to the southeast, beyond the Palace and up to the Temple of Olympian Zeus, and also to the Ilissos River, the basic lines of which still exist today. This was the last plan implemented for the next 60 years (up to the 1920s) that included the central area of Athens. From then on extensions of the city plan took place on the outskirts.

Again there was a great outcry and resistance to the plan by landowners who would be displaced to make way for the new grid, and once again much was compromised. In parallel with—indeed, in spite of—these government-backed efforts, the city was growing and changing quickly due to private initiative. The city center was growing denser, in and around the isosceles triangle defined by Kleanthis, Schaubert and von Klenze, as hundreds of new private buildings were built, mostly on small lots to house one or two families. As Chastaoglou has noted, the Royal Decree of 1855 focusing on buildings outside the early plan introduced the idea of "legalization after the fact" upon payment of fines. Perhaps it was inevitable that this practice would survive until today, as we will see in later chapters.[9]

Despite all the great challenges to implementing new urban plans in Athens, between 1834 and 1912 plans for 176 new cities had been drawn throughout Greece, many of which were executed, even if in simplified ways.[10] And if we look carefully, at the plans of Athens today, we may still discern a triangle connecting the Acropolis, the Old Royal Palace (now the Hellenic Parliament) and Omonoia Square. We will also see a secondary grid that includes the present-day Klafthmonos and Koumoundourou squares and glimpses of the rational logic of the neoclassical city as first imagined by Kleanthis and Schaubert, inscribed within the seeming disorder of contemporary Athens.

History: The Neoclassical House and Nineteenth-Century Domesticity

The fascination with neoclassical architecture and planning ushered in during King Otto's reign brought with it a new urban domestic building type to Athens, also based upon European prototypes, and of very different morphology from the pre-revolutionary domestic fabric. Whereas pre-revolutionary houses were built as a series of rooms around a courtyard, the new Athenian neoclassical houses had a symmetrical, rational plan and facade. This new urban type had no tall walls surrounding it, and instead faced the street directly. Wealthier mansions were elaborately decorated and typically clad in beautiful Tinian or Pentelic marble. Despite the popularity of these new qualities, the neoclassical houses that spread quickly through Athens in the mid-nineteenth century were far from uniform, and even incorporated elements of previous Athenian domestic types. Many houses preserved a vestigial courtyard or at least some small outdoor area that had been typical of Athenian houses under Ottoman rule, although balconies in marble or other local stone appeared then for the first time.

Historians of nineteenth-century Athens have talked about the different European "influences" (Bavarian, French and Italian) and the corresponding "periods" of neoclassical architecture, ranging from divisions into "orthodox neoclassicism" and "free romantic or free neoclassical" (Kostas Biris); into "neo-classique" with influences from eighteenth-century Europe and "neo-antique" of the nineteenth century (François Loyer); and into a "first period" (1833–1863), and a "mature" period (1863–1897) (Xanthipi Skarpia-Hoipel).[11]

Initially, neoclassicism was used to give monumental form to public buildings and wealthy mansions self-consciously designed by foreigners or by foreign-educated Greeks; eventually middle-class, and even lower-middle-class, Greeks in Athens and elsewhere—including the countryside and the islands—began deploying aspects of neoclassical architecture as well. It was widely associated with a return to classical ideals and to what was rightly Greek, despite the fact that, initially at least, northern Europeans imported these ideas and they embodied the European perception of classical Greece.

Towards the end of the nineteenth century, the typical urban middle-class house in Athens was predominantly small in scale: two to three floors that housed one or two families. Middle-class Athenians often lived above their family stores, which were on the ground floor (such as the bakery illustrated on page 27). There was usually a basement level with one or two rooms that were used for laundry and storage. Symmetrically placed stairs led to the main domestic spaces, with these typically opening up to a rather long axial space that spanned the full depth of the house. In some areas this axial corridor was called *ondàs* and acted as both a single organizing corridor, connecting all rooms on the floor, and the main living volume.[12] It contained sofas and armchairs pushed against its walls, and was frequently "decorated in an Eastern manner, with large and multicolored carpets on the floor or hanging from the walls".[13] The main dining/living area of the house was at the end of this axial space with the bedrooms on either side of it. Continuing tradition, the main bedroom had to face east.[14] If there was a second family in the building, there was a separate entrance with its own stair, and an external metal stair for the service areas of the two apartments.

By the last decades of the nineteenth century, neoclassicism's acceptance among all social classes was so wide that it had become a popular architectural style. It is as if by adopting neoclassical elements, everyone could become (more) Greek—rather than an "Oriental barbarian"—but also more European, since everyday life in the neoclassical houses was to be modeled upon European prototypes. Ordinary builders—those with elementary or high school education plus some building training, or just experience in the field—at times working in collaboration with so-called practical architects or engineers, built humble neoclassical houses.[15] Some of the elements commonly found in more humble neoclassical houses included symmetrical facades, walls colored in pastel or bright colors, plaster architraves, pilasters and figurines. These were produced in local workshops and were relatively inexpensive, rendering neoclassicism even more accessible and pervasive.

Representation and Rituals

The Athenian neoclassical house enabled certain forms of modernization across social classes. The interior changed drastically from Ottoman times, reflecting the shifts in nineteenth-century everyday life in the modern Greek State that was now more influenced by European ways of life. In spatial terms, this meant a more rigid division of function for each room rather than the multi-use spaces of houses in pre-revolutionary times, where dining, sleeping and living used to typically take place in one large room in the top part of the house. The concept of "privacy", imported from Europe—to this

Operation being performed at the *kali kamara* of a neoclassical house in Thessaloniki. The patient's mother stands on the right of the image.

Children playing in the entrance room area of a neoclassical house in the late afternoon. Note the painted decorations on the walls (and most probably the ceiling) and the European-style furniture.

day there is no direct translation of this term in Greek—began to gain importance at this time. Unlike the pre-revolutionary period, by the mid- to late nineteenth century there was a great deal more movable furniture in the house, mostly imported from Europe. An interview with a person born circa 1890 shows the central role of the house in the organization of family life before the onset of modernization processes:

> The house was not just a refuge. It was the center of family life. Everything happened at the house: entertainment (people rarely went out for that), weddings, baptisms, funerals, births and even surgery. The middle classes hired a doctor by the year. He would visit the house at least once a month. Often the house was connected with a professional space. There would be family rooms upstairs, and a pharmacy or medical office or tailor's shop or millinery below.[16]

Unlike the flexible, less differentiated domestic interior of the pre-Independence period, the neoclassical house included rooms such as the *kali kamara*, or "best living room", modeled upon the Victorian parlor. Like in Victorian England and America, this room demonstrated the inhabitant's social status and aspirations. As with the parlor, this room was only used on special occasions, such as introducing a young girl to her arranged suitor, for weddings, medical operations, funerals and other get-togethers (*veggeres*) with friends especially during long winter nights.[17] It was situated to one side of the *sala* or "everyday living room" and was furnished carefully with objects imported primarily from Europe. The walls were often hand-painted with colors such as pistachio green or blue, and ripe cherry red was most often used for the bedcovers as well as for furniture, tapestries and carpets.

The furniture was heavy and arranged around the room rather than at the center, in symmetrical fashion. There was often a piano to indicate the hostess and her daughters' European education, plants, flowers, family photographs and photo albums. Children were rarely allowed in this room. As the editors of the exhibition catalog *Astiki Thessaloniki* comment, "everything was ruled by austere rules, from the arrangement of the furniture to the small spoon for dessert, to the special dress of the host and visitors to the serving of tea. In this space [there was no] spontaneity and naturalness."[18]

The "everyday living room" was less austerely decorated. Middle-class homes often had Thonet chairs (the Viennese Thonet factory was thriving at the time), a console (*konsola*) with a mirror, portmanteaus and enough gas lamps so that the family could gather and read, sew, knit and meet close friends and relatives.[19] In fact the family took its meals in this room rather than in a separate dining room or kitchen. As in the Anglo-Saxon Victorian house, the kitchen was only for servants and very young children. Aside from their bedrooms, the children could sit and play or read in the main axial living area with its fresco paintings and gentle afternoon light.

Household Technology

Domestic technology at the turn of the century was very basic in Greece compared to northern Europe. Electricity arrived in 1889, but did not become widespread until 1910–1915, when Athens became one of the better-lit cities in Europe, despite the extremely high cost of this service. Thus electricity remained a luxury until the late 1920s.

Piped, potable water infrastructure was only introduced into Greek cities after 1893. Bathroom facilities were extremely crude. Whereas every bedroom had a porcelain jug for the daily care of the face, the washing of the hair and the body from the waist up could be more easily done in the kitchen with help from the servants. The bathtub evolved slowly from a kind of large, rounded copper tub into a European-type bathtub by the early twentieth century.

The bathroom was the most isolated and darkest space of the house, often close to the kitchen. In most houses it was actually positioned immediately outside the main house. It was very small when used only as a toilet and more spacious if it shared a space with bathing functions. In a typical neoclassical bathroom interior,

> the floor was covered in square gray stone or white marble, or ceramic tiles in white and black or red patterns like the kitchen and bath... the walls were whitewashed with lime and later on, with ochers... on its narrow side it had a marble basin "à la turk" and next to it a small copper pot for local cleaning of the body, which was later replaced by paper hanging through a wire hook... a bucket full of water was always available for washing the basin.[20]

Immediately outside the door there was a basin to wash one's hands. The servants had their own bathroom, always positioned outside the main house. In fact, in some cities, especially Thessaloniki, people continued to use the public baths, a legacy from the *hammam* culture of the Ottoman Empire.[21] The whole family would go to the public baths once a week—usually on Saturdays—accompanied by a maid who carried clean clothes and other personal items and helped the children bathe. The house would be cleaned thoroughly beforehand while the family was in the baths so that their return would be more pleasant. Washing in the bath would take the whole day and "in anticipation of religious holidays cleaning and bathing would take on the character of a military campaign".[22]

The kitchen area of the nineteenth-century house had a fireplace for the stove with a chimney that worked with either coal or wood. It was typically decorated with colorful ceramic tiles and had a small shelf above for small pots and other decorative objects. There was a built-in, typically wide marble sink with ceramic ocher yellow or red tiles around it, wooden dish-shelves, and a built-in bench with storage underneath that might be closed off with curtains. The floor was covered in ceramic tiles and there was a gas or coal burner for heat.[23]

Another auxiliary space was the laundry or washing room. Every "good house" had one of these spaces, located in the basement or in a separate room in the courtyard: the washing room had to be bright and have a fireplace with built-in cauldron for heating water. In addition, as detailed in the *Astiki Thessaloniki* catalog,

> in this room ruled by the washerwoman there had to be space for the copper basins, buckets, copper pots, water jugs, stoups, buckets, wooden supports for the copper basins, the laundry baskets, bamboo baskets, baskets made of tree branches or tree bark for drying clothes on, moulds, white soap on the shelf, clothesline and clothes pins. This was the permanent scenery of this space.[24]

Building (since demolished) with "For Sale" sign on Frinichou and Aischinou Streets, Pagrati, Athens. Photograph by Stelios Skopelitis, 1975.

The washerwoman was usually the poorest of all servants, often a widow with children. She would be regularly employed in the same house to work for certain days every month for many years. The hanging of clothes had its own technique that had to do with displaying the pieces that one was proud to show off for their whiteness, such as embroideries, and concealing the older clothes that were permanently soiled. Lastly, the clothes had to be collected at the right time and placed in separate baskets for ironing, a task that was done by other servants, as well as sometimes by the lady of the house and her daughters. At that time a woman of a certain class did not work outside her house, for she was not supposed to have paid employment. Of course, at the same time, a middle-class woman could not get married without a house as part of her dowry or the corresponding value of the house in cash.[25]

By the early twentieth century, especially during the late 1930s and 40s, some intellectuals began openly to question the fact that the very concept of neoclassicism was actually "foreign-brought" (*xenòferto*), "imported" from the north. Understood as an importation, neoclassicism was consequently held responsible for the rejection of local culture and memory. This turn was articulated by Yannis Tsarouchis, a prominent artist and writer who was himself born in a neoclassical house in Athens' port city of

Film still showing nineteenth-century residential architecture being demolished to make way for post-Second World War *polykatoikìa*. This scene from *Teddy Boy My Love* (1965), a popular film, shows how the trauma of this destruction eventually became part of mass consciousness.

Photograph of demolition of an Athenian neoclassical house, ca 1979. The banner at the first-floor balcony declares "old building materials" for sale.

Pireaus in 1910. In 1963 Tsarouchis wrote with some irony about the ways in which the neoclassical house participated in the construction of a bourgeois class modeled upon European prototypes, a class that did not exist in Greece prior to Independence. For Tsarouchis, this new middle class played make-believe with other cultures:

> Good families lived in neoclassical houses with high ceilings, cool in the summer, kept very dark [...] with white embroidered curtains of heavy cream colored linen, white covers on the furniture of their sparkling clean rooms. Houses next to the sea with caryatids and balusters of clay. These houses had clay sculptures, probably from Italy: Hermes, Poseidon, Athena, the whole ancient world [...] This society was mad about European and Northern designs and ideas; the religious petit bourgeois ladies dressed like Russian princesses and the dark-skinned children of day-laborers [*viopalestwn*] wore clothes as if they were princes from the North.[26]

Tsarouchis here points to both the sense of pride shared by the upper middle class for their "European" houses, as well as to a degree of alienation commonly felt towards these houses by many educated Greeks of his generation. Yet Tsarouchis was also very critical of the almost wholesale destruction of the nineteenth-century neoclassical urban fabric that would occur during the postwar period.

Well through the mid-1920s, people continued to build in a neoclassical style, with columns, pediments and other classical elements appearing in both popular and elite residential and commercial buildings. After the defeat of the Greek army in Asia Minor in 1922 and the complete collapse of the so-called Great Idea—the attempt to expand Greek territories in Asia Minor and restore Constantinople as the center of Hellenism as it had been before Ottoman occupation—people gradually stopped building neoclassical houses. From the mid- to late 1920s and until the Second World War, popular modernist buildings rejected the decorations of the neoclassical facade, opting instead for plain rectangular volumes, flat roofs and rounded corner columns (a detail reminiscent of Stamos Papadakis's single-family house in Glyfada from 1932–1933, see photograph on page 70). The urban Greek home was evolving, replacing the more evocatively nationalist neoclassical house while keeping the symmetry of the facade and the tradition of courtyards or gardens. Eventually, in the postwar period these humble modernist houses would also gradually be replaced by the *polykatoikìa*.

The phenomenon of the near-complete destruction of the Athenian neoclassical domestic fabric that was to come—when most neoclassical houses were demolished to make space for the *polykatoikìa*—intensified during the two decades of rapid postwar urbanization (1952–1974). Tsarouchis wrote of this traumatic destruction of built culture:

> Pseudo-classical they were called... as if searching for the primitive, organic and practical, they managed to demolish them, to make them disappear. While looking for truth they brought about the Middle Ages of Greek architecture. [...] From the war on, demolitions were so frequent you didn't have time to draw these buildings—not even to photograph them—before they disappeared. And photographs cost a lot of money at that point. The neoclassical houses were like the dead from an epidemic, thrown into a common grave.[27]

Writing after the Axis occupation (1941–1945) and the Civil War (1946–1949), Tsarouchis's image of a "common grave" is extremely touching, for clearly this was nothing less than a violent cultural upheaval. These buildings that were a palimpsest of memory were suddenly lost and reduced to rubble, their mnemonic embodiment metaphorically and literally liquidated. Looking back at this moment, one is compelled to ask not only what drove this wholesale destruction of the "traditional" urban fabric but also, what did this violent process signify? Can we understand it through Pierre Nora's conceptualization of memory as living "in permanent evolution" and "unconscious of its successive deformations"? And how did this process fit into the larger trajectory of Greek modernization? The requiem, as it were, for the neoclassical house constitutes a background against which to discuss the transformations of domestic urban life in the postwar period.

1   Nora, Pierre, "Between Memory and History: *Les Lieux de Mémoire*", *Representations* (special issue, *Memory and Counter-Memory*), no 26, Spring 1989, p 8.

2   The Greek War of Independence is conventionally said to have begun in 1821. Greeks turned to the Great Powers for help, especially after 1825 when Mehmet Ali, ruler of Egypt, and his son Ibrahim Pasha became involved in fighting for control of Crete and other territories. For more on the role of European powers in the instating of the Greek monarchy, see Richard Clogg, *A Concise History of Greece*, Cambridge: Cambridge University Press, 1992, pp 42, 45.

3   As Otto was a minor when he first arrived in Greece, "the new kingdom was ruled between 1833 and 1835 by a regency council made up of Bavarians. Between 1835 and 1843 he ruled as an absolute monarch. Following a bloodless coup on 3 September 1843, Otto was forced to concede a constitution. [...] He was overthrown in 1862." Clogg, *A Concise History of Greece*, p 219.

4   On the topic of "cleansing" of classical sites and monuments in the nineteenth century see Kostas Biris, *Ai Athinai apo ton 19o–20o aiona* (*Athens: From the 19th to the 20th Centuries*), Athens: Melissa Publications, 1966, and Eleni Bastéa , *The Creation of Modern Athens: Planning the Myth*, Cambridge: Cambridge University Press, 1999. Bastéa's innovative use of nineteenth-century print publications in her research and analysis significantly enriched our understanding of the city's growth, particularly in terms of the intricate relationship between urbanism and national identity. Her work is also referenced in chapter 3, pp 60–61.

5   Chastaoglou, Vilma, "The Urban Planning of the New Kingdom", *Otto's Greece and the Construction of the Greek State* (*I Othoniki Ellada kai I Sygkrotisi tou Ellinikou Kratous*), Alexander Papageorgiou-Venetas ed, Athens: Odysseas Publications and Goethe Institute Athens, 2002, p 305. See also Bastéa, *The Creation of Modern Athens*, especially chapters 3–6.

6   Kallivretakis, Leonidas, "Athens in the 19th Century: From Regional Town of the Ottoman Empire to Capital of the Kingdom of Greece", based on a conference on the "Archaeology of Athens", National Hellenic Research Foundation (NHRF), 1994, http://www.eie.gr/archaeologia/En/chapter_more_9.aspx.

7   Biris, Kostas, "The First Athens Plans", *Athinaikai Meletai* (*Athenian Studies*) [Athens], vol 1, 1938, p 16.

8   Kallivretakis, "Athens in the 19th Century".

9   See Chastaoglou, "The Urban Planning of the New Kingdom", pp 207–309.

10   For more on the nineteenth-century urban plans, see Bastéa's *The Creation of Modern Athens: Planning the Myth*.

11   Dimitris Philippidis gives a list of all these different interpretations in his *Neoelliniki Architektoniki: Architektoniki theoria kai praxi (1830–1980) san antanaklasi ton ideologikon epilogwn tis neoellinikis koultouras (Modern Greek Architecture: Theory and Practice (1830–1980) As a Reflection of Ideological Choices of Greek Culture)*, Athens: Melissa Publications, 1984.

12   *Ondàs* from the Turkish meaning "room for guests". (Note also the term *mousafir-ondàs* meaning "guest-room" in Turkish. The term *mousafiris* is still used to mean "guest" in demotic Greek.)

13   *Astiko Elliniko Spiti Thessalonikis 1880–1912* (*The Urban Greek House in Thessaloniki 1880–1912*), exh cat, Thessaloniki: Laographiko-Ethnologiko Mouseio Makedonias, 1985, p 63.

14   The practice of positioning bedrooms at the east end of the house continued in many post-Second World War *polykatoikìa* apartments. Although I am not certain, I feel that this had to do with the symbolism of the altar in the Greek Orthodox church which also faces east.

15   As explored in more detail in the next chapters, the tradition of "practical architects or engineers" continued well into at least the 1920s and 30s. The term in Greek is *embeirikos architekton*, or *embeirikos mixanikos* (engineer), collectively called *embeirikoi* (experienced ones) from *embeiria* (experience).

16   *The Urban Greek House of Thessaloniki 1880–1912*. See the chapter on *Thessaloniki*, transcript of an oral history, "From 'N.K.M.'", p 28.

17   On this occasion there was a specific ritual of *kerasma*, or "treat", whereby the young woman would offer her suitor a specific dessert made by her own hands. Her whole family would be sitting in this room as well watching: "this was the hostess' chance to show her ability as a housewife [*noikokyrosyni*]." This ritual persisted well into the twentieth century in the living rooms of the new *polykatoikìa* apartments and is explicitly featured in popular films of that time.

18   Like the Victorian parlor, this room was meant to impress and to show the culture and taste of the new urban middle-class families. *The Urban Greek House of Thessaloniki 1880–1912*, pp 31–35.

19   According to Sigfried Giedion, Thonet showed a bentwood chair at the London Exhibition of 1851. By 1871 there were stores that sold Thonet furniture from Moscow to Madrid and New York. Le Corbusier famously praised the simplicity and mass production of the Thonet chair and included it in his prototypical dwelling unit designed for the 1925 International Exhibition of Modern Decorative and Industrial Arts in Paris, the Pavillon de l'Esprit Nouveau.

20   *The Urban Greek House of Thessaloniki 1880–1912*, p 52.

21   The *hammams* were in turn adopted from the Roman *thermae*. According to Giedion, the word *hammam* means "dispenser of warmth" and derives from the Arabic *hamma* (to heat), and the Hebrew *hamam* (to be warm). Giedion notes that "even in America which was later to surpass all countries [in baths within the dwelling], the tub remained a luxury until the twentieth century". *Mechanization Takes Command: A Contribution to Anonymous History*, New York: The Norton Library, 1969, first published 1948, pp 637; 659.

22   *Astiko Elliniko spiti Thessalonikis 1880–1912* (*The Urban Greek House of Thessaloniki 1880–1912*), p 49. Although there were certainly public baths in Athens, they were not used to the same extent as in Thessaloniki. Note also that in Paris and London public baths were used well into the 1960s.

23   This is exactly the kitchen arrangement as featured in the film *O Thisauros tou Makariti* (*Dead Man's Treasure*) by Nikos Tziforos, 1959, discussed again in chapter 6.

24   The laundry room was called *plystario* or *plyntirio* from *pleno*, "wash". *The Urban Greek House of Thessaloniki 1880–1912*, p 46.

25   The dowry document (*proikosymfwno*) was a legal document that outlined all of a woman's possessions and their monetary value in great detail, and is therefore a valuable source of study for historians.

26   "Mathima Alitheias Ap to Mono Neoelliniko Theatro" ("Lesson of Truth from the Only Modern Greek Theater"), *Theatro* (*Theater*), 1963, p 10.

27   Tsarouchis, Yannis, "About Neoclassical Houses A" ("Peri neoklassikwn A") reprinted as a preface to the first edition of SB Skopelitis's *Neoclassical Houses of Athens and Pireus*, Athens: Dodoni Press, 1975, p 176.

Women walking in a
central Athens street, ca
1915. Note the neoclassical
houses on both sides of
the street and the wide
tree-lined boulevard.

Chapter 2: The Old Athenian Houses

Histories and Memories, Preservation and Repression

The most vocal architectural critic of domestic neoclassical architecture was the architect Aris Konstantinidis (1913–1993). Born in Athens, Konstantinidis was educated in Munich, Germany. He returned to practice in Greece in 1936. His works are regarded as iconic masterpieces of modern Greek architecture. He wrote numerous, remarkable books of which *The Old Athenian Houses* was one of the earliest, published in 1950.[1]

In this complex work Konstantinidis protests against neoclassicism as a foreign importation. He wants to show that there was an alternative, autochthonous but intellectually neglected tradition that had been overshadowed by the adoption and adaptation of neoclassicism. I should be careful to note that my intention in discussing Konstantinidis's work here is not to place blame for the destruction of Athens' neoclassical houses. Konstantinidis's book in fact remained a relatively obscure document and certainly had no wide appeal. At the same time, it is an important document, emblematic of the deeply rooted cultural conflicts experienced by Greek intellectuals when confronted with processes of modernization in the mid-twentieth century.

In *The Old Athenian Houses*, Konstantinidis considered the neoclassical architecture that abruptly replaced pre-Independence domestic typologies not only as a projection of the European values onto Greek culture but also as a violent importation superimposed upon a still very young and vulnerable nation. He proposed that Athenians should return to what existed before the imposition of neoclassicism, what he called the "old Athenian house", examples of which could still be found in the 1940s, the time when he was researching his book.

Konstantinidis carefully documented these houses in sketches, plans and photographs and argued that this was the only authentic form of Greek domestic architecture. The "old" Athenian house he described was composed of a series of rooms ranging from one to two stories in height around a courtyard. When two stories high, these would often feature a glass loggia above and a semi-covered space below. These houses were mostly built of stone augmented by wooden framing and wooden columns for the support of the loggia. Typical features included an external staircase, a well in the courtyard and a high wall secluding and protecting the house from the gaze of the passerby.

In praising the architectural merits of pre-Independence houses, Konstantinidis engaged in a critical cultural reversal: according value to a humble residential pattern not usually regarded as a worthy expression of native culture, thereby repudiating the still-commonly held notion that neoclassical buildings symbolized Greek nationhood. He endowed these humble houses with a new value, treating them as irreplaceable repositories of memory—even "anchors" in Pierre Nora's sense. Konstantinidis

From Aris Konstantinidis,
The Old Athenian Houses,
34 Aeschylou Street,
photograph and plan
showing the buildings
around the courtyard.

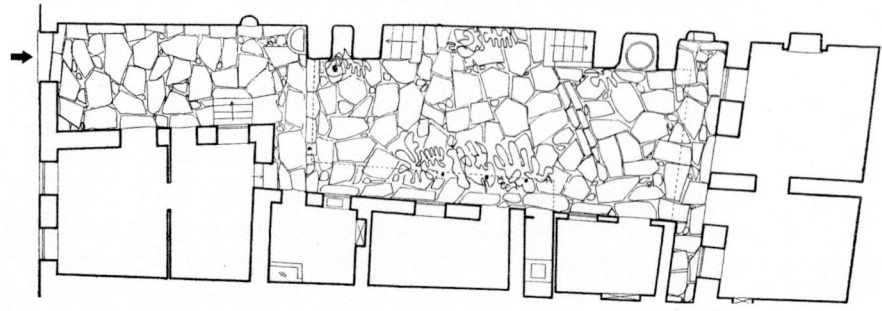

Photograph of a courtyard
facade on Panos Street.

Right: The plan of a house
on Asomaton 30 and
Psaromilingou Streets,
drawn by Konstantinidis
in the 1940s, published in
The Old Athenian Houses.

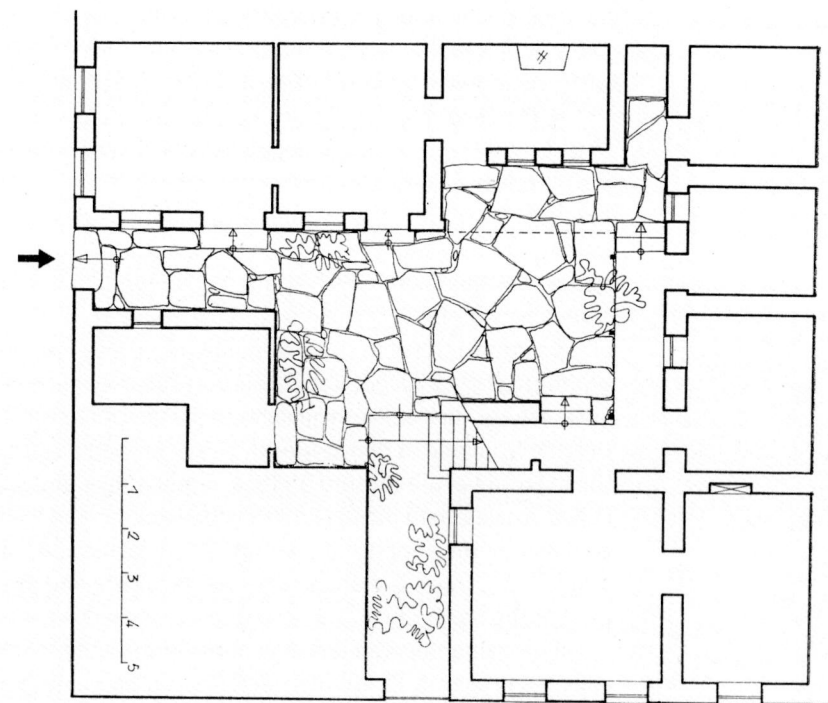

contrasted these "modest" Old Athenian Houses with the elaborate neoclassical buildings constructed after 1834. He insisted that the newer public and domestic buildings had nothing to do with what was truly Greek architectural culture. For Konstantinidis, the way in which neoclassicism was adapted to become a "national" idiom was misplaced or misconstrued by the zeal of philhellenes and other nineteenth-century European and European-minded Greeks.

Using architecture as an example, Konstantinidis was one of the first to suggest that neoclassicism idealized, mimicked and appropriated aspects of Greek culture in order to fulfill the Europeans' own quest for origins. The idealization of ancient Greece was central to philhellenism, the movement for independence initiated by the Greek diaspora and by European intellectuals in the late eighteenth century. In fact the European cultural identification with ancient Greece was indeed nowhere more pronounced during the nineteenth century than in Germany.

From the Romantic poetry of Hölderlin and Schiller to Humboldt's classical *bildung*, Greek antiquity was admired, even idealized by Europeans:

> In the Greeks alone we find the ideal of that which we ourselves should like to be and produce [...] They move us not with compulsion to be more like them but with inspiration to be more ourselves.[2]

More than 50 years later, examining these same issues through literature, Stathis Gourgouris perceptively noted that having "colonized their ideal", Europeans remained uncomfortable with the concept of a modern Greek culture. Moreover, Gourgouris detected "a co-incidence" between philhellenism and Orientalism, despite the fact that "the love of Greece is the love of the West and as such [apparently] incompatible with the Orient":

> [But] this is another trick of nineteenth-century European history, and a sly one at that. For, precisely in dissociating itself from the Orient, Philhellenism reveals its ultimate discomfort with modern Greece, at least with modern Greece as a cultural reality.[3]

One could see this idealization of classical Greece as an Orientalist trope often manifest in the process of colonization, but the primary difference in this case was that this progressive syndrome was somehow understood to have originated from Greece itself. And while the nineteenth-century Europeans had become Greeks, in their eyes post-Independence Greeks had turned into savages. During the 1830s, after a long period of war and centuries of foreign rule, Greece was indeed impoverished, its monuments looted, its population largely uneducated and its future more than uncertain.

Rather than helping Greece to address its many problems, for Konstantinidis the same "great" European powers that helped Greece become independent also sought their own dream of a classical revival worthy of their projected ideal image. Konstantinidis argued that this image was actually foreign to the indigenous culture of pre-Independence Athens. Karl Friedrich Schinkel's painting *The Apogee of Greece* of 1825 and his outrageous—in Konstantinidis's opinion—1834 proposal for the palace of the new king on the Acropolis Hill, built as a one-story Roman villa, were emblematic of the fantastic European "reconstructions" of classical Greece.[4]

Karl Friedrich Schinkel (1781–1841), proposal for Otto's Palace to be constructed as a Roman villa on the Acropolis, 1834.

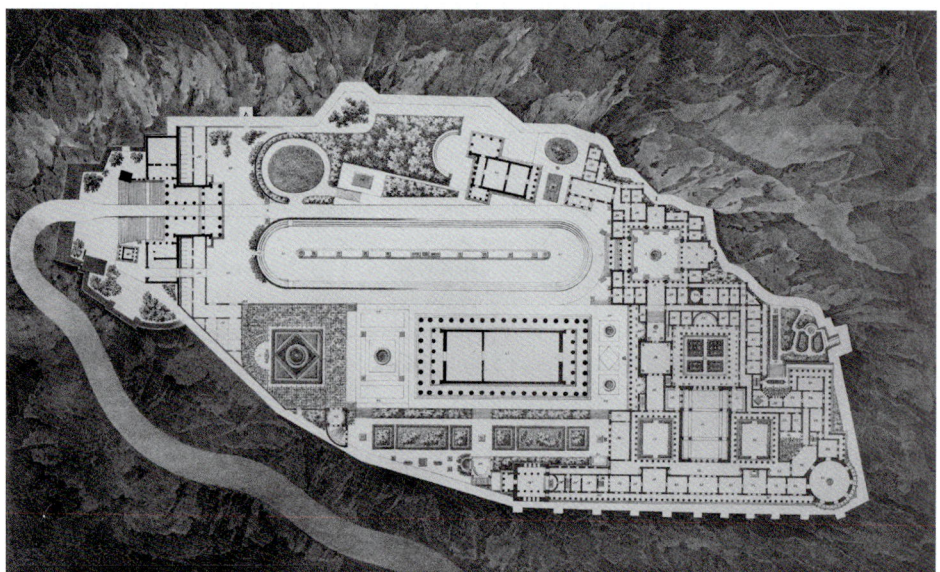

The architect Leo von Klenze, who produced one of the first urban plans for Athens, also drew and painted fantastic reconstructions of ancient Greek scenes. Back in Germany he designed the Walhalla, built 1830–1842, a copy of the Parthenon on the Danube that was supposed to be a monument to the German nation, or as his patron, Ludwig I, wrote, "to make us profoundly aware of our German nationality".[5]

While accusing the Germans and other Europeans of misunderstanding Greece's architectural heritage, ironically Konstantinidis probably had greater intellectual affinity with his European contemporaries than he was willing to admit. European—specifically German—modernist thought dominated his language and the terminology he chose to describe these houses. For instance, one of the ways in which he described these Old Athenian Houses was through the notion of "type", a concept that he used in a manner reminiscent of the Werkbund debates of 1914. Like these German thinkers with whom he was likely to be familiar through his education, Konstantinidis praised the "old" Athenian houses as having achieved the status of "the typical", that is, the "purely essential and functional in their architecture".[6]

And like other European thinkers of the first half of the twentieth century, Konstantinidis "read" these houses as the core of demotic Greek culture. Although the Latin-derived term "vernacular" does not correspond exactly to the equivalent Greek term, the essence of Konstantinidis's argument mimics the use of the word by twentieth-century European architects—particularly Adolf Loos—who discussed the vernacular in terms of rootedness, authenticity and timelessness.[7]

Perhaps without necessarily realizing it, Konstantinidis tried to translate some of the thoughts of European modernists into the Greek context, a process that was problematic, or at least somewhat awkward. Modern architects like Loos and Le Corbusier were very interested in the vernacular, not just intellectually. What they characterized as "vernacular" architecture provided their work with important formal precedents. Konstantinidis, too, while analyzing the Old Athenian Houses was also studying them with a trained modernist eye—and indeed his own work from this period was influenced by this research, particularly his Weekend Houses, 1942–1945, and House with Guest Quarter, 1943, in which the formal similarities are evident.

By recording the pre-Independence buildings in numerous drawings and photographs, Konstantinidis suggested using memory as a tool to bring them back to "life". He used the term "memory" often in his book, writing for instance that "the pursuit of form is the pursuit of memory", and "the belief and love for a contemporary architectural ideal will open up our vision for an appropriate and true memory".[8] In sum, he wanted to remember these particular domestic buildings as the only "true" Greek domestic typology. In this sense, Konstantinidis's book reminds us of another important German cultural document, Nietzsche's *Untimely Meditations*.[9]

In the second of these meditations Nietzsche suggested that too much history hinders man's development. He attacked the stifling historicism of the nineteenth century (what he called the "superhistorical"). Similarly, Konstantinidis wrote against the historical fever that gave birth to neoclassicism in Greece, helping to legitimize the very existence of the modern Greek State upon what he regarded as inauthentic foundations. Nietzsche had proposed that men should live "unhistorically"—not without history, but inventing a more vital form of history that is akin to our idea of memory: a selective process of reconstructing the past according to the needs of the present.

As Andreas Huyssen has commented, in terms of his view of history,

> Nietzsche was a utopian modernist, standing at the beginning of an intellectual trajectory from Bergson to Proust, from Freud to Benjamin, that articulated the classical modernist formulations of memory as alternative to the discourses of objectifying and legitimizing history, and as a cure to the pathologies of modern life.[10]

For Konstantinidis, the memory of the "old" Athenian house offered an alternative to the imported neoclassical style, which he implied was going to remain forever foreign.

Konstantinidis's prediction proved to be incorrect; by the end of the nineteenth and early twentieth century, these humble neoclassical houses had become a new urban tradition in Athens. This new, popular—in the Greek sense of the word, *laiki,*

Neoclassical houses in Athens (above) and Aegina (below). From Aris Konstantinidis, *The Old Athenian Houses*. Konstantinidis considers this domestic example with neoclassical elements such as pediments and columns as "false", "shallow" and "scenographic" architecture. These images were added in the second edition of the book (1981) confirming the author's views unchanged to that date.

A drawing of a pre-Independence house by Yannis Tsarouchis, which was probably exhibited at the 1928 Untrained Artists exhibition in N Velmos's Asylon Technics (Art Haven). The drawing records a neighborhood that was wholly demolished in 1930 to make way for the reconstruction of the ancient *Agora* by the American School of Classical Studies. From *Houses of Old Athens*, The Historical and Ethnological Society of Greece, Athens, 2006.

meaning "of the people"—architecture, had quickly been disseminated all around the country, always associated (as Konstantinidis rightly pointed out) with the idea of national rebirth. Similarly, the global architectural phenomenon we broadly name "neoclassicism" might have had parallel ideological underpinnings in many contexts, but it was not by any means expressed everywhere in the same way.

And even though Konstantinidis scathingly calls neoclassicism "the first International Style", this does not mean that buildings in Paris, Vienna, Munich or Copenhagen were exactly the same as those in Athens, even when built by the same architects. This is as true of the monumental government buildings as it is of domestic architecture, even in buildings far away from Athens. It was during the mid-nineteenth century that humble domestic buildings in Aegina, Crete and the Aegean islands, for instance, began to acquire their own versions of neoclassicism.[11]

Domestic neoclassical buildings in Athens were strikingly different from those of northern Europe in terms of scale, materials, color, techniques, details and execution. In addition, despite Konstantinidis's alarmist descriptions of a sudden and devastating invasion of neoclassicism from Europe, other historians have claimed that there was a gradual process of incorporation of these imported "foreign" aspects into Athenian architecture; they argue that the nineteenth-century neoclassical house in Athens combined both Eastern and Western influences in new ways, particularly in the interior.[12]

For Konstantinidis, neoclassical houses signified the non-indigenous, and therefore "false". The artist Yannis Tsarouchis, who used neoclassical houses as the backdrop of many of his own paintings, and who also documented "old" Athenian houses earlier than Konstantinidis, similarly believed that neoclassical houses represented "Europe" (his quotation marks) in the average person's mind. He also considered them a European transposition. Yet Tsarouchis's assessment of these houses was perhaps less conflicted; he was able to appreciate the transformation of the neoclassical house into a popular Greek form. In fact, Tsarouchis documented another great architect and intellectual of the previous generation, Dimitris Pikionis (1887–1968), expressing a similarly positive attitude:

> One evening in Syntagma Square [Pikionis] explained to me how beautiful the neoclassical houses were at night, with their soft lighting. He compared old plaster to human skin. In this dim light, these old houses looked like great works of art as well as architecture.... [Pikionis] was very interested in the variant of neoclassicism created by local craftsmen that gradually established itself after the departure of the Bavarians. [That night] he spoke about examples of how a local, Greek neoclassicism materialized, pointing to a single-family house with three windows on its facade and an inner courtyard.[13]

Unlike Konstantinidis, Pikionis had recognized that the broad term "neoclassicism" no longer had one meaning in Greek architecture. By the early twentieth century, even if it was still associated with symbols derived from classical Greece that were re-introduced by the Europeans, neoclassicism had also acquired a distinctly local dimension exactly because architecture was overwhelmingly a popular undertaking, practiced by simple builders and technicians. This was a factor that Konstantinidis was unwilling or unable to appreciate.

Which brings us to another important dimension of the pre-Independence, pre-neoclassical houses that Konstantinidis did not mention: the "common" or "shared" construction language (*koini*) that came beforehand, which was used throughout the Ottoman Empire by the traveling guilds of craftsmen called *isnafs* (Turkish) or *kompanies* (Greek). In their domestic buildings, built regional differences stemmed more from availability of materials and climate than from any significant ethnic, stylistic or typological concerns, although there were some differences between Christian and Muslim houses based on religious custom and belief.[14]

But there was yet another issue that makes Konstantinidis's book intriguing and points to the ways in which he used memory rather than history in order to construct an identity for the pre-Independence house. After completing his descriptions, as if stemming from an afterthought, or as if he were just emerging from a dream, Konstantinidis read these "old" Athenian houses as if they were a direct continuity of the domestic architecture of classical Greece. He sought to "recover" or "reawaken" what he saw as an originary Athenian architecture from the darkness of history, treating them as repositories of memory:

> And how strange, this arrangement [of the rooms around a courtyard] reminds us of something... in reality the courtyard of the [old] Athenian house is nothing other than the ancient atrium. And the *hayiati* or glass wall (with the shed formed underneath) is but the ancient stoa, the "peristyle": the two basic elements of Hellenic architecture from the oldest times.[15]

Konstantinidis's realization about the true nature of the Old Athenian House implied a direct "continuity" between classical and modern Greece. The question of "continuity" has been a recurrent one in Greek cultural life since the inception of the modern Greek

State. The argument of genetic as well as cultural continuity was initially "imported" from the West: it was a significant factor in the ideology of philhellenism.[16] In other words, whilst once more trying to "correct" European misconceptions about Greek culture, Konstantinidis unconsciously repeated or reiterated yet another European interpretation. Seeing the whole of neoclassicism as a utopian and therefore "untrue" and even a dangerous "romantic dream", he suggested a process of correcting modern national identity and culture through the rediscovery of the architecture of the Old Athenian House. This was no less utopian: it was the memory of the Athenian house, at least to a certain degree constructed or "created", and as Pierre Nora has remarked, "vulnerable to projections of all kinds".

In this light, to what extent is Konstantinidis's own claim about the architecture of the "old" Athenian houses historically correct? Even if there are indeed certain elements that have existed in Greece since antiquity, whether or not these Athenian houses were purely "Hellenic", as Konstantinidis wanted to believe, is difficult to discern. There is no doubt that the courtyard was in fact an element that has existed in domestic architecture since antiquity, as excavations have repeatedly shown. But this was also an element that appeared throughout the Mediterranean—a topic Le Corbusier was interested in as well.[17] Other elements of the Old Athenian House that Konstantinidis highlighted also appear in classical examples. But at the same time, the short "note" that Konstantinidis quotes at length in his own text, from an earlier Athenian scholar Dimitris Kambouroglou, also resonates with another kind of memory, not only of Western antiquity but of Eastern influence:

> In the upper floor decorated by an ornate corridor (the *hayati*) is the parents or the grandparents' room and the guest's room. The guest is led there and they offer him coffee, sweets, and a hookah if he wants [*nargile*]. The guest room has a large fire, wide and low *sofas*, high lights which color the interior with their *multicolored glass*.[18]

More than the memory of a classical past, this text resonates with traces of the Ottoman occupation on the level of everyday life. This is evident too, in the terminology used to describe some of these spaces, which is no longer of Greek origin. For example, the term *hayati* appears and reappears in studies of so-called "traditional" Greek architecture, derived from a word meaning "life" in Turkish, and corresponds clearly with a space found in Ottoman architecture which we could call the main "living" room. The "low sofas" (*sofa* is also a Turkish term) may be related to the benches found around ancient Greek symposia rooms, but they also recall interior arrangements of the Ottoman house; the "multicolored glass" as well as the particular rituals to welcome guests—coffee, sweets and hookah—are certainly related to the Ottoman past. And an image found in Bernard Rudofsky's *Prodigious Builders*, 1977, showing a pre-Independence interior (not shown in textbooks of Greek architecture, while exterior views by the same engraver, CM Stackelberg, are common), illustrates Kambouroglou's point: the idea of an Oriental lifestyle was an important factor that shaped the inside of these houses.

Stackelberg's engraving reinforces the Oriental nature of everyday life in Konstantinidis's Old Athenian Houses, which Konstantinidis neglected to acknowledge. Not having much movable furniture was indeed an Oriental way of inhabiting the interior.

An early nineteenth-century Athenian interior from an engraving by CM Stackelberg, 1831, as it appears in *The Prodigious Builders*, where Rudofsky's own caption reads: "Before their liberation (in the 1820s) and subsequent westernization, the Greeks were devoted to an Oriental lifestyle of scrupulous cleanliness in uncluttered houses. The elevated living room with a continuous dais that served as a divan was out-of-bounds for boots and shoes." Rudofsky adds: "As in Japan, street shoes were not tolerated indoors. Although the neo-Greeks in the picture were diehard Europeans, they had sense enough to see merit in the Turkish oppressors' custom. Yet as soon as the country was liberated and made safe for European civilization, they forgot all about uncalled-for footwear and furniture, gave up their regal bearing, and took to chairs."

Rudofsky pointed out that domesticity under Ottoman rule was not that different in Greece than it was elsewhere in the Ottoman Empire. The engraving shows men clothed in Eastern attire, having removed their shoes and sitting on low-elevated continuous seats around the periphery of the room, which couldn't be more indicative of such an Oriental way of life.[19] Yet the cosmopolitan Austrian's caption to Stackelberg's image is enigmatic, implying that prior to liberation Greeks lived in a more ideal state, since they were apparently cleaner and "less cluttered"—adding yet another layer of foreign misinterpretation.

While he explicitly tackled European neoclassicism and its relationship to modern Greek culture, Konstantinidis preferred to completely overlook the four centuries of Ottoman rule, as if they never existed. He entirely repressed any memories that might have been evident from the Ottoman occupation in the architecture of the "old" Athenian house. Or—to invoke Freud—he fled from them and at the same time silently condemned them.[20] Strikingly, for Konstantinidis the Ottoman occupation did not enter his otherwise thorough research, as if it was completely missing from his consciousness. Anthropologist Michael Herzfeld has broached the issue of the relationship of Greeks to the years of Ottoman occupation in a particularly perceptive way:

> Greeks tend to regard the Turkish elements in their culture as the results of a *kind of original sin* attributable to the Fall of Constantinople, which in turn is analogous to that original Fall from grace to which are attributed all common social ills [...] elements of Turkish culture spoil the purity of every man's Hellenism.[21]

On the other hand, Konstantinidis was not able to see that neoclassical houses had become a local Greek phenomenon through the ongoing processes of assimilation and adaptation. Even though public neoclassical architecture remained "foreign" in its references, domestic architecture in particular had become incorporated into a popular Greek architectural idiom that varied from place to place, carried out by small craftsmen and their informal building processes.

The ways in which Greek culture "took" things from other cultures—Oriental or otherwise—was also part of the colonial experience and was critical in the process of modernizing Greek architecture. Neoclassicism replaced what was there before, what was apparently more indigenously Greek. Yet the irony in this account is that the pre-Independence city was no more "purely" Hellenic than the neoclassical one—in fact, it was quite heavily influenced by Ottoman architecture and lifestyle.

Konstantinidis was unable to see this precedent for the adaptation and assimilation of European neoclassicism. His so-called "old" Athenian house more closely resembled the Turkish house than any other European or classical archetype. However, in modern Greece this conversation remained a taboo for intellectuals and perhaps partly accounts for why neither Konstantinidis nor other Greek scholars of "traditional" architecture have been able to carry out this kind of research more openly.[22]

Karagiozis

One cultural artifact that openly kept its links to its Ottoman past, and may help us understand the conflicts over identity in *The Old Athenian Houses*, was the dramatic shadow theater tradition of Karagiozis. Thought to have originated in China, Karagiozis held sway for centuries in many lands from Manchuria to the Adriatic Sea, and in each country it molded itself to the ideas and manners of the inhabitants. While in Turkey it had a lewd character, "among the Greeks", travel writer Patrick Leigh Fermor informs us, "it took on a lively, witty, parabolic turn".[23] Every play is about the poor, ugly, physically deformed Karagiozis (who has one extremely long arm) and his struggle to keep himself and his family fed and sheltered.

In each performance, by some ruse he fools the ruler into believing he is something he is not: a baker, a pharmacist, a captain, a doctor. He then improvises, blundering his way through the story, claiming each profession for his own until he is caught and punished, though not before he has made fun of the authorities and managed to have a meal or two. As Fermor notes, "ragged, barefoot, illiterate, nimble and versatile, he is a fast, pert and funny talker, his speech is full of comic mistakes. [...] he is a willing thief [but] is often caught".[24]

The Hellenized version of this anti-hero was a constantly hungry and impoverished uneducated Greek who, despite his lowly status and even monstrous appearance, succeeded in tricking and undermining the Ottoman authorities. The mentality of the trickster was enormously appealing to the public as it confronted the reality of living under an authority perceived as foreign—indeed an early shadow puppeteer noted that, unbeknownst to the Ottoman authorities, Karagiozis performances doubled as sites where leaders of the War of Independence would gather and plan their attacks.[25] The main plots were developed in the nineteenth century: this is important because, as

A Karagiozis performance
set within an urban context,
painting by Fotis Rammos.

literary scholar Stathis Gourgouris has noted, "the peak years of Karagiozis theater, when its classical repertory was being created, ie 1830–1920, was the very time when modern Greek culture was being formulated".[26] Later, we will see how this figure helps us understand the power dynamics in the twentieth-century city.

Whereas intellectuals since Independence were actively trying to assemble a "high" modern Greek culture by repressing and even cleansing away the centuries of Ottoman rule, Karagiozis's popular art form was able to address this fundamental schism underlying Greek cultural life in less conflicted ways. The irony of these two very different perceptions of Greek culture was very close to the surface, at least for some observers. Yannis Tsarouchis perceptively contrasted the new "Europeanized" ways of the middle classes with the more authentic or authentically Greek world of Karagiozis: "In [the early twentieth-century neoclassical city] as soon as night fell you would hear a male voice, magical, imposing, as if the voice of the great Pan, full of merciless irony. It was the voice of the Karagiozis puppeteer."[27]

If by day Greek intellectuals were busy trying to construct a new post-Independence life based on European prototypes, by night Karagiozis was wandering the streets reminding them of a past they were still uncomfortable with. It is of course ironic that Karagiozis as an art form was initially imported to Greece from the culture of the oppressor. It worked by appropriating and changing the Ottoman prototypes enough so that Greeks recognized it as their own; it was then used as an instrument to mock and to resist its "original" (Ottoman) culture.

Karagiozis theater articulates some fundamental oppositions in Greek culture that came about as a result of modernization processes—the gap or schism between the culture of East (Ottoman times) and West (modernization processes underway), but also the different ways of thinking between the popular/working class and that of the intellectuals, as well as the differences between the rural and urban worlds. Every play reinforces the idea that the East (Karagiozis's hut, the village, an older way

Karagiozis troupe of main characters, with Karagiozis himself and son on the left near their shack. The opening scene of every Karagiozis popular shadow theater performance shows the Greek hero's hut on the left, and the Ottoman ruler's palace on the right. The hero literally and symbolically travels between the two buildings that represent two separate worlds, as shown in this image. Figures by well-known Karagiozis player Y Haridimos.

A Karaghiozis-troupe with the shack of Karaghiozis on the left and the sarai of the Pasha on the right. By Y. Haridimos.

of doing things) was in essence much closer to the average person's everyday life than that of the West (the palace, official ways and "Europe"). Even Karagiozis's words and familiar objects are full of Turkish terms, so much so that old recordings of the plays are difficult for a contemporary listener to understand. In Karagiozis plays the "East" had become part of indigenous culture, a fact that—as we've seen with Konstantinidis's *The Old Athenian Houses*—was hard for many Greek intellectuals to acknowledge and even harder for them to accept.

Language

We will return to Karagiozis and the mechanisms of mimesis and appropriation in chapter 5 in our discussion of the postwar *polykatoikìa*. For now, let us turn to another crucial manifestation of the opposition between the "high" constructed culture of intellectuals and that of everyday popular art forms: language. The debates over the "proper" Greek language centered around the question of whether to use *katharevousa*—the official post-Independence Greek language constructed in the early nineteenth century, supposedly cleansed of non-Greek elements and therefore closer to ancient Greek—or the spoken language, the demotic, which continued over most of the twentieth century and is still spoken today.[28]

From its inception, the Greek State showed an elite concern that architecture and language were both functional and symbolically correct. The importance of the debate over language—*katharevousa* versus demotic Greek—cannot be overestimated. As literary scholar Karen Van Dyck has commented, language has "a privileged status" in Greek culture "across class barriers":

Ever since the War of Independence in the 1820s, political changes have been

> proposed in terms of linguistic changes. [...] Whether in the formal terms of the language question, or more generally with regard to how language identifies people according to region, class, gender, trade, and so forth, the question of language consumes Greeks in their newspapers and everyday interactions... the power of the word has a claim on the Greek national imagination which provides a striking contrast to the status of language in many other Western countries where linguistic issues are often debated only among small groups of intellectuals.[29]

In fact, there are fascinating parallels between the so-called language question and the ways in which Konstantinidis read *The Old Athenian Houses*. Konstantinidis was not only an ardent demoticist but his insistence to equate the popular Athenian house with "truth" might be compared to another great Greek modernist: the poet, critic, Nobel laureate and immensely influential figure in Greek letters, George Seferis. The way Seferis theorized the demotic, identifying it with "life" and demoticism with a search for "truth", closely parallels Konstantinidis's own thoughts on the superiority of popular/vernacular architecture.[30] For Seferis the demotic was "the living tongue" or the "voice of life", while he acknowledged that for many centuries "the only true poets of the Nation ... [were] the anonymous and illiterate people [*laòs*]".[31]

Like Seferis's famous re-appraisal of the illiterate revolutionary General Makryiannis, who "acquired quality not through dictionaries and grammar manuals... but through the living nature of his race", Konstantinidis wrote:

> For what reason are these old "popular" [Old Athenian] houses Hellenic? Was it because their authors had studied the old "rhythms" or because they sought to bring and understand closer the external formal aspects? Of course not—it is because—even if subconsciously—they held within *themselves* the deeper unity of the most essential tradition of our land [...] And the most simple popular/vernacular house would stand now like another Hagia Sofia or another Erechtheion, that is to mark in its form and type *the same unbroken Hellenic principle*, the same synthetic ability, the same simplicity and quality of a marvelous interior spiritual law.[32]

In performing an aesthetic as well as a selective and ideological reading of these houses, Konstantinidis acted like other great Greek modernists of the so-called Thirties Generation. It was also during the Second World War that Seferis "recovered" the memoirs of the illiterate hero of the War of Independence, General Makryiannis (and later the works of the naïf painter Theophilos), so as to elevate him within what he called "a *Greek* Hellenic" artistic ideal.[33] Like Seferis, who looked upon Makryiannis's "coarse" writings with an almost idolatry respect, Konstantinidis appreciated these stylistically unsophisticated yet "dignified" buildings for their aesthetic content, something he tried to interpret in a contemporary way.

At the same time, much like Seferis's texts from this period (*Dokimes)*, his work betrays a struggle for the construction of both a modern and a Hellenic identity, one that would be powerful enough to endure the impact of an approaching and uncertain period of modernization. As in the debates about the *katharevousa*, architects and other intellectuals deplored neoclassicism's "archaeolatry", or "ancestor worship", which seemed to suggest a kind of colonial mimicry rather than a "true" national architecture. If the language debate asked "what kind of Greek should we speak?", the architecture debate during this period asked "in which style should we build?" —a question that was also at the root of debates elsewhere in Europe, but with very different cultural references.

In her reading of another important earlier demoticist writer and professor of Greek language and literature Yannis Psycharis (1854–1929), Van Dyck has argued that the very process of moving between different forms of Greek and European languages, as Psycharis and other nineteenth-century diaspora Greeks did, is very significant as an example of many "conceptual models for grappling with cultural displacement".[34]

Van Dyck perceptively notes that the structure of *katharevousa* was not only based on ancient Greek but was also "syntactically and semantically modeled on French, German and other European languages". Thus when the French-educated Greek Psycharis tried to read a Greek newspaper in a Constantinople reading room, he experienced to his great dismay the sensation of reading in French:

> If I read a word written in Greek, I thought the same moment that I read it in French. Everything came through in French; the type was Greek, but the words were French, the meaning French. It all came to me in *frangika*. What unpleasant work! I was furious and I grew impatient [...]. The more I continued the more exasperated I became; without wanting it, without doing it on purpose my eyes brought out from under the Greek letters French phrasing, a foreign language![35]

The image of this polyglot trying to come to terms with what was Greek and what was foreign evokes, for me, the ways in which Konstantinidis cast his gaze on the neoclassical house. It seems that for him, too, the neoclassical house stood for a kind of *katharevousa*: appearing to be "Greek"—even classical Greek—but actually constructed by European-educated Greeks based on German and French prototypes. When most people gazed at the neoclassical house they "saw" classical Greece, but Konstantinidis, in their neatly symmetrical facades, read the influence—or, metaphorically speaking, the syntax—of western Europe.

Katharevousa was eventually scrapped after the fall of the military junta in 1974. It has now all but disappeared after almost 150 years of national debate and deliberation.[36] One could see the disappearance of the neoclassical idiom in architecture as a similar process of *katharsis*, an almost necessary step forward toward the modernization of Greek domestic culture.[37] However, intellectuals were unable to recognize this fact during the early years following the Second World War and the Civil War, and this contributed to its demise. The language question was a constant backdrop to debates about architectural culture, which might start to explain why both were so fiercely contested; what was at stake was not simply language nor the formal qualities of Greek architecture, but Greece's national cultural identity during the time of the Cold War. In fact, the very language used to discuss architecture at the time became the site of a similar conflict. Like in many other aspects of Greek culture, architecture too, had a "double" language: that of "the people" and that of the trained "scientists" (*epistimones*). Like in art, theater, literature and other cultural forms, in architecture there was a way to say something in the "popular" or demotic language, and another way to say the same

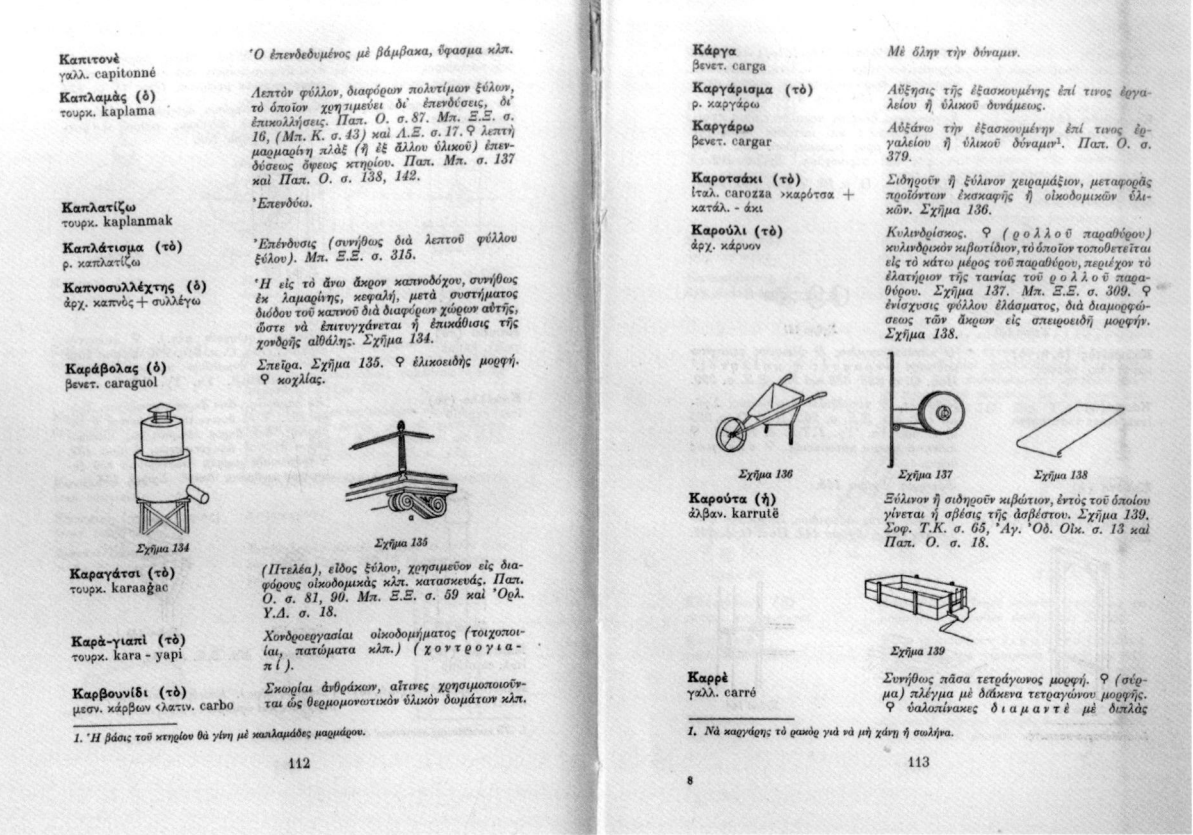

Zisimos Tzartzanos's *About Popular Technical Terms of Building*, updated and republished in 1981 with new terms, images and, importantly, no longer written in *katharevousa* but wholly in demotic Greek. Thus on the left there are still the builder's words and etymology from an older building tradition, and on the right translations in contemporary spoken Greek, or what Peter Mackridge has called "Standard Modern Greek". (See *The Modern Greek language: A Descriptive Analysis of Standard Modern Greek*, Oxford: Oxford University Press, 1985.)

thing in *katharevousa*.

An architect who tried to recover some of the hidden layers of Athenian architectural language in the postwar period was Zisimos Tzartzanos. His PhD dissertation, privately published in book form in 1961, attempted to excavate the history of architectural terms literally and discover their lineage.[38] In *About Popular Technical Terms of Building (Of Large Urban Centers) With a Dictionary of Terms*, Tzartzanos's goal was to trace the ancestry and layers of history in each "common" or "popular" building term. Unlike some other intellectuals of his generation, Tzartzanos's research did not culminate in the idea or claim of an "unbroken continuity" between ancient and modern Greek culture—although he didn't preclude that. Through this archaeological work with the language of architectural terms, Tzartzanos tried to make history more explicit.

By structuring the dictionary as a translation between "popular" or "common" technical or building terms and "scientific" building terms, Tzartzanos indicated not just ancient Greek links to popular terms, but also Turkish ones, as well as those coming from western Europe and elsewhere. His book was intended as a practical manual to ease the transition of recent university graduates into their "everyday" work on the building site.[39] The very fact that Tzartzanos conceived of the construction of this dictionary and why "popular" technical terms had persisted in Greek society was a symptom of a deeply rooted divide towards building. The relatively late onset of architecture as a profession taught in its own right at university level (1918) and not as part of engineering (1897), played a part in the persistence of a "double" language of construction. More than that, the split between a high and low building language represented the actual differences between a much older way of doing things that was contingent, as Tzartzanos discussed in his introduction, on the language of itinerant builders and master craftsmen, yet another legacy of the long Ottoman occupation.

Tzartzanos's book starts to articulate and to confront these oppositions—even schisms—in Greek society, between "low" and "high", "informal" and "formal" or "official" by his attention to the "popular" and "scientific" approaches to building. At the same time, by tracing the origins of each term carefully, Tzartzanos opened them up, expanding their claims of cultural continuity. Rather than having two worlds, "East" and "West", "traditional" and "modern", Tzartzanos showed us the multiple origins of building tools and techniques through his linguistic research.[40] He showed that neither was more completely or truly "Greek" than the other. Instead they all co-existed, like in the Greek language (demotic and *katharevousa*), Greek theater, (Karagiozis shadow theater and Western theater), art (popular/naïf art and Western-style painting) and so many other aspects of modern Greek culture.

In his dictionary, Tzartzanos provides equivalences for each term—as if once these were settled, all conflict between opposing sides of Greek culture might finally be resolved. But his efforts were destined to remain marginal. Like in the debates about language, the debates about architectural culture were never really settled, but rather were gradually forgotten. The attempt to create a national modern Greek language and culture with direct ties to the ancients could not be reconciled with the popular cultural forms and their characteristic resistance to authority, continuities with village ways, and informal or non-professional activities. Yet this everyday popular culture was somehow less conflicted than that of the intellectuals. This helps us see why for them it was possible to somehow sweep away a whole period of modern Greek architectural life—the neoclassical house—in order to replace it with modernist prototypes. The intellectuals were implicated in this (as Tsarouchis has suggested), but their influence or effect was really very minor.

1   Konstantinidis's very first book published privately was Dyo "Choria" ap' ti Mykono (Two "Villages" from Mykonos), in 1947. Some of his other books include Toicheia Autognosias—Gia mian alethine architektoniki (Elements for Self-Knowledge—Towards a True Architecture), 1975; Meletes kai Kaskeues (Projects and Buildings), 1981; Gia tin Architektoniki: Dimosieumata 1940–1982 (About Architecture: Publications 1940–1982), 1987; Ta Prolegomena (Forwards from Forthcoming Books), 1989; I Architektoniki tis Architektonikis: Imerologiaka simeiomata 1937–1990 (The Architecture of Architecture: A Journal 1937–1990), 1992; Ta Theoktista (Godbuilt), 1993.

2   Von Humboldt, Wilhelm, Geschichte des Verfalls und Unterganges der griechischen Freistaaten, 1807, cited in Stathis Gourgouris, Dream Nation: Enlightenment, Colonization and the Institution of Modern Greece, Stanford, CA: Stanford University Press, 1996, p 123.

3   The rest of this paragraph is also very revealing: "we can speak of two moments in Philhellenism […] whose inherent antithesis will eventually display overtly the 'anti-Hellenic' essence of its discourse: First, […] a Philhellenism of ancient traces, which seeks and enjoys its intoxication amidst ruins and legends—this constitutes Philhellenism's explicit utterance. Second, […] a Philhellenism of a contemporary resurrection of ancient traces, if you will. Byron exemplifies this second site, which is inextricably interwoven with the Oriental. In both cases […] we have to do with 'dead Greeks'." Gourgouris, Dream Nation, p 139. See also chapter 4, "The Punishment of Philhellenism", pp 122–154.

4   About this project, architectural historian Barry Bergdoll writes: "The ancient monuments were to be relandscaped with gardens, including a great sunken hippodrome, drawn from Schinkel's reading of Pliny, that served as a link between the picturesque order of the ancient Acropolis and the new propylaeum entry to the villa-palace." Karl Friedrich Schinkel: An Architecture for Prussia, New York: Rizzoli, 1994, p 217.

5   As Konstantinidis suggested, the ideological relationship between German neoclassicism and Greek culture is complex and perhaps still not sufficiently explored. David Watkin and Tilman Mellinghoff have touched upon the strange circuitous path between Greek and German national identities as expressed in architecture in the nineteenth century: "As Ludwig had made Munich the Athens of the nineteenth century, so Otto may be said to have started the process of turning Athens into a second Munich." German Architecture and the Classical Ideal, Cambridge: MIT Press, 1987, p 162.

6   Echoing Adolf Loos in particular, Konstantinidis also wrote "only the temple (house of God) and the tomb have the right to be monuments", The Old Athenian Houses, p 27. In a manner reminiscent of Le Corbusier's writings and drawings, Konstantinidis discussed using contemporary materials—especially glass—to "bring the landscape inside the house to the most hidden corners", The Old Athenian Houses, Athens: Agra Editions, 1950, p 45.

7   Konstantinidis was educated in Germany exactly at that moment when Heimatstil (Paul Schultze-Naumberg, Heinrich Tessenow, et al) was being advanced as the residential format of the Volk as opposed to the Schinkelesque Neo-Grec classicism reserved for the buildings of the State. Some scholars, like Sokratis Georgiadis, have speculated on the extent of Konstantinidis's affinity with some of his Munich professors who were influenced by the Heimatstil and its nationalist overtones although the evidence does not seem conclusive. (From a lecture delivered at the colloquium, "Aris Konstantinidis: The Building and the Land", held at Princeton University, 14 February 1998.)

8   Konstantinidis, The Old Athenian Houses, pp 26 and 21 respectively.

9   Nietzsche, Friedrich, On The Advantage and Disadvantage of History for Life, Peter Preuss trans, Indianapolis, IN: Hackett Publishing Company, Inc, 1980. It is highly possible that Konstantinidis would have had knowledge of or read the original German text during his studies in Germany or later on.

10 Huyssen also noted: "Here memory was always associated with some utopian space and time beyond what Benjamin called the homogeneous empty time of the capitalist present." Huyssen, Andreas, Twilight Memories: Marking Time in a Culture of Amnesia, London: Routledge, 1995, p 6.

11 In Aegina, the wealthier houses lining the main port are built in a neoclassical style as well as many small dwellings in the countryside (some of which appear in Konstantinidis's book). These houses have brightly colored facades rather than the more pastel hues of Athenian houses. In contrast, on the Aegean island of Sifnos there is one settlement built by wealthy diaspora Greeks from Egypt (Artemonas) where the houses utilize neoclassical morphology and plan, but their facades are white like all the other "Cycladic" buildings around them, a decision that surely had little to do with European influence and much to do with how neoclassicism had by then become adapted to and absorbed in the local building culture.

12 See Kostas Biris, "The Athenian House of the Classicist Period" ("To Athinaiko spiti tou klassikismou"), Athenian Studies Journal (Athinaikai Meletaî), vol 1, 1938. In the third volume of this same journal (1940), Biris wrote that "the house of classicist Athens may be thought of as a totally new and local creation" and, similar to Konstantinidis, he pronounced:

"the recreation of Athens coincided with the period of great ancient-worship and of romanticism". Biris, Athenian Studies Journal, vol 3, 1940, p 26. Biris ended this 1940 article by saying that "generally the atmosphere of the interior was cold and melancholic, so much so that one would think that the people of that time built their house only so that they could admire it from the outside rather than live comfortably in the interior", p 26.

13 Tsarouchis, Yannis, Dimitris Pikionis, 1887–1968, Athens: Bastas-Plessas Publications, 1994. Architect Dimitris Pikionis wrote numerous texts addressing what constitutes "popular art" and "popular architecture", however I have found no texts by Pikionis specifically about neoclassicism. See the beautifully produced collection of Pikionis's writings, Keimena (Collected Texts), Athens: Morfotiko Idryma Ethnikis Trapezis, 1985.

14 See for instance, Nikolaos Moutsopoulos's study Ta arhontika tis Siatistas (The Stately Houses of Siatista), Thessaloniki: Aristotle University of Thessaloniki, 1965, pp 83–85, 91–92. For more on the isnafs and the professionalization of the Greek building trades, see chapter 3.

15 Konstantinidis, The Old Athenian Houses, p 40. This is a trope used as an analogy of the whole state of Greek culture/the nation during the Ottoman occupation by intellectuals since the Greek Enlightenment. For instance, see George Seferis's phrase "the awakening of the race" in an essay dating from 1938–1939, Dokimes A, translated as On the Greek Style: Selected Essays in Poetry and Hellenism, Boston, MA: Little Brown and Company, 1966, p 93.

16 Konstantinos Paparrigopoulos (1815–1891) was the first Greek historian to articulate a "unity" or "continuity" from ancient times through Byzantium to the present. In his History of the Hellenic Nation, Paparrigopoulos linked the Hellenism of the Middle Ages to that of classical times. For example, Paparrigopoulos compared the Parthenon to the Hagia Sophia both in content and in the architects' intent. Literary critic Stathis Gourgouris has stressed the reliance of Paparrigopoulos on Humboldt and on the German bildung: "[Paparrigopoulos] in fact saw "the same 'essential continuity' between Germans and Greeks… he figures the Neohellene as German", partly by arguing for an affinity between Greek and German philology as well as between Greek and German ancient tribes. Gourgouris, Dream Nation, pp 254–255.

17 All sorts of courtyard design, varying according to local climate, mores and materials can be found throughout the Mediterranean. This does not necessarily discredit Konstantinidis's attempts to arrive at a more generic, accessible, sustainable

residential modernity. In a later text, Konstantinidis compared the Old Athenian House to other courtyard-type buildings, including domestic architecture from India and China, but conspicuously, not to any domestic types from neighboring Turkey. See "*Dochia zois I to provlima gia mian alithini architektoniki*" ("Vessels for Life or the Problem for A True Architecture"), *Gia tin Architektoniki: Dimosieumata 1940–1982* (*About Architecture: Publications 1940–1982*), Athens: Agra Publications, 1987. The older architect and author Dimitris Pikionis was also very interested in "the East". He too, used this term specifically about the Greeks of Asia Minor or alternatively, India and Japan (the Far East), not that of neighboring Turkey.

18 Note 13 in *The Old Athenian Houses*, p 35, found in Dimitris Kambouroglou, *Ai Athinai pou feugoun* (*Fleeing Athens*), Athens, 1933.

19 This image matches other "traditional Greek" interiors, particularly from northern Greece. A permanent exhibition of reconstructed interiors of the "traditional" northern Greek house at the Benaki Museum in Athens uses original features that look remarkably similar to Stackelberg's engraving.

20 Briefly, this is how Freud explains the mechanisms of repression. See Sigmund Freud, "Repression", 1915, in *General Psychological Theory*, New York: Simon & Schuster, 1991.

21 Herzfeld, Michael, "Within and Without: The Category of 'Female' in the Ethnography of Modern Greece", *Gender and Power in Rural Greece*, Jill Dubisch ed, New Jersey: Princeton University Press, 1986, pp 227–228.

22 This situation has been changing since the late 1990s with more scholarship dedicated to the topic of Greek culture under Ottoman occupation. See for instance Christina Koulouri, "The 'dark' ages of our Ottoman past", *To Vima* newspaper, February 2000, a report on "Historiographic Approaches to the Ottoman Past (nineteenth to twentieth centuries)", a symposium held at Panteion University in Athens, January 2000.

23 Fermor, Patrick Leigh, *Roumeli. Travels in Northern Greece*, London: John Murray Publishers, 2004, p 101.

24 Fermor, *Roumeli. Travels in Northern Greece*, p 102.

25 Mollas, Antonis, *Theatro,* no 10, Athens, reprinted in *Einai pou oneirevomai san ton Karagiozi* (*Because I Dream Like Karagiozis*), project anthology, Athens, 2010.

26 Gourgouris, Stathis, "I Mythoplasia tou Karagiozi kai to Ethniko Asynideito" ("The Mythmaking of Karagiozis and the National Unconscious") *Planodion*, no 7, Summer 1988, p 358.

27 Tsarouchis, Yannis, "Lesson of Truth from the Only Modern Greek Theater" ("*Mathima Alitheias Ap to Mono Neoelliniko Theatro*"), initially published in *Theatro*, Athens, 1963, p 10.

28 Demotic (from *demos*, "the public"); *katharevousa* (from *kathari,* "clean", "purified"). *Katharevousa* was an archaistic language put together by intellectuals such as Adamantios Korais (1748–1833), based upon the Hellenistic *Koine* (common language) of the years immediately before and after the birth of Christ, the same language in which the New Testament was written. According to linguist Peter Mackridge of Oxford University: "what Korais thought he was doing was to start with modern Greek and systematically and progressively 'correct' its features according to the ancient model. This 'correction' was carried out notably in the area of orthography and morphology, with the result that every *form* of a word that was written down was supposed to *look* as if it were a *plausible* ancient Greek form. (The form didn't actually have to be attested in ancient sources.)" Peter Mackridge, correspondence with the author, June 2006.

29 Van Dyck, Karen, *Kassandra and the Censors, Greek Poetry Since 1967,* Ithaca and London: Cornell University Press, 1998, p 14.

30 Seferis was not the originator of this discourse, which was already used a generation earlier by people like Elisaios Gianidis and Alexandros Delmouzos. Here I am comparing Seferis's own formulation of these issues and showing how Konstantinidis borrowed from him. See for example Seferis's passage: "Meanwhile, let us remind the younger generation that if the movement towards the use of the demotic language is for us one of the major events in our national history, this is because, above all, it symbolizes the first step and turning point towards the *truth.*" Seferis, "Dialogue on Poetry: What is Meant by Hellenism?", *On the Greek Style.*

31 Seferis, "Makryiannis", *On the Greek Style*, p 60 and Seferis, "Costis Palamas", *On the Greek Style*, p 217 in the original Greek edition *Dokimes A.*

32 Konstantinidis, *The Old Athenian Houses*, p 46.

33 The "Thirties Generation" or "the Generation of the Thirties", is a (contested) name given to writers and intellectuals like Seferis, Elytis, Ritsos, Sarandaris, Randos, Embirikos but also painters like Ghyka and Tsarouchis, while the only architect usually mentioned in connection to this loosely defined "group" is Dimitris Pikionis, who was one of the publishers of the important cross-disciplinary *The Third Eye* journal during the 1930s. Opposed to the extravagances of lyricism in poetry and literature (such as Karyotakis's work) the "thirties generation" were knowledgeable about the European avant-garde artistic movements of their time; this interest was reflected in their work. Their influence upon Greek letters was extremely powerful—even hegemonic—and in many respects is still felt today.

34 Van Dyck, Karen, "Tracing the Alphabet in Psycharis' Journey", *O Psycharis kai I epoxi tou: Zitimata glwssas, logotexnias kai politismou* (*Psycharis and his Era: Issues of Language, Literature and Culture*), Georgia Farinu ed, Thessaloniki: Institute for Modern Greek Studies, 2005, p 137. Van Dyck tries to complicate any direct analogies between language and nation, insisting instead on the productive aspects of the "diasporic and linguistic disorientation" she reads in Psycharis.

35 Psycharis, Yannis, *To Taxidi Mou* (*My Journey*), Karen Van Dyck trans, "Tracing the Alphabet", pp 144–145.

36 According to Peter Mackridge, *katharevousa* did not exactly disappear completely; rather for him it survives "like a virus" in the contemporary spoken language. Correspondence with the author, June 2006.

37 Unlike *katharevousa,* which remained the language of the elite, by the early twentieth century neoclassical architecture—especially on a domestic scale—had in fact become a local or vernacular Greek expression.

38 Title in Greek: *Peri twn laikwn texnikwn orwn tis oikodomikis (Twn megalwn astikwn kentrwn) Meta lexikou autwn.* Tzartzanos's PhD advisors at the National Polytechnic in Athens were professors Panagiotis Mihelis and Kyprianos Biris.

39 Note that Tzartzanos was the son of important grammarian, student of ancient and modern Greek language, Achilleas. In fact in the first pages of this book there is a dedication, which reads, "in my father's shadow".

40 Tzartzanos's work also elaborates what Van Dyck refers to as the "multilingualism of diglossia" into architectural discourse.

Petros P Poulides,
Orphans under care of
American Near East Relief
exercising at ruins of the
Temple of Jupiter, Athens.
In the background; the
Acropolis, published
between 1921 and 1922.

Chapter 3: Before the Athens Charter
Modernism Travels to Greece

As indicated in the previous chapter, following Independence there was much conflict in everyday life between the lower social classes (*laòs*) and the urbane middle and upper-middle classes. Where the Greek elite tried to emulate Europe in every conceivable way, from clothing to domestic life, and above all through education, for many others this identification was virtually impossible to achieve. As a result, a large part of the population felt alienated from their own civilization and a more autochthonous way of life. The growth of Athens paralleled and also complicated this split.

During the early decades of its life as a modern city, some proclaimed that Athens looked European. Kostas Biris concluded that in a certain moment in the late nineteenth century, Athens' appearance was even "superior" to that of other European cities. For Biris, unlike elsewhere in Europe, Athens' own "neoclassical rhythm" was "infused with spiritualism, grace and tastefulness, reflecting its genuine roots, local conditions and Athenian emotion".[1] In his lively style, Biris also claimed that by the 1920s Athens was a "typical" European city. Writing in 1966, Biris noted that:

> After Independence the new city of Athens did not in any way, not even in its poorest neighborhoods, remind us of the meager cities of the East. It was in all respects a newly built European city, without its medieval heritage, except in some isolated monuments and in the labyrinthine plan of the old city. It lacked organization because it was still a newly born city in a poor country. [...] Many people from all over the country came to Athens. They would stand on city streets and cry their wares: Thessalians chestnuts... yogurt and a very sweet milky drink typical in Turkey [*salepi*] at nights.... Epirots exclusively ran the bakeries and sold bagel-breads in the streets. Arcadians... were newspaper men [...]. Those from the islands worked as technicians and in construction. These island men with their worn clothes, knee breeches, belts, fez, headbands added a paradoxically colorful tone to the buildings' scaffoldings. All barbers were almost exclusively Cephalonians. They would also give guitar, violin and mandolin lessons and would work as nurses/medics: they would undertake to apply dry and wet cupping, leech extractions and small operations.[2]

Like Aris Konstantinidis in 1950—even as he employs a language that describes a much older way of life—Biris, an architect from an educated upper-middle-class family, was unable or unwilling to acknowledge any connection between early-modern-day mid-twentieth-century Athens and its past as part of the Ottoman

Empire. He could not see the Ottoman influences in his very own description, claiming that Athens was immediately, suddenly, quintessentially European. But the issue of Greek modernization with regard to a mythical European cultural identity was far from being resolved as quickly as Biris wanted to believe.

Instead, each segment of the population responded differently to the processes of modernization. In the words of theater scholar Theodoros Chatzipantazis, two distinct and essentially unequal cultures co-existed in Athens in the last decades of the nineteenth century: the "urban-European" and the "popular-eastern Mediterranean". This cultural schism was partially played out through the relatively anarchic way in which the city came to be developed. Chatzipantazis's observations emerged out of his study of Karagiozis plays that expressed many aspects of this enduring cultural divide. Chatzipantazis notes that the "ruling classes" felt very disdainful towards the local, popular "urban-Mediterranean" culture, which Karagiozis represented. He thinks that part of the reason for this discomfort was the popular classes' involvement with the "unwanted" ethos of the eastern Mediterranean, and with it "the suspect ties with many peoples of the Ottoman Empire and the Near East".[3]

Whereas the educated elite—the professional classes—tried to enforce their way of doing things that involved a rational, organized and centrally controlled overview of the city, the lower classes refused to comply with this regulated approach. As elsewhere in Europe, the most primary class distinctions were based on access to higher education. For whereas the upper class was invariably well educated—their children sent either to Europe to study or into the Greek university system, loosely modeled on Germany's—the lower classes were, initially at least, excluded from both options.

Where the upper classes became European-style professionals, the lower classes continued to rely on orally transmitted, craft-based trade education. For Chatzipantazis, these two sides of Greek culture already manifest in the late nineteenth and early twentieth centuries were not only totally independent from one another, but were at times in direct conflict, exactly because "one was not in any natural way the development of the other, and because the transition from the eastern (oral) to the European (written) was made rashly and even randomly by a conscious choice of the ruling classes".[4]

The architectural historian Manos Biris has also shown that "social shifts towards urbanization happened overwhelmingly in an artificial manner"; after all, urban planning was initially introduced by the Bavarian architects and military engineers who accompanied Otto, as well as by the powerful representatives of the educated Greek diaspora.[5] This privileged class, which also included a very small number of local "noblemen", was isolated from the majority of the people. To realize the dynamic between these two sides of Greek culture is an essential step toward understanding the reasons why, for over two centuries, urban planning has failed to work effectively in Greece.

The very discipline of planning was imported directly from the West, and for that reason had always been subject to a certain recalcitrant reception in Greece. On the one hand, planning was welcomed as a heroic projection, evocative of the antique past and thereby contributing to the "re-awakening" of the Greek nation (a concept articulated in the previous chapter). At the same time, planning was equally subject to strong grass-roots resistance. As Eleni Bastéa has shown in her book *The Creation of Modern Athens: Planning the Myth*, from the very outset of its history, Athens had a particularly problematic relationship to planning that was also due to the State's own irregular, contradictory and discontinuous efforts of implementation.

For instance, in the first 14 years of the founding of the modern Greek State, there were 8 consecutive plans for Athens: by Kleanthis and Schaubert, Leo von Klenze, Lieutenant Weiler, architect Stauffert, engineer Hoch, and Gregory Petimezas with surveyor J Beck, whose plans were amended twice more but were not approved by Otto. All this created confusion because no one knew exactly how each plan would— or could—relate or co-exist with the others. In Bastéa's words, "it seems that at times the regulatory plan of Athens was anybody's best guess".[6]

On the one hand, Athenians welcomed formal planning, since to have a rectangular city grid rather than the narrow streets of pre-Independence Athens meant becoming more civilized, more "European". On the other hand, many reacted against the widening of streets because it meant relinquishing their properties, which the State was often unable to compensate them for. Reading press from the time, particularly the popular press, Bastéa shows that during the nineteenth century the subject of urban planning and development was always widely discussed. She reveals a whole range of informal behaviors already in operation in the nineteenth-century city that we might have thought were only characteristic of the postwar period—particularly with regard to a specifically local attitude towards authority and the informal relationship between government and people.

Popular reactions included trying to "reveal or fabricate personal moving stories to secure a planning variance" and "attacking the government with ferocity". This range of behaviors against State-organized plans meant that:

> Many buildings went up without the appropriate permits, some on lots that were reserved for future excavations or designated as public land for squares, parks and civic buildings. The Engineer of the City of Athens Ioannis Genisarles wrote several letters to the Ministry of the Interior, deploring this culture of *lawlessness* [...].[7]

Bastéa documents not only the different ways the public related to authority (the State), but also the State's own difficulties: it often seemed unstable, not wholly authoritative, contradictory, and discontinuous. Since the nineteenth century, land belonged primarily to individuals. This fact alone would be a major contributing factor to the ability of the State to enforce its policies, as many have pointed out over the years.[8] Due to the small size of plots as well as to the generally anarchic conditions prevalent in the newly independent city of Athens, as early as Otto's time most building activity was completed on an individual basis. According to Manos Biris, "in no other European city was there a similar phenomenon to the same extent".[9] More than in any northern European or even southern European country, land was segmented into small-scale private plots. Typical Athenian single- or two-story houses of the nineteenth century were built upon plots that measured between 6 and 10 meters wide, and 12 to 15 meters deep. As we will see in chapter 5, it was from these dimensions that the postwar *polykatoikìa* would emerge.

In addition, whereas construction in other major European cities was already organized and executed by large companies in the nineteenth century, in Athens it continued to stem from private initiatives, organized by small builders and developers.

Partly as a result of the long Ottoman occupation, modernization processes in Greece differed from those in western Europe in many other respects. Industrialization happened late and industry has never played as large a part in the Greek economy as it has in northern Europe. Since there were no large industries and no expanding industrial cities, the idea of social planning, although it did exist, was never a major discourse in the same way that it was in France and in England. The invention of a modern economy that went hand-in-hand with modern planning in northern Europe was formalized and articulated very differently in Greece. Urbanization was defined by polarized, unequal and interdependent relationships between the capital city and the countryside.[10] Unlike northern Europe, there were no long-standing market towns, no regional university centers and no explicit or professionally independent guild system. There was also no well-defined urban architectural tradition—neither public nor private—as there was in nearby Italy, for instance.

The perennial tension between the form and scale of urban planning compared to individual development or informal activity became even more dramatic in the early twentieth century. At that point, not only did private individuals consistently execute their own plans without proper authorization, but also the very government agencies in charge of planning were repeatedly established, abolished and re-constituted again under new guises and with different titles.[11] When the Public Works Agency took over from the military engineers, it had to operate under great political pressure. The uneasiness of official structures related to planning—compounded by the Greek public's defiant relationship to them—was not only reflected in the long and tortuous processes to obtain a building permit, but also in the gratuitous institution and dissolution of agencies charged with overseeing the work. As if in a humorous play, the boundaries between those in power and those who managed to have their way in the end have always been unclear.

The fact that the repeated failure of planning processes has been such a reliant topic of lively discussion among Athenians surely reveals the importance of both planning and architectural considerations in the collective consciousness. We can almost hear the laughter of the common person towards such confusion at the top—indeed there was a great deal of spirited debate in the press about planning and its failures, specifically with regard to Athens, from the nineteenth century onwards.[12]

The generally chaotic state of affairs at the turn of the twentieth century was exacerbated by the fact that the swift expansion of Athens' city limits between 1880 and 1907 was initiated by wealthy private individuals, despite the existence of the planning arm of the Municipality. During those years *geometers* dominated the planning process.[13] Individual developers would approach *geometers* to prepare plans for their clients' land. Biris notes that he met one such person in 1925 "who boasted that he was the planner of large section of Athens [...] among others the plan of Kypseli [a particularly dense, now central urban area] and its extensions".[14]

Not only would *geometers* prepare individual plans, but they would also demarcate roads, without necessarily making provisions as to how they would connect to the rest of the city. By 1900 there were at least 100 private roads: even though this practice was prohibited in 1907, the government kept granting building permits on plots upon some of these roads. In this way the government essentially legitimized their construction, reversing their earlier decision and demonstrating the fluidity of official structures. As a result, even more private roads of poor quality were created in the ensuing years.

During this early period of exceptional growth, not only was it common for individuals to sidestep government officials, but in addition, the land they developed was often outside the province of the City Plan. This land was sold for relatively low prices. When buyers wanted to build they would have to first "legalize" their land by applying political pressure on the appropriate agencies, a process that continued to survive through to the late twentieth century—another indication that despite routinely negative assessments of postwar urbanization, these kinds of phenomena had a longer and more complex history.

In the 1920s, the government of Eleftherios Venizelos (1864–1936) wished to study the "Athens Problem", inaugurating the first official use of what would become an often-used phrase to address this "urban anarchy". In his first term as Prime Minister (1910–1920), Venizelos acted to constitute a committee under the chairmanship of civil engineer Petros Kalligas to restore order to the city's development. The so-called Kalligas Committee, which included prominent architects, was founded in 1919.[15] The Committee's report, published in 1924, was influential in establishing a large expansion of the city to the north and northeast of the Acropolis, a considerable part of which was to be put aside for archaeological excavations. In spite of all its efforts and the large number of proposals that it produced, the Kalligas Committee failed to see its plans through to realization. The report was critical of the many ad-hoc extensions of Athens that were made without any prior thought, resulting in neighborhoods growing side-by-side without proper connections between them, in locations where existing urban infrastructures such as the provision of public utilities—water and electricity, for example—were already strained. In a characteristic political pronouncement Petros Kalligas reported:

> Athens' urban network was not formed according to a pre-designed and unified plan, but instead is composed of many systems in parallel, vertical, and diagonal relationships to each other. It seems that these systems were put in place due to vested interests of existing small settlements [and have remained] even if their spatial relations and positions are at odds.[16]

The Catastrophe

Informal tendencies and attitudes toward building were strengthened by the influx of refugees following the war of 1922 and population exchange with Turkey. In Greece this is referred to as the "Asia Minor Catastrophe". At that time, Athens' population of about 300,000 suddenly almost doubled due to the arrival of 250,000 traumatized and distressed people who had left everything behind.[17] A refugee relief fund was quickly established through both individual donations and government resources to develop unbuilt areas rapidly in the outskirts of Athens with small, simple, timber and masonry houses that were arranged as a series of rooms, one room per family, with common kitchens, bathroom facilities and water fountains. Those who were unable to find a place there had to build shacks for themselves.[18]

In terms of our discussion of the failures of planning and the cultural reasons behind it, it is telling that the government's first efforts to help refugees by building modest

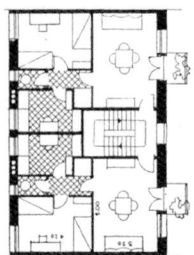

Photograph and typical
plan of refugee housing
on Alexandra's Avenue,
Athens, 1933–1935,
by Kimon Laskaris and
Dimitrios Kyriakos.

shelters were not coordinated with the Municipal Planning Agency. In the following year, 1923, Greece received foreign aid for refugee relief from both England and the US in order to set up the Committee for the Rehabilitation of Refugees.[19] With this new influx of funding, a decade later, the government hired architects to create prototypical housing. Some of this housing, like the example illustrated here, has survived to this day.[20] However these formally interesting, even innovative buildings, influenced by German *Existenzminimum* housing, were only a minor aspect of the effort to house the refugees. Demand for housing continued to be very pressing.

Between 1923 and 1928, vast new areas sprang up on the edges of the existing City Plan, built mostly by "unknown" people. Kostas Biris, then head of planning for the Municipality of Athens, claimed that these people were a new breed of small entrepreneurs craftily mimicking the development initiated by the government for refugees. Under the pretext of a government decree of 1926 to benefit refugees, these businessmen, whether owning small plots of land or working with individual owners at the limits of the City Plan, would cunningly put together their own proposals for a "self-functioning settlement" without submitting their plan to the Ministry of Public Works first.[21] Remarkably, they were typically successful in having their plans approved after the plots had already been divided, and whether or not their developments met the requirements set out by the law. Biris writes that, once approved, these businessmen would then place

Opposite: Refugees
in front of the ruins of
the temple of Theseus,
Athens, 1923.

outrageous advertisements in the daily press, selling what was ostensibly farmland or even mountainous inaccessible land as plots fit for building. Thus in the space of a decade the new areas of Kypriadou, Psychiko, Ilioupoli, Cholargos and Gargitos, the wrongly named Vrilissia, were created. Of these only Psychiko and Ilioupoli had

Refugee self-built housing
in the center of Athens,
probably around Lofos
Nymfon. Photograph
taken in 1956 by
Dimitris Harissiadis.

Typical street grid, refugee area, here showing the neighborhoods of Korydallos, Nikaia, Pireus and Aghios Ioannis Rentis.

known designers (Alexandros Nikoloudis and Aristomenis Valvis respectively).[22] This practice of selling plots on mountainous, inaccessible and not entirely legal areas to build on, such as sensitive seaside areas, would be one of the key features of the postwar urbanism that was already well established during the interwar period. In parallel to this quasi-illegal plot-selling (*oikopedembòrio*), according to Biris there was also a common practice of illegally selling lots at the limits of the existing City Plan or in the zone just beyond it.

By 1930, whole suburbs had been built without any planning on land that was not legally designated for urban development. They were often known by the name of the developers themselves, or by names they devised and announced with a great deal of exaggeration in advertisements in the press, such as "New Switzerland" ("*Nea Elvetia*"). After 1925 these kinds of semi-illegal negotiations only increased, and there was a boom of land exchange and development. As Biris wrote, this building activity continued to such an extent that by 1952,

> it is believed that 43,000 plots, supposedly fit to build, had been sold under illegal conditions outside the allowable City Limits, for between 40 to 100 golden sovereigns each. This meant an extremely high profit [for businessmen]. If they were real plots of land—that is accessed by necessary infrastructure such as streets, light, transportation, water, sanitation services—would be one thing. But at this point the sellers actually received a portion of income *as if* they provided these services. Often the buyers would have to get together and to contribute new funds for these very basic services.[23]

Biris rightly claims that at that point it would have been both "futile and unfair" for the government to try to stop people from buying plots in these new areas, because it had not been as active as it should have been in providing housing for refugees and the working class in general. From his position working for the Municipality of Athens, Biris tried to articulate his anxiety about these developments with a series of articles in the press. Later, in his 1966 book he wrote:

> The founding of these new suburbs or settlements [*synoikismoi*] both urban and at the edges of the city, had very important and very negative consequences for the demographic and urban development of Athens. The capital was enlarged with such a terrible layout that it will probably never be possible for Athens to be properly planned nor will it be possible for the city to undertake enough infrastructural works to support all this expansion.[24]

It was therefore during the late 1920s and early 30s that the confusion or even reversal of power relations between the "small" or "weak" (the crafty businessmen-developers) and the "great" or "strong" (the State) became a firmly rooted aspect of Greek urban cultural life. In fact, to understand this key aspect of urbanization that persisted throughout the postwar period, we need to trace the contested history of the professionalization of architecture in the twentieth century. The ways northern European professional life evolved from the nineteenth to the twentieth centuries are well documented. Much less research has been published on the evolution of southern European professional life—particularly in respect to architecture—and to the impact of this major issue on the processes of modernization and urbanization. Kostas Biris, himself so involved with municipal structures of power, strongly hints at this in his book, but as he was writing in the postwar period, he did not have the benefit of hindsight and comparative studies we have today.

Modern Architecture

Although lessons in architectural composition were part of the engineering curriculum in the School of Civil Engineering of the National Polytechnic School, founded in 1887, there was no specialized School of Architecture until 1918, almost 90 years after Independence.[25] The frenzied building activity of the interwar period was already underway when the first students graduated from the School of Architecture, the first class of architects in Greece, in 1921. The Association of Architects was founded in 1922. The Technical Chamber of Greece, an association of those who qualified as "engineers"—a term spanning surveyors and civil and mechanical engineers as well as architects—was founded in 1923.[26] The Technical Chamber of Greece was to function as an authoritative consultant to the government throughout the interwar years (and to a lesser extent, up to today).

    In the early 1920s there was an explosion of modern architecture in Greece, built both by locally trained architects and others who, as was often the case at the time, trained in Europe, working primarily for the upper and middle classes. The availability of reinforced concrete was key in helping to disseminate the ideas of the modern movement. The first use of reinforced concrete in Greece was as early as 1902 in the construction of two bridges over the Kifissos River in Athens. The first privately owned building that used reinforced concrete was a four-story hotel with street-level commercial space, belonging to Alexandros Afendoulis, built in central Athens, in 1906. The study for this

The first building using reinforced concrete in Athens. The image above shows it during construction with reinforcement rods. The study was completed by Hennebique in Paris, Elias Angelopoulos was the civil engineer in charge of construction; the building belonged to Alexandros Afendoulis. It was a hotel with stores on the ground floor and it still survives today.

Kyriakos Panagiotakos's 1932–1933 school on Liossion Street with *"compliments de Le Corbusier"* inscribed on its wall. This building contained two separate schools sharing a playground, dining room, kitchen and gym. All the classrooms were oriented south or east; there were large accordion doors between them so that larger areas could be created at will. The flat roof was to be used for assemblies or as a play area.

building was made by the office of François Hennebique in Paris (who had patented the first reinforced concrete system in 1892). The Greek civil engineer Elias Angelopoulos supervised its construction.[27] The urgent need for building production after the 1922 refugee crisis meant huge leaps in the production of cement, one of the very few local industries and the main material needed to produce concrete.[28] Reinforced concrete became so easy to produce that by 1925 its use was routine not only for public but also for domestic buildings.[29]

By the time the delegates of the CIAM IV Congress arrived in Athens in August 1933, Greek architects proudly showed them several examples of their own modernist work. Patroklos Karantinos organized the first exhibition of modern Greek architecture at the School of Architecture, in parallel to the CIAM Congress exhibition, prior to the participants' departure to the Aegean islands aboard the *SS Patris II*. The response was enthusiastic: Alberto Sartoris included Stamos Papadakis's single-family house in Glyfada, 1932–1933, in his *Gli Elementi dell'architettura funzionale* of 1935, and Le Corbusier scribbled *"compliments de Le Corbusier"* on the freshly finished white wall of Kyriakos Panagiotakos's elementary school in Liossion Street, 1932–1933.

There was wide acceptance of modernism among the country's architectural elite. Even the most academic of professors, Anastasios Orlandos, gave a sincere welcome to the delegates and even vowed to embrace "the modern spirit" himself.[30] The exhibition of modern architecture from Greece displayed the innovative school building program, one of the most interesting moments in Greek architecture of the interwar period. It was initiated under Prime Minister Venizelos's second term in government, 1928–1935, by his Minister of Education Georgios Papandreou, and continued up until the Second World War despite the Metaxas dictatorship during 1936–1941.[31] By creating a new post of Director of Architecture for the aforementioned school building program, and giving this appointment to the talented architect Nikos Mitsakis in 1930, the Venizelos

Patroklos Karatinos's Kalisperi Street Elementary School, 1932. This reinforced concrete building contained six classrooms facing south with a corridor on the north side. The upper floor was organized around a free plan with movable wooden partitions between rooms. A documentary of the CIAM IV Congress by László Maholy-Nagy shows the delegates visiting this building, strolling on the roof.

House in Glyfada by Stamos Papadakis, that had just been completed around the time of the CIAM IV Congress. As head of the Greek delegation of architects, Papadakis delivered the Congress' opening and closing statements. The delegates went to see the house, and it appears in Maholy-Nagy's documentary of the Congress. Earlier projects by Papadakis were the only examples from Greece included in Alberto Sartoris's *Gli Elementi dell'architettura Razionale*, 1932.

government endorsed modern architecture as a direct expression of State culture. As a result of this program, an estimated 4,000 modernist, reinforced concrete frame schools were built throughout Greece. It also had the effect of familiarizing people all over the country with the formal vocabulary of modern architecture.

The Polykatoikìa

Although a number of multistory public buildings were constructed in Athens during the early 1920s as housing prototypes during the Asia Minor crisis, architects had to campaign to have the *polykatoikìa* become socially acceptable for domestic life. One of the problems confronting the two largest cities in Greece, Athens and Thessaloniki, was that they were too sparsely populated. In 1929, in the professional journal *Erga*, architect Stamos Papadakis wrote, "even the center does not present any density. Buildings are low and do not fulfill even the most basic needs."[32] In the same issue of *Erga*, the Chief Engineer of Thessaloniki, Nikolaos Pappas, argued that multistory buildings "make sense". Pappas reasoned that with multistory housing (*polykatoikìes*), cities will achieve greater density of population, and be potentially better designed, with more green areas.

He claimed that *polykatoikìa* for domestic use makes financial sense for the municipalities since they are "two and a half times" cheaper than the average single-family house. Apparently Pappas preferred *polykatoikìa* housing for yet another reason, which was that the older fabric, in Thessaloniki at least, was too "Turkish". He wrote:

> close to the limits of the old town (that which today we call 'old Thessaloniki') and near the new multistory buildings, there is still a zone of the city which differs completely from the new part built after the fire of 1917. This *destroys its prestige* and nice impression because it is composed by really very old buildings semi-wooden and low, in *an old Turkish rhythm*.[33]

Similarly, the fact that the few prototypical multistory houses were specifically constructed for refugees who were poor and desperate, and perhaps because they were too close to Turkey from a cultural standpoint, made middle-class Athenians regard multistory domestic buildings with suspicion. This discomfort with Turkish influence was rarely stated explicitly of course, but at the same time remained at the core of much repressed feeling about the evolution and development of Greek architecture, as we saw in chapter 2. Aside from issues of identity, it seems that upper-middle-class Greeks were initially skeptical of the *polykatoikìa* because it represented communal life associated with lower social classes and with that, the loss of privacy. In 1944, architect Ioannis Vassiliou was still trying to convince his readers that:

> Life in a *polykatoikìa* makes men more sociable. Living in a tall building is more pleasant. There are ample amenities for household work distances [for daily cleaning] are shorter. The prejudice that when one lives in a *polykatoikìa* apartment one loses one's independence is not correct. Often families who live in the same building have no contact and may not even know each other.[34]

By 1929 there was a new law instating an administrative structure that ensured the future proliferation of the *polykatoikìa*, when the Venizelos government passed the Law of Horizontal Ownership. The law aimed to facilitate urbanization, and in particular, help house the refugees from Asia Minor; it decreed that for the first time people could own individual floors of a building. Scholar Theano Fotiou has pointed out how this was "a calculated political move" on the part of the Venizelos government. According to Fotiou, some of its goals were "to encourage individuals to become involved in housing so as to provide a new field of investment; to increase the density of the capital [that was until then problematically spread out]; and to modernize or 'Europeanize' Athens".[35]

The 1929 law was soon followed by two equally influential legal documents: the introduction of the first General Building Code (also 1929), and a decree about maximum heights in 1934. This decree was voted on at the suggestion of architects, primarily in order to ensure that the modern city would not end up overwhelming or even hiding the Acropolis Hill. The maximum height of buildings in the center of Athens was not to

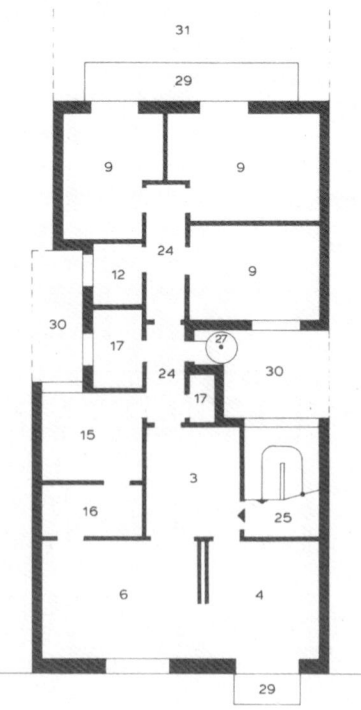

exceed 14 meters.[36]

Architects discussing the *polykatoikìa* in the press and professional journals, like Kyprianos Biris and Kostas Kitsikis, presented it as being an idea coming from northern Europe, showing examples primarily from Germany. Yet when the Greek versions started to be produced, they were totally different. First of all, as already mentioned, the Athenian *polykatoikìa* were built on comparatively tiny urban plots, of the same size as the older neoclassical one- or two-story houses. Continuing a Greek urban tradition dating back to Otto's time, nearly all property—particularly domestic buildings—was privately owned. Unlike northern Europe, there was no standardization of parts and no standard grid of construction; instead, housing construction continued to be largely craft-based. Although there were a few construction companies in operation in Athens, there was nothing like the organized construction industry of Europe, neither in the interwar period nor in the postwar period.[37]

As scholar Manolis Marmaràs has shown in detail, the first interwar *polykatoikìa* buildings belonged to the wealthy urban classes. While both upper and middle classes inhabited the earliest *polykatoikìa* from 1919 to 1924, after 1924 they became exclusively the domain of the upper classes until the onset of war in 1941 after which everything changed.[38] Almost from the beginning, the *polykatoikìa* signified a new way of life and was linked to the elusive idea of Europe, as we can see from some of the French and English terminology used to describe some of the *polykatoikìa* rooms. The apartments initially contained elaborately planned spaces such as "pre-vestibule", "vestibule", "coat room" (*pro-hall, hall, vestiario*), "saloni" (drawing room), "family room" (*kathimerino*), "study" (*grafeio*), "office" (pantry area), "studio" (transliterated in Greek characters from Italian), "boudoir" (transliterated from French), "pendoir" (transliterated from French), "douche" (transliterated from French), "cellar", "maid's room", "ironing-room/linen room", "main stairs", "service stairs", "guest room", etc, indicating the upper-class status of their inhabitants.[39] The typical *polykatoikìa* comprised of one, or at most two, large apartments per floor. A writer from 1957 charting one of the first histories of the *polykatoikìa* noted that the early *polykatoikìa* buildings were equipped with so many individual amenities (an individual entrance, individual stairs, individual laundry facilities in the basement, separate spaces in the terrace for clothes' lines and separate heating facilities) that it was "as if they were single-family houses built on top of one another with the only common factor their foundations".[40]

Examples of early upper-middle-class *polykatoikìa* buildings from the 1920s and 1930s include works by architects Kostas Kitsikis, Kyprianos Biris, Nikolaos Nikolaidis, Vassilios Tsagris, Vassilis Kouremenos, Thoukididis Valentis, Kyriakos Panagiotakos and Renos Koutsouris. These *polykatoikìa* apartments provided a new array of comforts to the Athenian household, particularly central heating and elevators. Reinforced concrete was always used, first for flooring and later for the structural skeleton, which enabled architects to design large window openings. With their elegant facades, interesting rectangular and curved enclosed balconies (*erker*), large, well-designed lobbies, pergolas and plentiful fenestration, these apartment blocks were successful examples of an indigenous modernist Athenian domestic architecture.

In terms of financing these new apartments, a 1920 law that innovated company structures facilitated more organized capital going to building construction, especially from 1925 to 1940. There were a few different ways to build *polykatoikìa* in the

Fokionos Negri Street,
Athens, ca 1965, showing
different *polykatoikìes*
from the 1930s with the
characteristic *erker*,
rounded balconies,
rectangular protrusions
on the facade and timber
pergola on the flat roof.
The image suggests that
the *erker* did not disappear
completely but rather
transformed into the more
rectangular and simplified
semi-outdoor spaces of
the postwar *polykatoikìa*.

interwar period: first, the person who financed the building would own it in its entirety. Secondly, a group of (upper-middle or middle-class) people who planned to live in the new building would pool some capital to fund design and construction. Thirdly, a builder could finance the building entirely in order to sell it, utilizing a system then called the "*fatura*", whereby the future owner would purchase all building materials to prevent the builder and his crews from making a profit on them. This system made crews more independent since they did not have to come up with capital in advance. The owners themselves (typically upper-middle or middle-class professionals) would usually oversee the construction.

This *fatura* system was the precursor of the *antiparochè*, a similar financing system, which thrived in the postwar period, as we will see in the chapters that follow. Thus, according to architect Pavlos Lefas, for the first time in around 1932, the owner of a plot of land would be involved in the process of its production, offering his plot as a business venture and taking parts of the finished product in return.[41]

Architecture's Other Professionals: The Interwar Builders

A combination of a lack of planning and tacit government policy following the Asia Minor Catastrophe brought about new threatening conditions for architecture professionals, motivating their ongoing search for legitimacy. Since there was a great need for shelter, the government, unable to respond alone, was eager to find ways to attract more people in construction. Prime Minister Eleftherios Venizelos began allowing all kinds of tradesmen and contractors, as well as graduates of the so-called "Site Management Schools", new legal rights. In contrast, and as a consequence of this decision, trained architects just graduating from the recently founded school became less instead of more instrumental in shaping the city. The situation only worsened for architects: in 1930 a law passed mandating that for "simple" architectural and building works of up to two stories, one did not need to have the title of "architect" or "engineer" to file for permit, a law that amazingly survived for decades.[42]

Architects and civil engineers who had trained at the university, either in Athens or abroad, fiercely resented this new law. However, perhaps the reason that trained professionals felt so threatened was that there was already a strong tradition of such non-university-trained building professionals in place. Until the early to mid-nineteenth century, the building trade was based on rigorous on-site training, observation and oral instruction. In this tradition, groups of builders were organized in strict hierarchical order under one "master builder" (*prwtomastoras*) who was also responsible for finding work and for negotiating the terms of each building contract. Teams of builders and craftsmen—the *isnafs* or *kompanìes* discussed in chapter 2—would typically convene each spring and travel to all regions of the Ottoman Empire seeking work, returning to their own villages and families for the winter. These Greek builders designed and executed both private and public buildings throughout the Balkans and modern-day Turkey's eastern coast—as far east as Anatolia. The *kompanìes* system survived through the nineteenth century and even up to the beginning of the twentieth.[43] Specific regions of Greece were known for specific building trades; for instance the Epirus region in northwestern Greece was famous for its stonemasons. Young apprentices had a very tough life of long hours and

Middle-class three-story
building from the 1930s,
possibly designed by
a "practical architect",
showing *erker* protrusions
on its facade flanked
by earlier humble
neoclassical buildings on
either side, ca 1956.

not much pay. In contrast, the figure of the master builder inspired fervent respect, as can be seen in folk tales that tell us of his prowess.

Up to the mid-twentieth century, everyday domestic architecture throughout Greece was still produced by the so-called practical architects or "experienced craftsmen", who were in a way the successors of the *kompanìes* system. They relied on practice and experience over academic training or licensure.[44] Architects consistently tried to stop them from participating in the profession, but this proved to be no easy task. The split between those with "scientific" (university) education and those with practical training (oral instruction and local technical school) remained deeply ingrained in all aspects of Greek life—and in building practices in particular, as Tzartzanos's dictionary attests—well into the early 1960s.

In 1917, one year before the founding of the School of Architecture, the government tried to bridge the chasm between the two still-distinct domains—that of the "experienced" (linked to Eastern traditions) and that of the formally educated (to European standards)—by instituting a new School of Site Management (*Scholes Ergodigwn*). This school accepted students who had completed a minimum of two classes of high school education, and aimed to create a new area of expertise, hoping its graduates, the "practical engineers", would assist architects with on-site construction work.

But as we read in the journal of the Technical Chamber of Greece, these new graduates—presumably able to meet the average client's needs more economically—suddenly started replacing, rather than helping, university-trained architects and engineers as the government had planned. Vassilios Tsagris wrote that of the 4,000 building permits issued in 1934, 3,400 (90 percent) came from such "practical engineers". Even though they were instructed to practice in the provinces, as the Technical Chamber of Greece repeatedly countered, in reality they also practiced in cities, particularly in Athens.

Of course this divide between university-trained and practical architects was also a thinly veiled issue of class. Practical electricians, architects and engineers did not have the privilege of university education—especially historically, as there were no architecture schools in Greece prior to 1918 and only the very wealthy could afford to study abroad. As much as the lower classes tried to step into the roles that the educated elite believed rightly theirs, so did the elite mistrust local popular culture. For one thing the craft-based education of these practical builders held, in their eyes, suspect links to an older, pre-Independence way of life.

One of the ways that the intellectuals tried to cope with any aspect of Greek culture with ties to an older way of life was to try to find ways to claim that it too, was rooted in classical Greece. For example, in a series of essays published in 1952, Kostas Biris suggested an ancient Greek ancestry for Karagiozis, linking the cunning anti-hero directly to the Eleusinian Mysteries and Aristophanes's comedy.[45] While there might be some conceptual similarities, the way in which Biris denied Karagiozis any links to an Eastern popular culture—which after all was Karagiozis's immediate predecessor—was also indicative of Biris's desire to "cleanse" the hero's identity.

As we might expect, Biris mistrusted and disliked the practical engineers, blaming them for all ills associated with architecture and planning in the 1920s and 30s. Throughout his book, Biris used the term "intruders" or "interlopers" to refer to those with practical training. They not only improvised at the scale of the city but also at the scale of the architectural object. For Biris, practical architects "improvised *tasteless* decoration" in domestic architecture of the 1920s, "mimicking foreign-educated architects" especially from France. With irony, Biris notes that the neoclassical rhythm gradually turned into "neo-baroque" by utilizing new, cheaply produced, plaster moldings on domestic facades.[46]

Yet today we may look at this conflict as a process of adaptation from "high" architecture to less elite, "everyday" buildings, being worthy of attention in its own right. During the 1830s, neoclassicism was the architectural style that quickly became the most widely emulated; during the 1930s it was modernism. As Panagiotis Tournikiotis has shown, this adaptive process already had a historical precedent. Tournikiotis notes:

> If for the 19th century, we can speak of popularizing the neoclassical style in the simple homes and public buildings of Greece, we can speak in approximately the same terms of popularizing modernism in the middle of the 20th century. Until the 1920s simple houses built by unschooled but experienced engineers and simple contractors in Kypseli or Pagrati had neoclassical elements. After the 1930s they acquired, in almost all the new neighborhoods (Patissia, Kallithea, Chalandri, Glyfada), modern elements: simple cubic shapes, flat surfaces without decoration, parapets, vertical windows, circular windows with simple iron work. [...] Neoclassical folk architecture was transformed into modern folk architecture.[47]

During the 1930s, the two- or three-story buildings in middle-class areas like Kypseli and Pagrati, built of concrete and finished in "*artificièl*", exhibited certain characteristics borrowed and adapted from architect-designed wealthier prototypes. One such formal characteristic was the concrete "pergola" over flat roofs, a feature particularly despised by Kostas Biris. Another, perhaps the most recognizable, was the *erker* (oriel or bay window). Introduced by French town planner Ernest Hébrard during the 1920s, the *erker* was one element that came to be associated with modern architecture by all classes of builders. However, after the Second World War the *erker* started seeming too northern European—specifically, one suspects, too Germanic—and thus became extremely undesirable. Under pressure by influential architects like Kostas Biris and Kostas Kitsikis, the *erker* was duly revised in 1947 on the pretext that people were "abusing" it and extending their properties well over the street.[48]

The elimination of the *erker* began an overall simplification of the typical *polykatoikìa* facade in both architect and non-architect designed buildings. In fact, we may think that an analogous process was happening on the "high" end among the wealthier client base: an architect like Kostas Kitsikis, who was enormously successful and worked for conservative postwar upper-class clients, also consciously worked towards a formal simplification of modernist ideas, presumably for different reasons.

The Second World War, the Axis occupation and subsequent Civil War intensified the confusion of categories in the building trades and gave a firmer hold to the non-architects. In 1941, under the Axis occupation, the "semi-professional" schools were re-named as Schools of Sub-Engineers (*Scholes Ypomixanikwn*). Despite the prefix "sub", these new graduates were somehow suddenly perceived as being closer to real engineers, as the new name tried to suggest. In fact this new school was quickly baptized as "Small Polytechnic" in colloquial language. Its graduates, as of 1930, were now legally allowed to design and build "simple" constructions, defined as one- to two-story buildings in reinforced concrete. Yet, as the Technical Chamber repeatedly insisted already in 1937:

> How can we be sure what exactly "simple" construction and "two stories" means in architecture? What if there is a basement? Then it's already more like semi-three stories. What if there are two basement levels? Then there has to be a proper structural study.[49]

This sense of blurring of boundaries, status reversal and "confusion" (*sygxisi*)—a term found again and again in architects' letters to the journal of the Technical Chamber—was not unique to the architectural profession. Aliki Vaxevanoglou's work shows that similar tensions existed in other fields of professional expertise, even in the highly technical field of electrical engineering in the 1930s. Vaxevanoglou has also pointed out that the figure of the "engineer" was seen both with great admiration and a great deal of resistance or mistrust. She has shown how it was the practical engineers who, because of their "capacity for adjustment", managed to prevail and be more successful professionally than the university-trained professional engineers.[50]

These kinds of confusions in terms of everyday street life were performed in a remarkable Karagiozis plot that further articulates the oppositions between the elite educated professional urban classes and the essentially illiterate, newly urbanized classes of early twentieth-century Athens. In *Karagiozis Grammatikòs*, the devious hero announces himself to be a writer. He sits in a city street and calls out to people who want to send letters to their loved ones back in the village to come to him for assistance. Not knowing how to spell, Karagiozis proceeds to inscribe illegible marks on paper until he is finally discovered and beaten up. Theater scholar Yiannis Kiourtsakis has noted that:

> What is also raised with this scene [in *Karagiozis Grammatikòs*] is the issue of the professed literate and all kinds of pseudo-professionals or semi-professionals of Greek cities taking advantage of the illiterate world of the countryside. This in turn makes us think of the sense of alienation felt by people when modernization invades violently in a traditional society.[51]

This scene also instills some comedy into the issue with which we began this chapter: the contrast between the illiterate world of the village and oral tradition (in fact, in the play, an uncle who doesn't understand the function of writing expects Karagiozis to actually cry as he writes a sad letter for him), and the world of the city with "properly" trained professionals and European ways. Anthropologist Loring Danforth has interpreted Karagiozis's "status reversals" using Mary Douglas's research on laughter and jokes, to claim that there is a correspondence between the structure of the joke and the structure of the social organization in which the joke takes place.[52] Similarly, Patrick Leigh Fermor offers an apt description:

> However absurd and monstrous Karagiozis's behavior we are always on his side. He is deeply likeable, a comic David surrounded by Goliaths. A small man pitched against intolerable odds, he corresponds to something in all of us; a pin thrust again and again into the balloons of vanity and self-importance; he is a perfect manifestation of the passion of the Greeks for mocking themselves

and each other.[53]

This mockery is a signal of a victory for the less educated and less privileged social classes in Greece, who succeeded in building vast urban areas in their own manner, over those bearing university degrees from upper social strata, the professionals, who were pushed aside. This situation, which continued through the early postwar decades, was exposed in a vivid text from the first issue of the Greek *Journal of the Association of Architects* in 1948:

> From those legally practicing the profession of architecture in Greece, only ONE TENTH [his emphasis] are in fact architects—that is people who studied architecture from a young age, who trusted it and dedicated themselves to it due to their emotional and spiritual development and interests. The other NINE TENTHS [again, his emphasis] of those legally practicing architecture are all kinds of intruders [*pareisaktoi*], with no specific training or interest whatsoever other than taking advantage of [this profession] and abusing it. Civil engineers [...], mechanical engineers, surveying engineers, sub-engineers [*ypomixanikoi*], site technicians [*ergodigoi*], draftsmen [*sxediographoi*], geometers [*geometrai*], practical architects [*embeirotexnai*], military officers, and all other persons or classes able via their political standing and votes to terrorize those who are vulnerable, declare themselves 'architects' via a simple ministerial decision.[54]

Far from being totally resolved, there was instead a constant interplay between these different groups in the postwar period, and perhaps some traces of that struggle survive to this day. Architects perceived themselves as the only rightful actors in the field of architecture, but for the majority of people they were perceived as "intruders" and agents of modernization processes vis-à-vis the structures that were in place before. Indeed the government facilitated more confusion by tasking different municipal agencies with planning at different points in time, an unhelpful practice that only seemed to encourage these improvised actions. Moreover, the various city agencies that were at different moments charged with planning, as we will see, did not necessarily cooperate smoothly—in fact they were often openly hostile to each other.

1 Biris, Kostas, *Ai Athinai apo ton 19o–20o aiona* (*Athens: From the 19th to the 20th Centuries*), Athens: Melissa Publications, 1966, p 247.

2 Biris, *Athens: From the 19th to the 20th Centuries*, pp 247–248.

3 Chatzipantazis, Theodoros, *I Eisvoli tou Karagiozi stin Athina tou 1890* (*The Invasion of Karagiozis in 1890s Athens*), Athens: Stigmi Publications, 1984, p 11.

4 Chatzipantazis, *The Invasion of Karagiozis*, p 19.

5 Biris, Manos, *Misos Aionas Athinaikis Architektonikis, 1875–1925* (*Half a Century of Athenian Architecture: 1875–1925*), Athens: TEE publications, 1987, pp 1–2.

6 Bastéa, Eleni, *The Creation of Modern Athens: Planning the Myth,* Cambridge: Cambridge University Press, 1999, p 111.

7 Bastéa, *The Creation of Modern Athens*, p 133.

8 Both Kostas Biris and later Doxiadis (in his 1961 lecture and booklet *Our Capital and its Future)* urged the State to take hold of greater sections of urban land so that it could manage it better.

9 Biris, *Half a Century of Athenian Architecture*, p 17.

10 For a thorough analysis of the relationship between the Greek city and countryside during the Ottoman period, see Dimitris Oikonomou, "*I poli kai oi sxeseis polis-upaithrou kata tin periodo tis tourkokratias*" ("The City and the Relationships between City-Countryside during the Ottoman Period"), *The Greek Review of Social Research,* no 60, 1986, pp 110–145.

11 Even a very brief look at the government agencies in charge of planning, illustrates the point of "confusion" at the top. Beginning in 1914, the first "Sector of Public Works" belonged to the Ministry of Transportation. By 1919 there was an individual committee for the planning of Athens (Kalligas Committee). In 1925 it was reconstituted as the "Agency for City Planning for the City of Athens", abolished in 1926 with the Pangalos junta. By 1934 there was a "Highest Urban Planning Committee", by 1936 an "Administration of the Capital", by 1937 a "Highest Planning Organization for the Capital". Then came war and occupation and the abolition of the Highest Planning Organization for the Capital. In 1944 the Ministry of Housing and Reconstruction was founded. In 1951 this Ministry was abolished. In 1954 the planning agencies moved into the Ministries of Transportation and Public Works. In 1961 these two ministries split up. In 1980 the Ministry of Planning and Environment was formed but "national planning" remained in the Ministry of Coordination. In 1985 the Ministry of Public Works and Ministry of Planning merged into the Ministry of Environment, Planning and Public Works (YPEXODE), and so on. This list is taken from "Public Agencies Responsible for Urban Planning", compiled by Giorgos Sarigiannis, published at "Planning in Greece 1949–1974", Second Conference of the Greek Society for Urban History and Planning, *Postwar Greek Planning Between Theory and Chance*, Volos: University of Thessaly Press, 2000.

12 Bastéa has highlighted the role of the press in the perception of planning practices in nineteenth-century Greece. Mihalis Lefatzis explores how planning was reported in the daily press in the twentieth century. See "Urban Planning in Greece Through Athenian Press 1944–1974", Second Conference of the Greek Society for Urban History and Planning, Postwar Greek Planning Between Theory and Chance, Volos: University of Thessaly Press, 2000.

13 *Geometers* would be close in expertise to today's surveyors. They studied in the Space-Measuring Section (*Tmima Chorometrias*) of the Old Polytechnic. It is possible that Italians introduced this term to Greece, as it is still used in present-day Italy.

14 Biris, Manos, *Half a Century of Athenian Architecture: 1875–1925*, p 274. Dimitris Philippidis estimates that geometers were around since at least 1835. *Neoelliniki Architektoniki* (*Modern Greek Architecture*), Athens: Melissa Publications, 1984, p 413.

15 Architect Kostas Kitsikis, who had studied in Berlin, graduating in 1914, was one prominent member of this committee.

16 From the Committee Report, 1924, as quoted in Pavlos Lefas, *Athina. Mia Proteuousa tis Europis* (*Athens: A European Capital. A Brief History of its Development from becoming a Capital City to Our Day*), Athens, 1985, p 92.

17 Pavlos Lefas notes one positive aspect of the Asia Minor refugee crisis, writing that for the first time in its modern history, in the early 1920s Athens was once again the center of the whole Hellenic world, from Constantinople and Smyrna to Ephesus and to the Black Sea. See Lefas, *Athens: A European Capital*, p 103.

18 At times these shacks sprang up in central locations where people lived in particularly bleak conditions (Ilissos and Lofos Nymfon, for example, two neighborhoods which were demolished in the postwar period).

19 Apostolos Doxiadis, father of architect Constantinos Doxiadis, was a pediatrician, dedicated to working with refugee children. He eventually became Minister of Social Welfare.

20 This particular example, in great need of repair, has been under the threat of demolition since 2004.

21 Biris, *Athens: From the 19th to the 20th Centuries*, pp 286–287.

22 Biris, *Athens: From the 19th to the 20th Centuries*, pp 286–287. Psychiko was one of Greece's earliest upper-class suburbs, inspired by Ebenezer Howard's "garden city" ideas. Philithei, another wealthy suburb, was founded in 1932. Papadakis, Stamos, "O Synoikismous 'Neas Alexandreias' kai I edafiki oikonomia twn Athinwn" ("The Settlement of 'New Alexandreia' and the Land Economy of Athens"), *Technika Chronika*, Athens, 1 April 1933, collection of the Library of the Technical Chamber of Greece, Athens, pp 361–364.

23 Biris, *Athens: From the 19th to the 20th Centuries*, pp 293–294.

24 Biris, *Athens: From the 19th to the 20th Centuries*, p 287.

25 The origins of the School of Engineering of the National Polytechnic School were both in engineering and in a "School of the Technical Arts" (*Scholeion twn Technwn*) founded in 1836. Kostas Biris wrote the first history of the school, *Istoria tou Ethnikou Metsoviou Polytechniou* (*A History of the National Polytechnic School*), Athens: NTUA, 1957.

26 In a 1949 article in the respected national paper *Kathimerini*, architect Kostas Kitsikis reported this situation with enormous frustration, typical of how architects felt at the time: "who is an 'architect' versus an 'engineer', an 'embeirotechnis', a 'site manager' [*ergodigos*], or a mastro-Kostas [a simple builder], what are the differences between them?... There are about 3,000 engineers with an enormous number of possibilities to find work, but who instead take over the work of some 400 trained architects. The Technical Chamber of Greece favors the engineers and represses the rights of architects!" *Kathimerini,* 19 July 1949, ELIA–MIET Archives.

27 See *Archimidis* magazine, no 11, March 1907, ELIA–MIET Archives.

28 The first Greek cement factories started operating in 1902; they appeared in western Europe as early as 1830, and in the US in 1870. By the postwar period, cement was one of the major national export products: between 1938–1952 the increase in production in Greece was 78 percent, compared to 55 percent in western Europe. Figures from *"I Elliniki Viomixania tsimentwn"* ("Greek Cement Industry") published in *Technika Chronika*, Athens, 1 March 1953, collection of the Library of the Technical Chamber of Greece, Athens.

29 Iron for reinforcement was imported from Belgium and Germany, as were timber for formwork and ceramics for domestic fixtures from elsewhere in Europe.

30 "*To IV Diethnes Synedrion Neoteras Architektonikis—I organiki polis*" ("The IV International Congress of Modern Architecture: The Organic City"), *Technika Chronika*, Athens, 15 October–5 November 1933, collection of the Library of the Technical Chamber of Greece, Athens.

31 For more on the school building program see Andreas Giacumacatos and Ezio Godoli, *L'Architettura delle Scuole e il Razionalismo in Grecia*, Florence: Modulo, 1985.

32 Papadakis, "The Settlement of 'New Alexandreia'...", p 361.

33 From "*I Euthini Astiki Stegi kai to Sxedion tis Polews en Thessaloniki*" ("Inexpensive Urban Housing and the Plan of Thessaloniki"), *Erga*, year IV, vol 95, 15 May 1929, p 691.

34 Vassiliou, Ioannis, *I Laiki Katoikia. Koinonikes Technikes kai oikonomikes apopseis—I laiki katoikia se diafores xenes chores kai stin Ellada* (*Popular/Low-Income Housing: Social, Technical and Economic Views. Popular/Low Income Housing in Various Foreign Countries and in Greece*), Athens, 1944, p 125.

35 Fotiou, Theano, "*Architectonika protypa stin sygxroni Athina. I periptwsi tis astikis polykatoikìas, I morphologia tis polis*" ("Architectural prototypes in contemporary Athens. The case of the urban *polykatoikìa*"), *I Neoelliniki Poli* (*The Neohellenic City*), Guy Bourgel ed, Athens: Exandas Press, 1989, pp 80–85.

36 In 1919 the tallest building was to be no more than 22 meters; in 1922 the legal height went up to 26 meters. Lefas, *Athens: A European Capital*, p 94.

37 Building technology remained extremely basic throughout the early postwar decades, a theme I explore more below. The very concept of standardization of construction does not appear anywhere in this period. Notable exceptions are the few architect-designed, state-funded housing in the postwar period, such as Aris Konstantinidis's work with *Organismos Ergatikis Katoikias* (*Organization for Workers' Housing*) from 1955–1957. In these reinforced concrete skeleton buildings, such as Nea Filadelfeia, 1955, Agiou Iwanni Renti, 1956, and Heraklion in Crete, 1957, Konstantinidis organized both plans and elevations around a recognizable grid. The concept of standardization in the sense of an improvement to building technology also appears in the work of other postwar architects, particularly in Takis Zenetos, 1926–1977.

38 These chronological categories are defined by Marmaràs according to social classes of inhabitants. See Manolis Marmaràs, *I Astiki Polykatoikìa tis Mesopolemikis Athinas: I Archi tis entatikes ekmetalleusis tou astikou edafous* (*The Urban Polykatoikìa of Interwar Athens: The Beginnings of the Intensive Development of Urban Space*), Athens: Politistiko Technologiko Idryma ETBA, 1991, p 190.

39 Detailed list of spaces from Marmaràs, *The Urban Polykatoikìa of Interwar Athens*, p 253.

40 Kitsikis, Kostas, *Leukoma Peninta Chronon* (*Compilation of Fifty Years Work*), Athens. Both Kitsikis and Biris claimed credit for the term *polykatoikìa*. See Thucydides Stamatiadis, "*I istoria tis polykatoikìas stas Athinas*","The History of the *Polykatoikìa* in Athens", *Architektoniki*, no 3, May–June 1957.

41 For more information see Lefas, *Athens: A European Capital*, p 164.

42 See the law 19304663 of 7.5.1930 Article 7, in Philippidis, *Modern Greek Architecture*, p 413.

43 According to Philippidis the *isnafs* disappear completely at the beginning of the twentieth century. See Philippidis, *Modern Greek Architecture*, p 411.

44 They were called *embeirotechnai*, from *embeiria* (experience) and *techne* (art and/or craft).

45 Biris, Kostas, "Karagiozis—The Greek Popular Theater", *Nea Estia* journal, vol 52, issue 600–609, July–November 1952. Biris wrote about ten articles on this topic that he later published as a book. Theodoros Chatzipantazis has written about Biris's work: "With etymological acrobatics, [Biris] then armed the two central heroes, Karagiozis and Hatziavatis, with a very respectable Byzantine ancestry. In this way this Eastern popular art not only ceased to be an obstacle to the establishment of a new non-eastern cultural identity of the Greek urban bourgeois class, but it also contributed positively to its foundation". Chatzipantazis, *The Invasion of Karagiozis*, p 15.

46 "There were suddenly a multitude of plaster workshops preparing and installing what they would call *pastes* both in interiors and the exteriors of buildings. The prototypes, if not copied from architects' works of that time, were created by cold outright and tasteless improvisation." Biris, *Athens: From the 19th to the 20th Centuries*, p 289.

47 Tournikiotis, Panagiotis, "Modernism and Modernization in Greek Inter-War Architecture" in *Urban Housing of the 30s. Modern Architecture in Pre-War Athens*, Dimitris Philippidis ed, Athens: Nereus Editions, 1998, pp 33–34.

48 Elias Constantopoulos claims that this "revision" took place in 1937. "From City-Dwelling to Multi-Dwelling", *20th-Century Architecture: Greece*, Wilfried Wang and Savas Condaratos eds, London: Prestel Publications, 1999, p 81.

49 Letter from the Technical Chamber to the General Dieuthynsis of the Ministries of Transportation and Public Works, 27 March 1937. From the TEE (Technical Chamber of Greece) archives, Athens.

50 Vaxevanoglou, Aliki, *I Koinwniki ypodoxi tis kainotomias. To paradeigma tou exilektrismou stin Ellada tou Mesopolemou* (*The Social Reception of Newness: The Example of Electrification in Interwar Greece*), Athens: Kentro Neoellinikwn Ereunwn, Ethnikou Idrymatos Ereunwn (Center of Neohellenic Research, National Institute of Research), 1996, pp 98–99.

51 Moreover, Yiannis Kiourtsakis writes: "Such a scene is reenacted in countless variations on the stage of our everyday lives". *To provlima tis paradosis* (*The Problem of Tradition*), Athens: Nefeli, 2003, pp 13–16.

52 Danforth, Loring, "Humour and Status Reversal in Greek Shadow Theatre", *Journal of Byzantine and Modern Greek Studies*, vol 2, January 1976, p 110.

53 Fermor, Patrick Leigh, *Roumeli. Travels in Northern Greece*, London: John Murray Publishers, 2004, p 102.

54 Siagas, Angelos, *O Architekton* (*The Architect*) no 1, 1948, p 3. Published by the *Journal of the Association of Architects with Degrees from Higher Institutions SADAS* (*Deltion Syllogou Architektonwn Diplwmatouxwn Anwtatwn Scholwn*).

German soldiers on the
Acropolis, 1941.

Chapter 4: War and Resistance

Far from being a dark and empty hole in the history of architecture in the twentieth century, the war was in fact a complex process of transformation, involving all the components of architecture in its total mobilization.[1]

During the decade of the 1940s, Greece found itself almost wholly at war: the Balkan Campaign of the Second World War began with the invasion of Greece by Mussolini in October 1940, followed by the Axis occupation (April 1941–April 1944). The Germans left Athens on 12 October 1944. British troops, who had played a key role fighting alongside the Greek Resistance against the Germans, arrived on 18 October to help install a provisional government under Georgios Papandreou and King George II.[2] The transition from occupation did not go smoothly. There was fierce fighting on the streets of Athens by December 1944. By October 1946 there was outright civil war that lasted until October 1949.

This was undoubtedly one of the most bleak and trying times in modern Greek history. During the Axis occupation Athens was purposefully isolated and left without food and supplies: through the particularly harsh winter of 1942, thousands of people died of hunger. As stated by John Nuveen, who would later become chief of the American "Mission" to Greece, "it is doubtful that any country in Europe, even Germany, suffered as great destruction in relation to its total resources as Greece in the Second World War and the guerrilla war that followed".[3]

In terms of the work and culture of architects during the war, as Jean-Louis Cohen has argued, there is still a lot to discover. According to Cohen, it was exactly at that time that "a dense network of episodes" on both sides of the Atlantic brought about vast technical and organizational advances. His research shows that it is as if the war sped up modernization; each country that was drawn into conflict adapted ideas and advances in its own way, in a subject that has only recently began to be explored. The one such Greek "episode" presented in Cohen's fascinating book accompanying his 2011 exhibition, is that of the work of Constantinos Apostolos Doxiadis (1913–1975).[4] This story, which has been forgotten or marginalized until recently, is a major part of Athenian architecture and cultural legacy that deserves more critical attention.[5]

Ordering: Akatastasìa and Chorotaxìa

To the great distress of the older Kostas Biris who, as we saw in the previous chapter, headed the planning office of the Municipality of Athens, Doxiadis became chief town planning officer for the Greater Athens Area immediately after returning to Greece

Constantinos Doxiadis in uniform on his way to the Albanian Front, 1940, with his wife Emma who served as a nurse during the war.

from his PhD studies in Germany in 1937.[6] He was only 24 years old. His work, and that of his many loyal collaborators, went against the long history of informal building that has been sketched out in the previous chapters. By temperament—and we suspect, reinforced by his northern education—Doxiadis was extremely critical of the state of affairs he found upon his return to Athens. In his numerous writings from that time, Doxiadis used the term "*akatastasìa*", which is most commonly used to describe a disorderly domestic interior, as if to say that the whole country needed tidying up. The use of this term among Doxiadis's otherwise detached "scientific" writing, indicates how jarring, frustrating, even exasperating, the state of affairs was in his view at the time he began work at his government post. To this end he set out to address the disorder on different levels: from the conceptual to the literal, from reorganizing ministry administration to re-ordering settlements.

On his initiative just before the war, in 1940, the government agreed to include the first housing census as part of the first General National Census. Doxiadis's involvement in this project helped him formulate his now well-known term *ekistics*, the science of human settlements, in the years that followed. Based on detailed questionnaires, his teams examined some 60,000 houses in great detail and produced "large multidimensional tables... that gave a highly interesting, original and very detailed picture of *ekistic* conditions in Greece" before the onset of the Second World War.

In addition to finding that in the countryside, up to a third of the population lived in single-room dwellings, the survey revealed that the housing situation in the greater Athens area was indeed dire:

20% of these houses were without kitchens, 9% without WC, 94% without bathing facilities, 11% had no adequate ventilation, 9% had bad lighting, 11% were totally unhealthy to live in, and 15% were visibly humid. From the total number of houses surveyed, 57% were comprised of only 1 room, whereas in some areas, such as Palaia Kokkinia, the single-room houses reached 71%. [...] The density of people per room was disheartening. From the total number of houses surveyed, 68% had more than 2 people per room. In 37% of houses, there were 3 people per room. In 20% of houses, there were 4 people per room, and in 10% there were 5 people per room.[7]

When Italy attacked Greece in October 1940, Doxiadis went to fight on the Albanian front.[8] Upon returning to Athens as a corporal in the Greek Army and resuming his government post, he undertook several clandestine activities, all of which were designed to help him achieve the sense of order that he sought but was unable to accomplish through official channels. The first initiative we will explore here was a series of weekly semi-underground meetings by the "Circle of Technical Specialists" (*Kyklos Technikwn*). The Circle was comprised of a loose group of architects and other intellectuals, mostly drawn from close associates in his government post. The aim was to start preparing for the postwar by conducting and presenting research on a series of "technical" but also interdisciplinary subjects: architecture, aerial photography, geography, map-making, statistics and language, with an emphasis on settlements. The Circle's findings were compiled in a publication, *Chorotaxìa*, a single copy of which still exists in the archives from 1942.

The term *chorotaxìa* literally means "bringing order [*taxis*] to space [*chòros*]". It embodies an ambiguity that Doxiadis was very fond of, namely the idea of planning at any scale: the terms *chòros* (space), *choriò* (village), and *chòra* (country) are etymologically so close. As his colleague John Papaioannou has shown, the idea for this term originated in his studies in Berlin, where he first became acquainted with the terms *Stadtebau* (city building) and *Raumordnung* and *Landesplanung* (land use, territorial planning), none of which had exact equivalents in Greek. For Papaioannou, *chorotaxìa* "was meant as an exact translation of the German *Raumordnung* with a side glance at *Landesplanung*".[9]

Doxiadis took on such translations as well as the creation of new terms throughout his career—as if accomplishing a linguistic fit might also bring about a successful real-life practice. In fact there appear to be important similarities between Doxiadis's earlier studies in Berlin, the substance of his dissertation and the ways in which he began to articulate the notion of planning during the war. In his dissertation, Doxiadis analyzed how ancient Greek temples were positioned in the landscape so as to set up certain visual relationships with other temples and important sites. In effect, he argued that due to their planning and positioning, these temples commanded a visual mastery of the landscape.

He "read" the positioning of these temples as having what Michel de Certeau would call a "panoptic view" used to "render and transform the uncertainties of history into readable space", a strategy typical of modernity.[10] For Doxiadis, planning would bring about such readable and visually accessible spaces in the cities of the future. It was as if, on one level at least, he wished to introduce a new language for an all-seeing, instructive, order-creating, disciplinary practice. Furthermore, his wish was to bring order to the city through both visual mastery (map-making, geography, aerial photography) and metaphorical mastery—that is to say, he saw planning as a new and precise language that could control and organize data into a coherent homogeneous whole. As he wrote in his introduction to *Chorotaxìa:*

> Planning is a completely new concept that represents a need that arose due to the chaos created on the surface of the earth by the *disorder* [akatastasìa] with which structures have been appearing throughout the capitalist period. This has started to become evident just in the last years and that's why there is yet no single international term for this concept and there is still some *confusion* even by specialists.[11]

In order to advance the concept of planning as a historically grounded discipline, during the Circle meetings Doxiadis expounded on its origins in Europe and argued for the need to adopt similar practices in Greece. He urged a greater study of geography, statistics, and surveying. He saw the aim of planning as being that of "achieving a harmonious union of the geographic landscape with the general economy, human settlements, aiming for a better distribution of population and thus for a better future for that population".[12]

Furthermore, Doxiadis tried to organize the Circle's research on settlements with a clear, panoptic overview. In the pages of *Chorotaxìa* there are reports on the impact of industrialization in England, France and Germany; a discussion of Engels's text "The Housing Question" of 1887, and a presentation of a variety of experimental ideas, such as housing cooperatives and other State-sponsored housing schemes that had been built or theorized throughout Europe, Russia and the United States during the 1920s and 30s.

Doxiadis himself presented a paper to the Circle about housing, "An Introduction to the Research of Popular Housing", contending that the Greek government had never taken up the issue of housing for the poor with adequate resolution.[13] He wrote that the fact that most such housing was built by individuals and not by the State was problematic. Even where the government had been more involved, it worked without an overall program and was not particularly effective. He wrote:

> The meaning of popular housing is colossal. Together with food and clothing, housing is a basic human need. Its quality influences people's health, family life, number of children, productivity, political situation of the tenant vis-à-vis the state. In this sense it escapes the narrow responsibility of the technical expert, and is of interest to the hygienist, the social scientist, the politician. It is a great problem of our country.[14]

He saw great advantages in the technology introduced by modern architects, "freeing architecture from its older types", and he was optimistic about the idea of prototypical housing but concluded that despite all these different possible approaches, there was still no "systematic research" and thus no clear architectural solutions. Documentation of these discussions shows that above all he emphasized architects' social responsibility to produce healthier and more economically viable forms of housing.[15]

Doxiadis thought that architecture and the question of housing ought not to be seen as isolated problems, but as part of larger social and cultural concerns. While the Circle meetings underlined the continuity of an emerging technocratic elite during the interwar period, they also indicate a shared belief in architecture as a cultural artifact, charged with social goals and responsibility. Indeed the relationship of identity to architecture, to models of living and ways of life, were of deep interest to the group of people who gathered to discuss how life could improve in the postwar period. In terms of housing, the Circle pursued two broad avenues of research: one was focused on western Europe and the other on Greek rural popular architecture. The thoroughness of presentations by Circle members is impressive and reminds us of Doxiadis's desire to organize wide-ranging fields of knowledge and to create order.

Some of the figures who participated in this research included Aris Konstantinidis, Angeliki Hatzimihali and John Papaioannou. Konstantinidis urged the collection of as much data as possible, and like in *The Old Athenian Houses,* which his contributions to *Chorotaxìa* anticipate, he spoke against "ancestor-worship" (*progonoplixìa*) and the Greeks' awe of western Europe (*xenolatrìa*), urging architects to try to focus on local, "Mediterranean" values:

> It is only at the moment when we will manage to throw off our shoulders the *horrible weight* [*to apaisio ekeino fortio*] that keeps us bowing and weak, the moment when we will find the courage and strength to raise our heads up high and to rid ourselves of all prejudice, ancient-ancestor-worship and foreign-worship, the moment when we will feel deeply inside ourselves the *Mediterranean* value of our land, that all our deeds and spirit will be able to justly be considered reborn.[16]

The Circle members were keen to explore how "popular" (*laikoí*) people lived, particularly in the countryside. In these studies, as with Konstantinidis's book *The Old Athenian Houses*, we see the difficulty of architects, who were aligned with the elite professional class, trying to understand and relate to the lives of humble people. Often it seems that they ended up idealizing these rather harsh indigenous or autochthonous ways of life, especially during times of war and conflict. For instance, in his contribution to the Circle discussions, Aris Konstantinidis noted that it is in this "architecture without architects" that we might discover "the *eternal* character of *all* architecture, that which is expressed differently in each age but that is in the end its most interesting aspect". Shelter was never created by architects alone; he claimed that "the house itself was also a kind of folklore *created almost by itself,* by people's hands, by simple builders and craftsmen".[17] To make the point, he elaborated on houses in ancient Greece, the Middle Ages, and the whole history of architecture. Citing Adolf Loos, whom we sense was a major influence on his thinking, Konstantinidis wrote that throughout history only palaces, religious buildings and monuments were designed by specialized, educated people. The rest were constructed by simple builders and by—one of his and Doxiadis's favorite terms—master builders (*protomàstores*).

We feel that many architects and intellectuals of the Circle, particularly Aris Konstantinidis, were caught between different worlds: between their own background and their subjects of study. A few years later in a beautiful, thin book called *Dyo "Choria" ap'ti Mykono* (Two "Villages" from Mykonos), Konstantinidis spelled this out, writing:

> We say "popular" architecture and our minds build an almost divine construction. Yet what is the meaning of this word and what justifies its existence? And which of man's works is the work of the people—therefore "popular"—and which one is not? And lastly which part of *ourselves* is popular and which is not?[18]

The top two photographs show images of interiors in rural houses in Thessaly; the one below illustrates a woman finishing the construction of an outdoor cooking area. Georgios Megas presented this material for the first time during the *Chorotaxìa* meetings, 1942. Megas, who wrote in *katharevousa*, noted down all the local terms for building materials, building terms, processes, as well as individual household items and equipment, and compiled a list or dictionary with these terms and their translations—from the language that rural people used to *katharevousa*—that he included in his book, *Thessalikai oikiseis* (*Houses in Thessaly*), 1949.

Ethnographic Flâneurs

The question of "popular" art and architecture was of much concern to the Circle members. In addition to architects, two other major figures were invited to participate, Angeliki Hatzimihali (1895–1965) and Georgios Megas (1893–1976), both "laographers". Rooted in the nineteenth-century tradition, the laographers of the Circle worked as ethnographic *flâneurs*, wandering in the Greek countryside, observing and recording aspects of everyday life in a kind of disengaged, defamiliarized way. What exactly were they gathering?

The Circle's desire to accumulate and classify cultural material needs to be seen within the larger project of certain prewar Greek intellectuals who tried to transcribe rural life—to literally write it down—to assemble as many expressions of local oral culture as possible and make it accessible to all, to save it for posterity. The effort was to turn the oral, ephemeral, informal *akatastasìa*—disorder and confusion—of Greek culture after centuries of foreign rule into something written, formal, orderly and also more permanent. The project was not unlike the idea of collecting intelligence and data, the difference being that these laographers were compiling cultural artifacts: fairy tales, demotic songs, poems, stories as well as the arts and crafts of the *laòs* (people).

Anthropologist Michael Herzfeld has argued that the reason this discipline was not called "ethnography" (*ethnos* denotes "nation" in Greek) was that during the late nineteenth century intellectuals felt that

> in order to justify the creation of the State (*kratos*) in terms of the ideology of philhellenism, it was necessary to show that *ethnos* and *laòs* were the same thing, with the sole difference that the *laòs* did not include the educated elite.[19]

Although laography is still a university discipline today, scholars are often critical of this term, arguing that historically, it exposed an explicit but unspoken ideological project to legitimize the Greek State by finding ways to establish continuities with ancient Greece. Anthropologist Alki Kyriakidou-Nestoros has noted that Greeks are not alone in this. There are strong parallels with other European states founded in the late nineteenth and early twentieth centuries—Germany, Hungary, Finland—that also developed strong folklore traditions when faced with defining their national identity given that they, too, had experienced long foreign occupation.

One of the most prominent laographers was Angeliki Hatzimihali, an upper-middle-class artist who spent much of her life in isolated rural communities living with those she observed and wrote about. From the 1920s to the end of her life, she worked to make everyday ordinary culture and lifeworld visible. She studied the Aegean islands, especially Skyros, as well as the Sarakatsani, a nomadic population now almost totally extinct, with an emphasis on the everyday life of women. Hatzimihali recorded domestic life, covering things like utensils, clothing, woodwork, embroideries, social life and rituals, celebratory dress, wedding beads, dowry items and so on.[20]

Georgios Megas, the other Circle laographer, was a diaspora Greek who, like Doxiadis, was born in Eastern Rumelia in Bulgaria. By the 1920s he was working on settlements and dwellings in northern Greece, and was editor of the Academy of Athens' *Folklore Archive*. His particular interest was in how houses were built, and he

This page: Photographs by Voula Papaioannou. Buildings and inhabitants in Kanalia, Volos, Thessaly, undated. Papaioannou visited the Greek countryside taking images of people and their everyday lives during the late 1940s and 1950s. She observed the harshness of the lives in rural Greece after the war, especially those of women: clothes had to be washed outdoors, there was no electricity, no toilet in the interior of the house, etc. Also note the small child who walks around barefoot.

Opposite: Maria Zagorissiou, settlement at Sella, province of Agios Vasillios, southern Crete, 1945. Zagorissiou was one of the architects working for Doxiadis, charged to bring back information about settlements in southern Crete. Zagorissiou writes that, despite the lack of time, whenever she could she would return to buildings she found interesting and add more details to her "hasty" sketches. We can see her interest in detail and in household objects in these drawings. Aside from buildings and interiors, she also made individual detailed drawings of chairs and other household objects and took photographs of people in these villages.

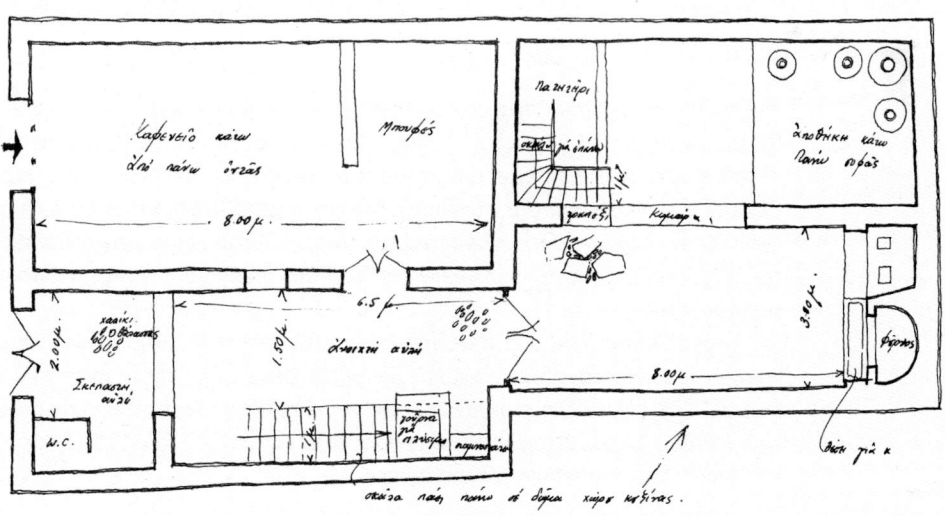

coined the term *laiki oikodomia*, or "popular building science".

In viewing the isolated communities they studied as carriers of "tradition", language, habits and rituals, Hatzimihali and Megas identified *laòs* with a romantic idea of the nation, the creators of a national heritage. Writing much more recently, anthropologist Kyriakidou-Nestoros argues that the claim of unchanging rural life was actually historically dubious in Greece: during the years of Ottoman rule it was the educated elite, particularly the upper tiers of the clergy, who held onto tradition and especially language, refusing any change. Instead, the popular tradition experienced many changes and shifts and constantly adapted to new conditions of life. As proof, Kyriakidou-Nestoros cites spoken demotic Greek, which never stopped developing, in contrast to the much older Greek still used in the Orthodox Church.[21]

Heavily influenced by German Romantic ideology of the nineteenth century—in particular Wilhelm Heinrich Riehl (1823–1897)—Megas considered the harsh everyday lives he studied in the rural north as living monuments, still connected to classical Greece. He thought of these rural people as repositories of some kind of national essence that they held onto through the years of foreign rule. This mentality is amply demonstrated by the following excerpt from a later Ministry publication, prefaced by Doxiadis, where Megas explicitly states that what makes popular rural dwellings so fascinating is that they are both "alive" and at the same time reveal to us what *ancient* Greek domestic architecture would have looked like:

> while ruins of ancient dwellings lie as silent and enigmatic as the remains of the life they sprung from, and mostly show intricate outlines of ancient Greek domestic architecture, modern Greek habitations being *alive and active expressions of popular art*, reveal by their bold shapes the *evolution of actual popular architecture, and thus assist us in our understanding of the ancient shapes*; this is the reason why the investigation of modern dwellings is of even greater importance.[22]

In his two texts from *Chorotaxìa,* "Settlements in Thessaly" and "Aims and Methods for the Research of Popular Building", Megas discussed the aims, methods and goals of the laographer and speculated on their relevance to the Circle's larger questions. Equally interesting for our purposes, Megas regarded architecture as a part of popular civilization (*laikòs politismòs*). He thus treated it the same way other laographers had treated other expressions of everyday life, such as demotic songs, customs, rituals and regional dress.

Megas established and defined the parameters of laographic study as being the "expressions of material and artistic life *of the people* and more generally the expression of creativity of the common people as well as of their technical civilization" (*technikòs politismòs*). He set up a clear framework of exactly what constitutes "popular building", and why a laographer should examine it:

> The laographer is interested in a building in as much as it reflects the abilities not of individuals but of a team of people who are carriers of popular civilization. For the purpose of laographic study a building is not only interesting in terms of its practical or aesthetic virtues—though those are also examined—but in terms of its historical and laographic character.[23]

Aside from these unspoken aims, Megas's work is particularly interesting today because it provides one of the first detailed studies of the material culture of common people in the countryside that includes a great amount of detail about buildings. His "method" for studying everyday building culture and his willingness to study even those buildings that did not seem artful or beautiful but were explicitly "mediocre or even minimal" is relevant to the manner of building that would define the postwar city, large parts of which were similarly built without architects and were accused of being "mediocre" and "banal".

The act of conducting ethnographic research in one's own culture meant that Hatzimihali and Megas worked as if they were scientists collecting data, or *flâneurs* with an eye and ear for local culture and language. There were so many features of everyday life in the countryside that were entirely unfamiliar to urban dwellers that a short dictionary of terms appeared in the back of *Chorotaxìa*, translating the various building components and themes the two laographers had collected into terms that could be more widely understood.

Like Hatzimihali, Megas visited the interiors of rural houses and recorded all kinds of domestic objects, utensils and ways of completing domestic work in great detail (we will return to Hatzimihali's careful work on interiors in chapter 6). Megas considered this research as an important step in the construction of a new postwar civilization. We might also note that a need to return to this kind of study also stemmed from the ongoing project of constructing a national cultural identity; that project, begun during the early years of Independence, would have regained significance at this moment during yet another period of war and foreign occupation.

Beyond communicating cultural information, Megas and Hatzimihali's contributions to the Circle reveal an interest in building a vocabulary of terms, as if to test and to expand the available language. They also evidence a larger modernization program envisioned before the end of the war. Proceedings from Circle meetings suggest that the languages of architecture and planning were still being developed, and the Circle contributed significantly to this effort. It is not by chance that language scholars were invited to participate; Doxiadis kept coining new terms: *chorographìa, chorognosìa,* and *anthropognosìa,* among others. This linguistic work continued in the early postwar period, when Hatzimihali and Megas produced more glossaries, Doxiadis continued constructing terms, and Zisimos Tzartzanos published his incredible dictionary of building terms, translating the "popular" terms of ordinary builders into "scientific" architectural language, as we saw earlier.

Another way we may understand this wartime activity is to consider that the work of modernization was imagined as or equated with linguistic work and struggle. Megas's ethnographic texts had an enormous influence on Doxiadis, who gradually created his own studies of *ekistics* using some of the very same methods and techniques, always starting with detailed analyses of local building culture in all the countries he was to plan and build for in the postwar period.

Scouts, Secrets and The Sacrifices of Greece

Another important activity undertaken by Doxiadis and a close-knit group of architects and other intellectuals during the war was active resistance. Doxiadis was part of a resistance group, Hephaestus, that belonged to the larger group Midas 614, headed by Major Ioannis Tsigantes. Doxiadis played a leading role in Hephaestus, organizing its members, architects and engineers, charging them to record the damages on the country brought about by war. The catalog we will discuss in this section, *The Sacrifices of Greece*, is a record of their clandestine research activities during this period. As London's *Morning Advertiser* newspaper reported in 1945, Doxiadis's direction of some 250 close collaborators in Athens was "perhaps the strangest underground organization in the whole of occupied Europe" during the war.[24] The US magazine *Architectural Forum* wrote that this team constituted a veritable "architects' underground", possibly the only one of its kind in wartime Europe. The team's activities were kept secret: they "kept their eyes and ears open and reported [only to him] what they saw and heard".[25]

The scouts' task was to gather as much information and data as possible regarding damages brought about by war in terms of housing, infrastructure and the general economy, in cities and throughout the countryside. Doxiadis was able to use his government post as a cover for these activities, turning his official position into an organization that provided information both to the Greek Resistance and to the Allies based in the Middle East. Due to these activities and to the vast amount of information they were able to gather, as soon as the war was over, Doxiadis and his teams produced several exhibitions in Greece and elsewhere that showed the effects of war on Greek life and economy. The first was set up in Athens one month after the Germans left, on view from November 1944 to early March 1945. Following the end of the war, Doxiadis traveled with this material to the war crimes exhibition at the Grand Palais in Paris in April 1945, London in May 1945 and lastly to the first UN Conference in San Francisco in the summer of 1945. This exhibition was reassembled with additional material that showed the extent of reconstruction work in 1949 and 1950.[26]

In July 1946, Doxiadis and his government office published the large-format catalog *The Sacrifices of Greece During the Second World War*, based on the material from the exhibitions, in a further effort to convince the Allies for help. He believed that the information would facilitate his work on national planning (*chorotaxìa*). For Doxiadis, only with a proper overview of the exact conditions of life and loss of resources during occupation could aid be adequately directed during reconstruction.

The material gathered by Doxiadis's group during the war was conceived with the idea of publicity in mind so that Greece could appeal to the Allies for help. To this end, *The Sacrifices of Greece* contained short explanatory texts in four languages (Greek, English, French and Russian) and included a staggering amount of data that showed the actual damage to the economy, infrastructure, building stock and human life during the war and Axis occupation with precision. The catalog also included striking visual data; most of this material was prepared in what seemed like a very short time, allowing Greece to be one of the first countries to ask for international aid. This small section from Doxiadis's introduction to the catalog gives a characteristically succinct and moving description of wartime conditions in Greece:

When the Axis struck at Greece, the whole Greek people fought as one man. [...] Then the occupation came. The country continued its struggle. It fought hard for the victory of the democratic camp. It waged a new struggle, the struggle of the home front. This struggle, too, was waged by the whole Greek nation. Men and women, old and young, both in cities and on the mountains, in the factories and in the secret printing presses, carried out sabotage or went on strike. Greek ore was no longer loaded on ships to be carried to the Axis countries and Greece provided neither soldiers nor workers for Germany. Not a single Greek fought the Russians, and not a single one helped in the German 'battle of production'. The supply lines of the Axis were cut. The Germans and Italians and the Bulgarian and Albanian satellites were forced to maintain in Greece considerable military forces. The Greek people, the whole Greek race, the country and the state paid dearly in its fight during the war and during the occupation. And the price was very heavy. Heavier than that of any other country in the world, and beyond the powers of the Greek people and of the state. The aim of this book is to give to the international public opinion a summary picture of the price paid by the Greek people in the defense of the great ideals of freedom and justice, which has so far remained practically unknown.[27]

The catalog was neatly and precisely ordered. It was comprised of 90 different segments, divided into six sections including: "Economic Warfare", "The Destruction of Public Works" and "The Sufferings of the Inhabitants". *The Sacrifices of Greece* revealed the state of the country as a result of war using concrete numerical data. During the war years Greece had lost 15 percent of the population from starvation, disease, executions and a fall in the birth rate. Its railroads were completely dismantled and the enemy took away 92 percent of Greece's railway stock. Two thirds of the merchant marine was

lost, some sunk in the harbors or stolen by the Germans. All but one of the larger Greek harbors were demolished. Farming and industrial production were decimated. The forests were laid to waste, bridges were burned, commercial plants were plundered and the telephone and telegraph services wrecked. The number of cattle fell to 40 percent of the prewar level. 23 percent of all buildings were destroyed, including about 400,000 houses of a prewar total of 1,700,000, and 1,200,000 people or 18 percent of the population became homeless. In some cases, whole villages were burned. Some 1,050 churches and 80 monasteries were destroyed.

The graphic presentation of the material was extraordinary, particularly given wartime conditions and the inevitable shortages of drawing and printing materials. For each of the 90 categories of information there was a unique graphic symbol: to explain losses in agricultural production, for example, there were drawings of cereals, beans, tobacco, cotton, olives, oil, grapes and currants. To describe the reduction of livestock, there were drawings of heads of sheep, goats, pigs and chickens. There were symbols for cars, trains, airplanes and boats to illustrate the losses in both military and civilian infrastructure. There were also symbols of bridges, men, women, old people, babies and homelessness.

It seems that alongside this catalog, Doxiadis tried to produce a separate one that had to do specifically with housing (both rural and urban) but was never fully completed. This one was to be entitled *Proposal for the Reconstruction of Settlements: Tables* and, with the same generous size and format as *The Sacrifices of Greece*, was to include 44 separate sections, with maps and tables showing nationwide information on demographics: "Average Income and Rent", "Settlements Provided with Electric Lighting or Not", "Building Activity 1923–1940 in Number of New Buildings" and so on.

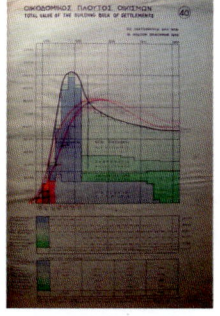

Graph showing the "Total Value of the Building Bulk of Settlements", from an unfinished volume entitled *Proposals for the Reconstruction of Settlements: Tables*. This is a large-format volume of roughly the same dimensions as that of *The Sacrifices of Greece*, which contains maps and working drawings of tables and graphs. Even though in a preliminary or working stage, it is bound with a linen cover and held with metal pins, perhaps indicating that this, too, was to become an official publication.

Only preliminary drawings and handwritten calculations have survived from this catalog. Nevertheless, by looking at these we can discern that Doxiadis and his team had concluded that the State would be unable to bear the expense of the vast new housing construction the country would need in the postwar period.

A Graphic Language: Otto Neurath

The material for Doxiadis's catalogs was not only remarkably rich factually—as data—but also visually, indicating a well-traveled and highly educated team who worked with Doxiadis at the Ministry.[28] It appears that one figure whose intellectual influence on this work is visible though, mysteriously, not explicitly mentioned, was the Austrian sociologist and political economist Otto Neurath (1882–1945). Neurath had been working on developing what he initially called the "Vienna Method of Pictorial Statistics", and later changed to "Isotypes" (International System of Typographic Picture Education). As the founding director of the Museum of Economy and Society in Vienna in 1925, he was driven to investigate how best to communicate social, economic and political information to a wider public. Working with an interdisciplinary team that included the later renowned German artist and graphic designer Gerd Arntz, and the talented Marie Reidemeister (who later married Neurath), Neurath developed a way to codify facts pictorially that is still enormously influential today.[29]

Doxiadis was certainly aware of Neurath's work, since the latter had participated in the 1933 CIAM IV meeting that took place in Athens at the School of Architecture when Doxiadis was a third-year student. Neurath's work on the visual representation of data was shown at the CIAM exhibition in the School of Architecture and was published as a separate article in *Technika Chronika*, the chronicles of Greek architects and engineers—a publication we know Doxiadis followed.[30]

Neurath's text in *Technika Chronika* was fully illustrated. Comparing the graphic system to hieroglyphics, he proposed that this work should be seen as a new visual "language" that would be accompanied in due time by a "new dictionary and illustrated catalog". He explained:

> We have created in Vienna a pedagogic method based upon 'visual presentation'... [so that] with the first glance we can obtain knowledge of main characteristics, with the second the secondary phenomena, and the third the details. If the fourth glance contains more information it means that the image was not satisfactory.[31]

Though the drawings in *The Sacrifices of Greece* did not replicate Neurath's symbols, they were certainly influenced by them, elaborating these same ideas in new ways. If Doxiadis was to use the data to solicit aid for Greece, it had to be well presented and universally readable, accessible to an international public. Some of the key graphic similarities with Neurath's pictorial "method" were the lack of perspective, the strong use of color against stark white or other monochromatic backgrounds and the idea that each two-dimensional symbol was a "unit" that represented a certain quantity of things. For instance, in the diagram explaining "Merchant Marine Losses During the War", each boat represents 10 vessels; in the drawing "Reduction of Beasts of Burden During the Occupation", each animal represents 20,000, and so on.

Neurath's overall philosophy and approach to town planning, which was one of the main areas where he applied his graphic vocabulary, was also a huge influence on Doxiadis. We might surmise that Neurath's belief in the power of the built environment to influence our everyday lives positively was particularly close to Doxiadis's own interests. In his pioneering Museum of Economy and Society, Neurath had created inventories for the achievement of a better standard of living, looking at variables such as clothing, housing, disease, criminality and death. Such quantitative research remained an important part of Doxiadis's own approach to planning throughout his career, starting with *The Sacrifices of Greece*.

Having proper mastery of the facts, Doxiadis believed that he would be able to be in a better position to coordinate, plan and manage the reconstruction effort most efficiently. Neurath understood the importance of logistical organization, particularly in preparation for war, as is evident in his 1939 book *Modern Man in the Making*, a book that Doxiadis might well have come across during his studies in Germany. Neurath's sections on "Mankind and the Preparation for War" and "Silhouettes of War Economy", together with their illustrations, might have directly inspired Doxiadis and his team.

Like Neurath, Doxiadis too shared an interest in understanding the deeper economic and sociological realities of modernity and was keen to explore and analyze architecture's role. In one of the public presentations conducted as part of the traveling postwar exhibition at the University of California, Doxiadis noted that:

> Whether we call it economic and social architecture or general science of settlements, that makes no difference. Let us proceed together. Let us build the new world of the United Nations. Let the architects play their big role.[32]

Doxiadis delivered another emotive yet dignified speech alongside the exhibition accompanying the Greek delegation to the United Nations Conference on International Organization in San Francisco of 1945 that led to the creation of the United Nations Charter. The delegation was there in part to solicit international aid. As a representative of the Greek delegation, in his speech Doxiadis linked the war that had just ended against the Germans to the Greek struggle for independence from the Ottomans:

> We are not asking for pity. Our only objective is understanding. We don't consider that we sacrificed ourselves, but that we offered as much as we could to the war effort. We are not exhibiting our wounds for show but so as to find the best way in which to cure them. We believe that we fought for the freedom of the world. Yet we paid for it dearly especially in terms of our housing. We have been fighting for this freedom since 1821 and we have been paying for it, we who live in the Balkans, more than any other region.[33]

This wartime material, largely forgotten today, seems to have moved and impressed the international press at the time. As *Architectural Forum* noted:

> The delegates in the crowded committee room at San Francisco had blinked at the sheaf of maps and plans which the Greek Delegation brought to the session on Economic and Social Cooperation. It was not hard to see, instead of the careful

This page: "As soon as the occupation began, the Greek people stopped producing as much as possible, so as not to help the Axis powers by providing them with supplies to continue the war. The land under cultivation and its returns by acre were considerably reduced. The squares indicate land under cultivation. The symbols indicate average annual agricultural production in tons."

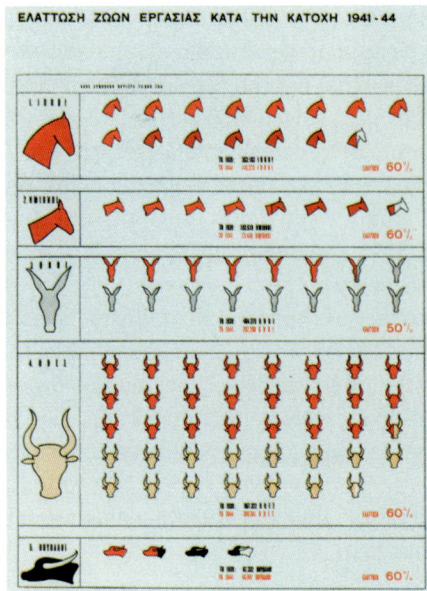

Reduction of Beasts of burden during occupation 1941–1944

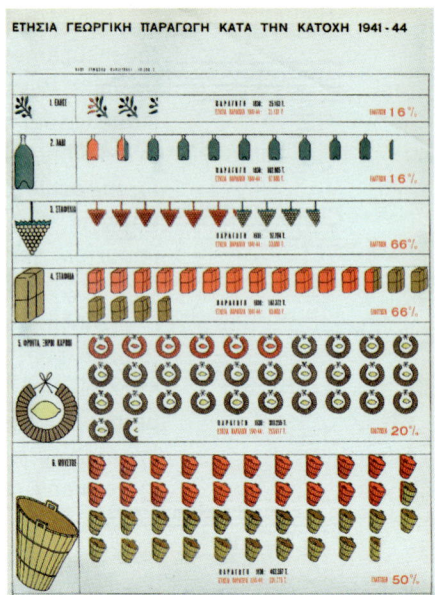

Annual Agricultural Production during occupation 1941–1944.

Opposite: *The Sacrifices of Greece* catalog, "Civil Aviation". The text in this section reads: "Though not extensive, the country's civil aviation served the needs of the country satisfactorily. But the war and occupation have dislocated it completely. Aerodromes, installations, factories, machinery." Losses: 100 percent.

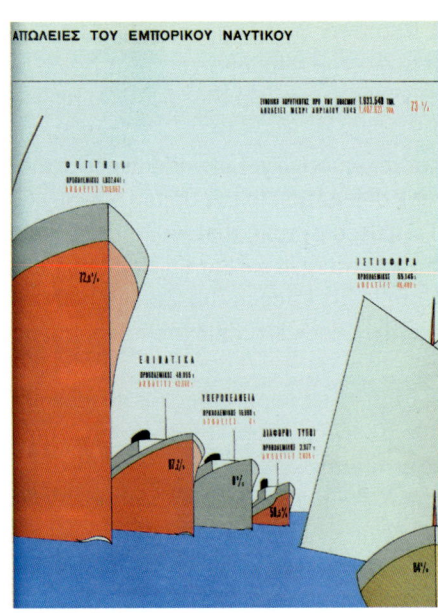

Losses in the Merchant Marine.

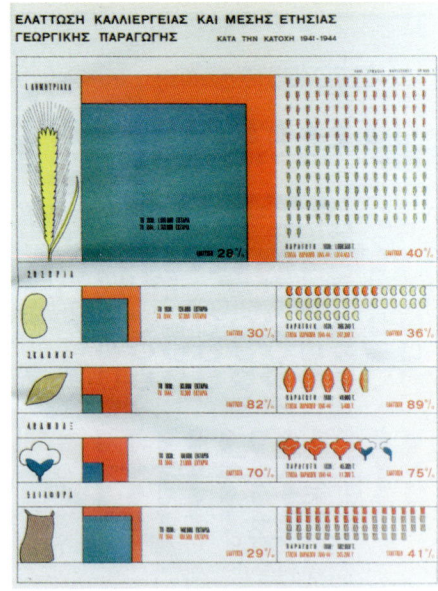

Diminution of Cultivation and of the Average Agricultural Production.

ΠΟΛΙΤΙΚΗ ΑΕΡΟΠΟΡΙΑ

figures, the faces of the 250,000 who had stood in Athens breadlines, the children who died in the streets, the smoldering ruins of a thousand villages.[34]

Reconstruction

Following the end of the war, Doxiadis became director-general of the Ministry for Housing and Reconstruction from 1945 to 1948. He continued to send out scouts to the war-damaged Greek countryside, with newly written detailed instructions on how and what information to collect. He then organized the material into a series of Ministry reports and publications. His model of secretive technical research developed during wartime—highly rational, strictly controlled for purposes of secrecy—resonates with the idea of the archive, a construction that he was clearly fond of. But his objectives were not quite as obvious or agreed upon in the postwar period and his methods were not as readily accepted as he had hoped.

In assessing Doxiadis's work at the Ministry for Housing and Reconstruction we must keep in mind that the majority of foreign aid in the early postwar period actually went to defense: less than a quarter of US aid was given to civilian purposes before the end of the Civil War.[35] If there was more intellectual work and planning than actual realized structures, this was at least in part due to the lack of funds for civilian purposes. In addition, reconstruction work had to take place in the midst of the Civil War. Those working to collect data needed for reconstruction often risked their lives doing so. It appears that the whole effort was tremendously challenging for another reason: there was intense pressure to spend the funds in a timely manner, at the risk of forfeiting the aid, an almost impossible task given the realities—particularly of rural Greece—at that time.[36]

There were two separate journals that regularly updated the public on the work of the Ministry: one was simply called *Reconstruction* (*Anasygrotisi*) and the other *Battle for Survival* (*Agon Epivioseos*).[37] The few remaining issues of these journals evidence the critical work done during Doxiadis's term as a public figure in postwar Greece. For instance, in *Battle for Survival* from 30 March 1949, seven months before the Civil War formally ended, we read about an extraordinary exhibition held in Athens, Greece's Survival Exhibition (*Ekthesis Epivioseos Ellinikou Laou*), which built on the material from the earlier exhibitions organized immediately after the end of the war. Organized by the Ministry of Housing and Reconstruction, this exhibition was conceived as a means to communicate the progress of the work of reconstruction to the Greek people: its goals, achievements and remaining work, which focused heavily on the countryside. It was also clearly geared to show the international community—especially the US—how the aid administered to Greece was being spent. After all, without the Truman Doctrine of 1947, and the large Marshall Plan aid funds that followed (1948–1952), Greece would have had an even more challenging recovery.[38]

The exhibition was extremely well attended: from the King and Queen, religious leaders and members of government, to the thousands of ordinary citizens who lined up patiently in order to see it, it is all the more remarkable that this momentous exhibition is missing from most accounts of Greek architectural history thus far. Recalling the exhibition's impact, Doxiadis appeared hopeful and proud, citing the national poet Dionysios Solomos:

Greece's Survival Exhibition was opened to the public on March 24th [1949]. Since then thousands of people from the capital have visited the exhibition daily. They have seen the exhibits and have learnt of the considerable effort that is being made, and the substantial results that have already been achieved, for the country's recovery. In spite of the ravages caused by the rebellion and in spite of opposition from her enemies Greece is treading steadily along the road to reconstruction. The verse of the country's national poet posted at the entrance of the exhibition will soon become a reality: '*The land the earthquake tore apart was filled at once with flowers.*'[39]

From the few surviving photographs, we can see that a large-format map dominated the space, showing the whole country in outline with notations representing different reconstruction works. The *Battle for Survival* claims that there was an extensive effort made around housing, whether helping to rebuild damaged homes or building anew, a fact that needs to be taken into account in future histories. It is also clear that the majority of housing projects were outside of large cities: only four projects appeared in the Attica region where Athens is located, and only one appeared in the area around the second largest city, Thessaloniki.

Placing an emphasis on rebuilding the countryside, which was particularly devastated during the Civil War, meant that there were fewer funds available for the reconstruction of cities, namely Athens. Yet Athens had not been bombed to the same extent as other European cities, and its housing stock—although inadequate and in need of repairs and expansion—was not in nearly as bad a state as that of the countryside. Instead, for evidence of the very difficult housing conditions of the Greek countryside immediately after the war, we may see the outstanding work of photographers like Dimitris Harissiadis and Voula Papaioannou, who documented both Athens and the countryside, as well as drawings and other data from Doxiadis's "scouts". One of Doxiadis's old scouts, Maria Zagorissiou, published some of her original sketches and photographs of rural Crete and rural Lesbos from this period, which give us a sense of the devastation and ruin.[40]

We can surmise from the material available that Doxiadis's effort toward rebuilding the countryside was in fact calculated as a way to convince people to return to it rather than flock to the city. Doxiadis believed in cities and in urban life, as we know from his private practice and writings later on, but like others in the late 1940s (such as Lewis Mumford in the US), he did not approve of over-populated city centers and increased congestion. Doxiadis thought that the countryside should absorb greater numbers of the population. Later on, in his 1961 paper "Our Capital and its Future", he proposed extensions away from the center and onto the larger Attica basin in the area between Menidi and Tatoi (in the north), accompanied by a perimeter of new roads, including roads that would serve the development of the entire Attica coastline. In fact, some of these roads were realized more than 30 years after his suggestion.[41]

To help prevent a large migration to Athens from the countryside, Doxiadis suggested building semi-temporary and temporary housing immediately, giving precise numbers of what he thought was needed.[42] Without abandoning his earlier, more analytic approach, and outlining a detailed series of problems related to housing caused by the war, Doxiadis proposed that inhabitants of rural areas should start creating nuclei of houses that would then be extended slowly in the future by their own initiative. After

Photograph of members
of the Greek delegation
at the opening of the war
crimes exhibition, May
1945 in San Francisco,
where Doxiadis (far left)
participated in the Charter
session of the United
Nations Organization.

Photograph from an
exhibition on war damages
held at the Grand Palais in
Paris, 1945.

all, this was how people built settlements in the Greek countryside for centuries. There were indications of how these buildings could look and function in drawings, made by a collaborator, the architect Solon Kyriakidis. Indeed, in the *Battle for Survival* from March 1949 we read that "15,000 dwellings have been built [in the countryside], and 57,000 families have been sheltered". In another source from 1955: "up to this point there are 29,000 new houses as well as houses which badly needed repairs, and they expect 28,000 more soon". [43]

Even though most of the reconstruction effort was given to rural housing, there was much more that the Ministry achieved. Many major infrastructural and industrial projects that could only be developed later on were initiated in this critical early postwar period:

> During 1948 agricultural production rose to 77% of the prewar figure, and industrial production to 87%. 1,037 kilometers of roads have been almost completely rebuilt. The harbours of Piraeus, Salonica, and Volos are again in operation. 585 of the 1,050 destroyed bridges have been restored. The Corinth Canal is again open to traffic. Our coastal shipping is now up to 65% of its prewar tonnage, and our deep sea Mercantile Marine is now greater than prewar. Ten civil airports have been repaired and six new ones have been built, and Greek civil aviation has three times as many planes as prewar. [44]

Lastly, an important part of Doxiadis's effort in reconstruction was to modernize ministerial bureaucracy and create a coherent planning policy initiated by the State to address the ongoing confusion between the various agencies in charge. The defeat he suffered in terms of this goal, however, is key in understanding the subsequent urban history of Athens. Doxiadis's belief in a technocratic elite that would be apolitical, and that would be able to improve the quality of life through science, industry and the rethinking of settlements was, as his rivals seemed to believe, perhaps unreasonable to start with. [45]

Doxiadis felt enormously disappointed in not having achieved all his goals at the end of his time in office. Writing his *Ekistic Policy for the Reconstruction of Greece and a Twenty-Year Plan* in 1947, he bitterly noted the disorganized, chaotic actions of different government agencies and ministries and the wasted efforts and funds that resulted. [46] One response might be that there was no structure in place for Doxiadis to implement his plans. There were limited resources, an unstable political situation, and a tradition of bureaucrats who were not only unable to implement, but also stood in the way of, his reforms. In other words, at that point Greek society was simply not ready for the level of planning that Doxiadis envisioned, let alone the kinds of tools he used. The extensive and comprehensive database that would encompass the totality of knowledge about the country, which he proposed in the earliest booklet published by the Ministry, *Ekistic Analysis*, 1946, seemed vertiginously complex—if not impossible—yet Doxiadis undertook the project in a typically self-assured manner. [47]

Doxiadis's wish for order and discipline, strengthened by his appreciation of wartime organization, inspired him to counterplan—that is, to plan for peace during the war. To add another level of irony, the fact that Doxiadis arrived in Greece fresh from his studies in Germany, and given his links with British and US intelligence agencies who trusted him implicitly, might have meant that his approach towards organized research

Battle for Survival, Weekly Bulletin of the Ministry of Coordination, Greek Recovery Programme Coordinating Office (GRPCO), no 71, January 1950. Below the photograph of a street with newly built, small-scale housing, a caption informs us in English that "The Greek housing problem is still acute [...]. The picture shows part of a new settlement in Keratsini, near Pireaus, where 500 families who had been left homeless during the war, have been given shelter."

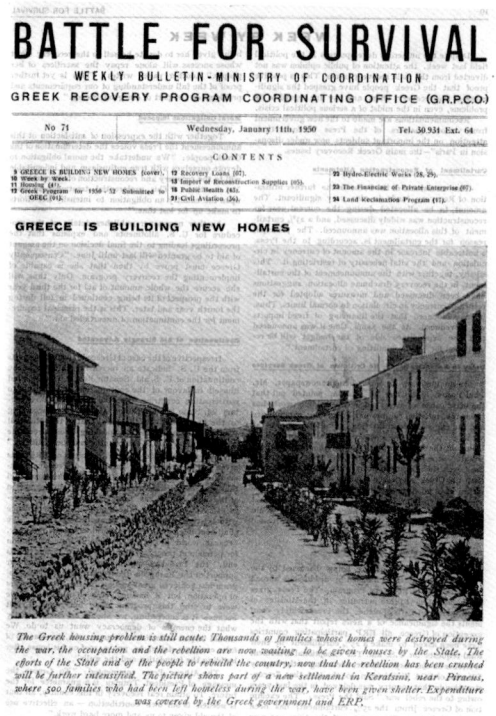

may have not only been misunderstood by his fellow countrymen but also perceived as an alienating imposition from hostile "foreign" powers.

The incompatibility between his way of working and that of his colleagues in the government, as well as the dire conditions at this point, was impossible to overcome. By December 1950, Doxiadis's term in the Ministry was abruptly cut short when Georgios Papandreou, then-Minister of Coordination, who had been a close associate and even a friend of Doxiadis prior to this point, called a special meeting of Parliament. There, rather than dismissing him in person, Papandreou abolished Doxiadis's post altogether. In a rather emotional letter to an American colleague, Louis Brownlow, Doxiadis explained that his dismissal was politically motivated:

> For the past week, due to political action, I have been dismissed from office, after the abolition of the post, and now find myself entirely out of service. [...] the conception of 'Permanent Under-Secretary' no longer exists, since it has been possible for five Deputies and the Minister of Coordination, in a two-hour discussion, to abolish and re-establish the post of the highest permanent civil servant. The first Permanent Under-Secretary for Coordination 'died' on the night of December 19th when in the Greek Parliament, in the presence of 42 out of 250 Deputies, five of them managed to pay me for my non-cooperation in their political plans.[48]

Since in Greece, civil service posts are for life, the way that Doxiadis was pushed away from his post was rather extraordinary. In his eyes it amounted to no less than a certain kind of "death": according to his close collaborator, architect Panagis Psomopoulos, "at

that moment he thought that his life was over". Plunged into deep depression, Doxiadis left Greece for Australia where he stayed for two years, never again to return to a public post.

"174 Millionth Ton of Marshall Plan Aid Reaches Greece", photograph by the Economic Cooperation Administration, 21 December 1949. The celebratory parade with the truck carrying grains covered by the Greek flag, and with the American and Greek flags on the nearby pole, is shown passing just in front of Greece's Survival Exhibition organized by Doxiadis and his team at the Ministry of Housing and Reconstruction, Athens, Stadiou Street, 1949.

1 Cohen, Jean-Louis, "Overture: The Test of War", *Architecture In Uniform: Designing and Building for the Second World War*, Montreal: Canadian Centre for Architecture, 2011, p 19.

2 King George II was an uncle of Prince Philip, Duke of Edinburgh. The British troops at that point were largely administrative, but the devious role the British government under Winston Churchill played in the Greek Civil War is well documented.

3 From John Nuveen's November 1949 address to an audience in Belgium, *Battle for Survival*, no 64, Wednesday 23 November 1949, p 163, Doxiadis Archives. British and US commentators, as well as Greeks from the Right, called the Civil War a "bandit" or "guerrilla" war—in fact it was not until 1989 that a law was passed unanimously by the Hellenic Parliament, formally recognizing the 1946–1949 War as a civil war and not merely a communist insurgency.

4 Cohen, "Overture". The eponymous exhibition was held at the Canadian Centre for Architecture in 2011.

5 The Doxiadis family founded the Constantinos and Emma Doxiadis Foundation, which has made the Doxiadis Archives available to scholars (see www.archive.doxiadis.org). The creation of the Archives has in turn helped foster a new and growing body of scholarship on Doxiadis's life and work, including a major exhibition at the Benaki Museum in Athens, 2006–2007.

6 Having completed his studies at the National Technical University of Athens in 1935, Doxiadis left to study for a PhD at the Berlin-Charlottenburg University. In 1937 his dissertation was published in German as *Raumordnung im griechischen Stadtebau;* it was translated into English by Jaqueline Tyrwhitt as *Architectural Space in Ancient Greece*, Cambridge, MA: MIT Press, 1972.

7 In the countryside 585,000 out of 1,740,000 people lived in one-room dwellings. "*To oxy provlima tis stegis*" ("The Grave Problem of Housing") uses this data and tells us that it comes from the first census. Unknown author, *Technika Chronika*, Athens, 15 December 1952, collection of the Library of the Technical Chamber of Greece, Athens, p 24.

8 Doxiadis fought on the Albanian front between November 1940 and May 1941. Aris Konstantinidis, too, fought on the Albanian Front. According to their writings, both Konstantinidis and Doxiadis were able to produce studies and drawings during this time.

9 Papaioannou, John, "C.A. Doxiadis' early career and the birth of statistics", *Ekistics*, vol 41, no 247, June 1976, p 314. My thanks to Panagis Psomopoulos for directing me to this issue.

10 Certeau, Michel de, "Making Do: Uses and Tactics", *The Practice of Everyday Life*, Berkeley, CA: University of California Press, 1984, p 36.

11 Doxiadis, Constantinos, "Introduction", *Chorotaxìa*, vol 1, manuscript from the Doxiadis Archives, 1942, p 1.

12 Doxiadis, "Introduction", *Chorotaxìa*, p 1.

13 The term "social housing" is not used in Greek. Instead the members of the Circle used the term "popular housing" (*laiki katoikia*). Teaming up the term *laiki* with *katoikia* was relatively new (rather than *laiki oikia*, referring to an individual house, and which was often used in the 1930s and 40s). In addition, before the 1940s, such housing made for refugees (discussed in the previous chapter), was explicitly called "refugee housing" (*prosfygikes katoikies*). During the 1920s there was also a discussion about "cheap housing" (*euthynì katoikia*) but not "social housing". This untranslatability connotes fundamental socio-cultural differences at that time between Greece and the rest of Europe, a fact that the Circle attempted to expose.

14 Doxiadis, Constantinos, "An Introduction to the Research of Popular Housing", *Chorotaxìa*, p 46.

15 Echoing Le Corbusier and other modernist architects, Doxiadis too was preoccupied with the subject of health in housing: "according to statistics the health of inhabitants is in direct relation to the degree of sunlight and the number of inhabitants per room and not of the density of the population or the number of people per building." *Chorotaxìa*, pp 46–47. There was another aspect to Doxiadis's interest in health; as we saw in the previous chapter, his father, Apostolos, had been a prominent pediatrician who had served as Minister of Refugees, Social Welfare and Public Health during the 1920s.

16 Konstantinidis, Aris, "The Problem of Architecture", *Chorotaxìa*, p 6, my emphasis.

17 Konstantinidis, "The Problem of Architecture", p 7. The phrase "architecture without architects" was famously used by Bernard Rudofsky in the 1961 MoMA exhibition of the same title; it seems that it has been generally used in the Greek context since the early 1940s. Konstantinidis used the phrase "eternal" in respect to architecture throughout his many later writings as well.

18 Konstantinidis, Aris, *Dyo "Choria" ap'ti Mykono* (*Two 'Villages' from Mykonos*), Athens: Agra Editions, 1947, p 12.

19 Herzfeld, Michael, *Ours Once More: Folklore, Ideology and the Making of Modern Greece*, New York: Pella Publishing Company, 1986, p 13. See also Alki Kyriakidou-Nestoros, "What is Laography?", *Laographika Meletimata* (*Laographic Studies*), vol 2, Athens: Poreia, 1993.

20 Hatzimihali's own house in the central historic area of Athens is now a museum featuring collections of artifacts from her studies and travels. The building, designed by architect Aristotelis Zachos, is called the Museum of Popular Arts and Traditions "Angeliki Hatzimihali".

21 Kyriakidou-Nestoros, Alki, "*Laographia: Proseggiseis stin Paradosi*" ("Laography: Approaches to Tradition"), 1983, in *Laographika Meletimata* (*Laographic Studies*) vol 2, Athens: Poreia, 1993, p 63. Moreover, she claims that the Greek "people were never totally uneducated and isolated rural people as the romantic laography of the 19th c. imagined" and "The history of Greek communities under Ottoman rule [...] shows that what mostly characterized their way of life was not stasis but change, constant change, movement", p 65.

22 Megas, Georgios, *The Greek House: Its Evolution and Its Relation to the Houses of the Other Balkan Peoples*, Athens: Publications of the Ministry of Housing and Reconstruction, no 37, 1951, in English, my emphasis. The preface is by *The Coordinator of the Greek Recovery Program*, Doxiadis. My thanks to Mark Mazower for lending me his copy of this remarkable book.

23 To show specific continuities between popular building culture and ancient Greece, Megas established a series of typological studies as tools of a developmental theory, "from simple to complex", which he used to "explain" not only twentieth-century Greek rural building, but also much of the buildings in modern-day Balkans as originating in classical Greece. In contrast, in his *Chorotaxìa* texts, Megas talked about a "variety of influences" on popular Greek building culture, including "ancient eastern cultures, Byzantine, old Slavic, western Mediterranean and mainland European". Like Konstantinidis's argument in *The Old Athenian Houses*, whether this kind of claim is absolutely "true" or not cannot be proved with such absolute certainty—at least not in the present study. The passage here appears in *Chorotaxìa*, p 41.

24 The *Morning Advertiser*, London, 6 April 1945. This excerpt was found amongst photographs and newspaper clippings about the 1945 Peace Conference of San Francisco at the Doxiadis archives. For his help during this period in 1946 he was awarded an OBE (Order of the British Empire).

25 From the Doxiadis Archives, Document 0647: "Behind Enemy Lines #91", by Fabry, source: Interview Broadcast [San Francisco] 22 May 1945, written 18 May 1945.

26 These exhibition panels have not survived, but as we can judge from remaining photographs, they contained almost identical information to the accompanying *The Sacrifices of Greece in the Second World War* catalog I discuss below.

27 From Doxiadis's introduction to *The Sacrifices of Greece in the Second World War* catalog, for an exhibition shown in Paris, London and San Francisco, during April, May and June of

1945. *The Sacrifices of Greece in the Second World War* was printed in Athens between June 1945 and July 1946. As Undersecretary of the Ministry of Housing and Reconstruction, Doxiadis produced a small-format publication using this same material and title also in 1946, in Greek only, with greatly expanded text and using very few of the illustrations in black and white. This was number nine of the series published by the Ministry.

28 The catalog notes: "The text was composed by the architect K. A. Doxiadis, who directed the whole work with the help of the architects of the Ministry of Reconstruction A. Skepers, J. Papaioannou, K. Krantonelis, G. Papageorgiou and A. K. Tsitsis, of the painter A. Stylianidis and of the draughtsmen M. Gavalas and S. Yannoulis."

29 See Nader Vassoughian's book *Otto Neurath: The Language of the Global Polis*, Rotterdam: NAi Publishers, 2008. See also Ellen Lupton's "Reading Isotype", *Design Issues*, vol 3, no 2, Autumn 1986, pp 47–58. On Doxiadis and Neurath see Kostas Tsiambaos, "Isotype Diagrams from Neurath to Doxiadis", *Architectural Research Quarterly*, vol 16, issue 1, March 2012.

30 Neurath, Otto, "A Proposal Towards Implementation of the Viennese Method of Symbolism for Town Planning and Plot Allocation", *Technika Chronika*, Athens, 15 October–5 November 1933, collection of the Library of the Technical Chamber of Greece, Athens. Jaqueline Tyrwhitt, later on an important colleague of Doxiadis's, was present at the CIAM conference.

31 Neurath, "A Proposal Towards Implementation".

32 Lecture notes to the students of architecture at the University of California, Summer 1945. From document found in the bound volume labeled "Office Archives, vol 8, 1945."

33 From the Doxiadis archives, G217 Or 32765. Fragile handwritten manuscript at the back of a thin paper, labeled "To Ypourgeion Sygkoinwnias, Geniki Dieuthynsi Dimosiwn Ergwn" (Ministry of Transportation. General Head of Public Works) from envelope labeled "Various from the Ministry of Transportation—General Direction of Public Works 1935–44", 1944.

34 *Architectural Forum*, New York, August 1945, Doxiadis Archives.

35 During the early postwar period, instead of using US aid for reconstruction of the economy and for housing, the Greek government used it to contain "the enemy within", communism: "By 1949 government military and security forces numbered approximately a quarter of a million. Much of the American aid that in western Europe was being devoted to economic development was channeled into military objectives". Clogg, Richard, *A Concise History of Greece,* Cambridge: Cambridge University Press, 1992, pp 145–146.

36 "Funding for housing that came from the US, had 'a basic prerequisite' which was that 'it had to be used within the same fiscal year [as the year it was donated]'. However this basic prerequisite obliged the agency to have a very rapid work rhythm, totally unknown to [Greek] public services. If these instructions were not followed, there was a danger that this free American Aid would be given to another country. Under these circumstances, the timely use of this aid was a national duty." Unsigned (most probably written by Doxiadis), "*I Ypiresia Anoikodomisews kai to ergon tis. Ekthesis tou Technikou Epimelitiriou*" ("The Reconstruction Agency and its Work. Report by the Technical Chamber of Greece"), *Technika Chronika*, Athens, 1 June 1955, collection of the Library of the Technical Chamber of Greece, Athens, pp 14–15.

37 *Battle for Survival* was published in Greek as well as English in its main sections.

38 In 1947, the US State Department formulated a plan for military intervention wherever it considered communism as a threat. President Truman, along with General George Marshall, convinced Congress to fund the European Recovery Program (ERP) for postwar recovery. Greece, Turkey and much of western Europe benefited from the Marshall Plan.

39 *Battle for Survival*, 30 March 1949. These documents are remarkably absent from Biris's contemporary account of Greek architecture as well as from most subsequent histories, since that the material was for a long time presumed lost.

40 Zagorissiou, Maria, *Folk Architecture In Crete*, Athens: Benaki Museum, 1995.

41 The Attiki Odos created before the 2004 Olympic Games works like the road network that Doxiadis envisioned. The coastline was in fact developed in the early 1960s, upon a more detailed plan by Kitsikis, Sfaellos and Karadinos that took the Doxiadis plan as a guide. A series of leisure hubs to serve Athenians and foreign visitors, with hotel facilities both austere and sensitive to the exquisite southern Attic landscape, were then designed by a team of gifted architects, headed by Vourekas, Sakellarios and Vassiliadis, with the artist Yiannis Moralis.

42 See Doxiadis's booklet *Ekistic Policy for the Reconstruction of Greece and a Twenty-Year Plan*, Athens: Ypourgion Anoikodomiseos, 1946, pp 14–15. Reprinted in *Ekistics*, vol 44, no 260, July 1977, pp 9–11.

43 Unsigned (most probably written by Doxiadis), "The Reconstruction Agency and its Work. Report by the Technical Chamber of Greece", pp 14–15. Separately, architectural historian Dimitris Philippidis writes that "the Ministry of Reconstruction coordinated rebuilding in the postwar period and until 1951, managing to design 150 agricultural settlements and around 200,000 houses", though he doesn't mention the source of this data. *Neoelliniki Architektoniki (Modern Greek Architecture)*, Athens: Melissa Publications, 1984, p 265.

44 *Battle for Survival*, no 30, March 1949, the issue which discusses the exhibition mentioned above.

45 Even those who were close to him thought of his Ministry's aims as at times "excessive". In an interview with his former colleague, Maria Zagorissiou, conducted in Athens in the fall of 2004, she described this as a typical reaction to the Ministry's work at the time. Yet despite that, many of Doxiadis's colleagues followed him loyally to the private practice, Doxiadis Associates, which he founded in Athens in the 1950s.

46 For his own comments, see *Ekistic Policy for the Reconstruction of Greece...*, pp 14–15.

47 On another level, Doxiadis's wish was simply to define the kinds of knowledge needed to produce large-scale planning, and to organize these fields appropriately. Arranged in a decimal system, ranging from "100000" to "397600" "so that all subsequent communications would be unified", Doxiadis divided and classified categories of knowledge into three large areas: ekistics, town planning and building science (*oikistikì, poleodomia, ktiriologia*). He proposed to study these categories in two stages: first by gathering existing data that included maps, photographs and other such sources, including oral history, and only then by analysis. Like Megas and Neurath, Doxiadis's proposed analysis was based on the empirical observation of daily life and local culture, paying particular attention to the history of everyday life. But it went much further than that, trying to construct a complete, exhaustive grid of knowledge. The futility of this effort especially at that time, did not escape his old rival, Kostas Biris, who wrote: "This [unnamed] person [clearly referring to Doxiadis since he is discussing the work of his Ministry], held the opinion that the planning and reconstruction of settlements should be done through the study of animals, plants, metals and men. He failed to recognize what was essential." From Biris, *Ai Athinai apo ton 19o–20o aiona (Athens: From the 19th to the 20th Centuries)*, Athens: Melissa Publications, 1966, p 358.

48 Doxiadis's letter to a Mr Brownlow of Washington DC is held in the Doxiadis Archives. Architectural historian Kostas Biris actively misread this episode and misled us in his established history. "Again, this person [no name], did not try to implement his program of study and *abandoned his post by his own will in 1951*. Subsequent to that, the Ministry of Housing and Reconstruction was scrapped and the task of planning after a short wandering through various ministries returned in 1953 to the Ministry of Public Works", *Athens: From the 19th to the 20th Centuries*, p 359.

Man contemplating
the expansion of the
twentieth-century city,
Athens, 1957.

Chapter 5: Building the Postwar City

Polykatoikìa, Mêtis, Processes and Fictions

In May 1956 Jacob L Crane, consultant to the US government and the United Nations on housing issues, came to Athens at the invitation of the National Land Bank (*Ethniki Ktimatiki*) to give his opinion about Greek housing policy. He was incredulous at what he saw. According to the report published in the journal of the Technical Chamber of Greece, Crane was amazed at the speed in which building was taking place in Athens:

> From 1950 until today, reconstruction of individual housing was a veritable *phenomenon*. Up until 1953, private housing constituted about 72% of the total new housing. [...] the largest percentage of construction was completely funded by individual savings of families who had collected them 'under their floorboards' and used them to construct or improve their own dwellings. In terms of total number of dwellings, between 1953 and 1954, there were about 50,000 new dwellings and about as many repaired and extended.[1]

Crane thought that this "phenomenon" could not possibly continue at such a pace and that there should be a more conventional "program of savings and loans" for "family housing" set up in Greece. He also suggested that the government adopt a unified policy on housing to resolve the "collision of responsibilities" between the multiple agencies in charge, which we saw Doxiadis complaining about repeatedly in the last chapter.

What ensued contradicted the American consultant's assessment and went against the expected patterns of urban development in Europe and the US. For despite the absence of bank loans, in Athens housing construction by individuals continued at a rapid pace throughout the 1950s, 60s and early 70s. Banks did not change their policies on loans until well after the fall of the military junta in 1974. There continued to be different and conflicting agencies in charge of planning, as there still are to this day. Despite all this, paradoxically, the processes by which this housing was produced worked as a mechanism for sharing wealth among the population and it even became, to some, "a form of resistance to extreme industrialization and proletarianization".[2] How was this possible?

The Postwar Context

As we saw in chapter 3, in the late 1920s and early 1930s, architects, many of whom had studied in Europe, designed the *polykatoikìa* housing for wealthy

Minister of Public Works soon to become the longest serving Prime Minister of the post-Second World War period, Konstantinos Karamanlis (front seat, on the left) inspecting new Public Irrigation Works in 1957.

Opposite: Athens, Survey Map, 1950, showing "the extensions to the Athens City Plan".

upper-middle-class clients. After 1950, however, the term *polykatoikìa* took on a different meaning; over the next 20 years, the appearance of *polykatoikìa* grew exponentially, becoming the basis of affordable housing in Athens, gradually metamorphosing into a local popular phenomenon.

In 1955, after almost a decade of political instability following the end of the war and subsequent Civil War, Konstantinos Karamanlis, a "bluff Macedonian" lawyer and Minister of Public Works, was chosen to become Prime Minister following the sudden death of Alexandros Papagos. Karamanlis proved a towering figure in Greek politics.[3] His policies of monetary stabilization, restrained inflation and investment in public works are generally credited as defining factors in bringing about postwar prosperity. He also promoted tourism and placed a great deal of emphasis on infrastructural networks, especially roads, irrigation, electricity and telecommunications.

In addition, already during his first term as Prime Minister between the mid-1950s and early 60s, Karamanlis initiated a series of important improvements for the modernization or—as it was called at the time—the beautification (*exoraismòs*) of Athens. The improvements included the installation of traffic lights that gradually replaced the ubiquitous traffic wardens and their booths; the electrification of public streets and squares; the widening of key avenues (such as Kifissias Avenue); the works for the improvement of key public squares (such as Syntagma, Omonoia and Klafthmonos squares); the development of the Athenian coastline; the purchase of new buses, including electric buses ("trolleys"); the restoration of important Byzantine monuments; and the construction of public amenities such as markets, post offices, cultural centers, music schools and concert halls.[4]

In addition, in a particularly inspired move, Karamanlis commissioned Dimitris Pikionis (1887–1968) for the landscaping of the Acropolis and Philopappou hills. Pikionis composed a work of immense sensitivity to the topography of the site, synthesizing marble and clay shards he had collected from demolished nineteenth-century buildings with new paving elements, composing the work piece by piece on-site with his craftsmen from 1954 to 1957. He also landscaped and planted the larger surrounding area of the Acropolis Hill that encompasses the ancient theaters of Herodes Atticus and Dionysus, and worked on the restoration of the nearby church of St Dimitrios Loumbadiaris.[5]

Karamanlis pursued an aggressive policy toward Greek membership in the European Economic Community (EEC), the precursor of the European Union, which he succeeded in initiating in July 1961.[6] This reflected the huge development of the Greek economy in the late 1950s. Largely as a result of Karamanlis's policies, per capita income quadrupled between 1953 and 1973.[7] As we read in anthropologist Peter S Allen's piece in *Ekistics*:

> The postwar performance of the economy was nothing short of spectacular. In 1950 Greece ranked 45th in the world with a per capita GNP of $239 [...] by 1979 the figure had risen to over $3,500, and Greece ranked 28th in the world having surpassed more than a dozen countries that were ahead of it in 1950.[8]

Even though this success was accompanied by well-documented, large-scale political oppression focused on containing the spread of communism, there was greater class mobility and class equality overall. And although gender equality did not advance significantly during the 1950s and 60s, women were allowed to vote for the first time in the elections of 1956. It was exactly during this period that for the first time in Greek history, the urban population surpassed that of rural areas or, as Richard Clogg has shown, the percentages of urban versus rural populations were virtually reversed.[9]

Athens absorbed 62.7 percent of the overall increase in urban population. Between 1945 and 1955, there were two main arguments or visions in terms of urban plans.

Aerial maps of the "downtown" area of Kypseli. On the left, from 1937, and right, the same area in 1974, showing the expansion and densification always on the same small plot footprints.

Kostas Biris's plan, which was first made public while he was Director of the Municipality of Athens, involved a widening of streets at the city center to ease traffic congestion, and more radically, the transfer of the whole administrative center to the west of Attica (Megaris). On the other hand, Doxiadis, while still head of the Ministry of Housing and Reconstruction, had countered Biris's plan with an idea of urban zones, perhaps inspired in part by Le Corbusier and the "Athens Charter". Leaving the center of Athens intact, Doxiadis proposed dividing the larger Attica region into urban, suburban, semi-rural, rural, industrial, commercial and public gardens or green zones, which would each be served by new road networks.

Neither of these plans were ever fully realized (although modified versions of some of Doxiadis's proposals were undertaken later on). Instead, unlike other European and American cities at that time, there were no significant new enlarged road networks cutting through the existing city, and even as the older networks became overburdened, ultimately that fact probably worked in Athens' favor. Overall, until the 1960s, infrastructure developed quite slowly compared to the explosive number of new buildings—particularly housing—under construction.

The Polykatoikìa

The basic structural diagram of all postwar *polykatoikìa* apartment buildings consists of a reinforced concrete frame with masonry infill. Critics have repeatedly written that this diagram is a derivation of the Corbusian Dom-ino system, but this is an exaggerated claim.[10] The reinforced concrete frame is indeed the basic format for virtually all *polykatoikìa* construction, but the technique had been widely used in Greece since the early twentieth century.[11] By 1925 reinforced concrete was routine in domestic buildings. What changed in the postwar period had more to do with the speed and efficiency of the construction process. As one architect wrote in 1957:

> The new movement for the reform of architecture and the wish of getting rid of the prejudice of old styles began in 1925 with the appearance of reinforced concrete, enclosed balconies, an effort for the greatest development of a given plot, mathematical types in the building code of $1/3$ of width and $1/6$ surface area. [...] as long as one knew the length of the facade ahead of time, one would also know what that facade would look like.[12]

The ground floor of *polykatoikìa*, regardless of the social status of its residents, would contain a lobby with Tinian or Pentelic or other local marble flooring, and marble-clad steps all the way to the top floor. Lobbies in upper-class and upper-middle-class neighborhoods were particularly spacious, with high ceilings and well-designed lighting, and would feature an elegant marble- or timber-clad desk area, for the *polykatoikìa* doorman. In upper-middle-class areas a *polykatoikìa* would usually be entirely residential. Everywhere else, a typical *polykatoikìa* was designed to accommodate commercial uses at street level, catering to all kinds of neighborhood needs: from doctors' offices to clothing, pharmacies, bakeries, family-owned fruit and vegetable stores (supermarkets did not arrive until 1970), and other small family-owned shops.

Polykatoikìa under
construction, January 1952,
showing the reinforced
concrete skeleton
construction, brick
infill, flat roof, large and
regular window openings,
balconies, and setbacks
on the top three floors,
imposed by code.

New *polykatoikìa* next
to an old single-story
"neoclassical" home.
Photograph by Dimitris
Harissiadis, 1971.

Middle and upper-middle-class apartments were roomier and had more access to natural light and ventilation. Each floor would typically contain between two and five apartments of different sizes, arranged along a corridor that acted as a spine with access points, stairs and elevators. Kitchens and bathrooms looked out into small private gardens at the back or had open-air shafts for ventilation.

Middle-class apartments contained a living room and usually a dining room; though separate spaces, these rooms were usually open and connected with each other. Due to the mild Mediterranean climate, Athenians have always spent at least half the year outdoors: balconies supplied the semi-outdoor spaces that in a sense replaced the traditional courtyard of older times. There were always balconies: the wealthier areas featured large, well-designed, marble-clad balconies that were veritable gardens with fragrant plants and flowers and outdoor furniture for family and friends to gather, especially in the summer months.

Certain interior areas became particularly desirable in the postwar years and appeared in most upper-middle-class neighborhoods, namely the hall, the maid's room and the *retirè* (from the French for "to retire"), or top-floor penthouse. The hall was the space of first impressions; often there was a hall even when the apartment was too small to warrant it. The maid's room, a space commonly found in upper-middle-class apartments, also appeared in less expensive apartments, where it would be little more than a closet with inadequate light and often awkward access through the kitchen. And whereas in the upper-middle-class apartment buildings of the late 1920s and 1930s the top-floor setback *retirè* or penthouse apartment contained primarily service and laundry areas, in the postwar period it gradually became the most prestigious space of the whole building; each floor came to have a different social standing, with the wealthiest at the top.

It was as if the section of each *polykatoikìa* cut across microcosms of Greek society.[13] Recent migrants to the city would often work as doormen for their first job in Athens, living in basement or street-level apartments with their entire families. The *retirè* was occupied by the more affluent, perhaps those who initially owned the land on which the *polykatoikìa* was built; everyone else lived literally in-between the two extremes. The *retirè* apartment would typically contain an open-plan living area, often functioning as a "bachelor pad". The usual balconies were transformed into wide and expansive verandas on the top floor that afforded city views—a feature of most urban penthouses throughout this period, with lush planting, even small trees.

In terms of formal attributes, the typical postwar *polykatoikìa* gradually became characterized by totally flat facades with continuous bands of horizontal balconies with glass and metal balustrades, losing even subtle traces of the outlawed Germanic *erker* that were still often visible in the 1940s. This process of formal simplification occurred in the *polykatoikìa* buildings of all classes, even while varying slightly in scale and quality of materials, all over the city.

The first law about "horizontal ownership", passed in the General Building Code of 1929, attempted to regulate the size of "leftover" spaces where individual *polykatoikìa* join on a given street or urban block. To ensure adequate light and ventilation, the 1929 law mandated certain proportions for these "uncovered" areas, gaps between built and unbuilt parts of a block, according to the height and width of individual building blocks. Even then, these regulations elicited strong reactions from owners who believed that they would lose usable floor areas, and who argued that this would eventually jeopardize

Architect-designed "Polykatoikìa For Income" ("*Polykatoikìa Eisodimatos*") by architect Dimitris Chelmis that would have utilized the *antiparochè* system of financing. The caption clearly captures the spirit of this building as financial investment: "Located on a triangular plot and at the corner of two streets... we tried to include small stores on the ground floor. On the four floors above we managed to create three complete dwellings on each floor taking full advantage of the space available so as to achieve the largest possible income for the owners since this is not a *polykatoikìa* that will be sold. There are service areas in the basement. The top floor contains a setback, large and comfortable apartment. We used reinforced concrete B120 and seismic design throughout. Our budget was quite economical."

ΠΟΛΥΚΑΤΟΙΚΙΑ ΕΙΣΟΔΗΜΑΤΟΣ
ΑΜΥΝΤΑ ΚΑΙ ΑΡΧΕΛΑΟΥ

ΑΡΧΙΤΕΚΤΩΝ: **ΔΗΜΗΤΡΗΣ ΛΑΖ. ΧΕΛΜΗΣ**
ΛΥΚΑΒΗΤΤΟΥ 6 — ΑΘΗΝΑΙ — ΤΗΛ. 614-182 & 99-333

ΚΑΤΟΨΙΣ ΤΥΠΙΚΟΥ ΟΡΟΦΟΥ

Α' Διαμέρισμα
1. Χώλλ
2. Σάλα
3. Τραπεζαρία
4. Κοιτών
5. Κουζίνα
6. Λουτρόν
7. Ὀφφὶς

Β' Διαμέρισμα
8. Προχώλλ
9. Χώλλ
10. Σάλα
11. Τραπεζαρία
12. Κοιτών
13. Κουζίνα
14. Λουτρόν
15. Ὀφφὶς

Γ' Διαμέρισμα
16. Χώλλ
17. Σάλα
18. Τραπεζαρία
19. Κοιτών
20. Κουζίνα
21. Λουτρόν
22. Ὀφφὶς

ΙΣΟΓΕΙΟΝ: *Καταστήματα*
Α' ΚΑΙ Β' ΕΣΟΧΑΙ: *Διαμερίσματα*

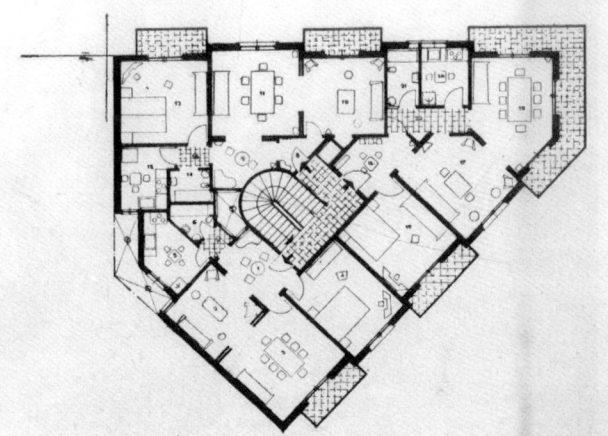

 Ἐπὶ οἰκοπέδου τριγωνικῆς μορφῆς καὶ κατὰ τὴν συμβολὴν δύο ὁδῶν, ἐν διαγωνίῳ ἀποτμήσει, ἐπεδιώχθη ἐν μὲν τῷ ἰσογείῳ διαμόρφωσις μικρῶν καταστημάτων εἰς δὲ τοὺς τέσσαρας ὑπερκειμένους ὀρόφους ἔγινε κατορθωτὸν νὰ περιληφθοῦν εἰς ἕκαστον τούτων ἀνὰ τρεῖς πλήρεις κατοικίαι, μὲ ἐντατικὴν ἐκμετάλλευσιν τοῦ χώρου, εἰς τρόπον ὥστε νὰ ἐπιτευχθῇ τὸ μέγιστον δυνατὸν εἰσόδημα ἐξ ἐνοικίων, δεδομένου ὅτι ἡ Πολυκατοικία δὲν προορίζεται διὰ πώλησιν διαμερισμάτων. Εἰς τὸ ὑπόγειον βοηθητικοὶ χῶροι, ὁ δὲ ἀνώτατος ἐν ἐσοχῇ ὄροφος μία ἄνετος μεγάλη κατοικία. Κατὰ τὴν κατασκευὴν ἐχρησιμοποιήθη σκυρόδεμα Β 120 καὶ ἀντισεισμικὴ ἐν γένει κατασκευὴ μετὰ τοιχωμάτων ἀκαμψίας καὶ ἐπετεύχθη κόστος οἰκονομικόν.

Builders in *polykatoikìa* construction, ca 1950s.

the growth of the city. Eventually, "the light-shaft, a luminous well with sandblasted windows, started to replace the [larger interwar] uncovered left-over spaces".[14]

In spite of the apparent formal similarities to modern architecture—white facades, flat roofs, horizontal lines and modern materials—the *polykatoikìa* is different in some important ways. It is a kind of simplified version of modern architecture that lacked the movement's political and aesthetic agenda. In addition, it was received and interpreted without the fundamental project of a radical break that modern architecture depended on—as we will see, there are many continuities between the *polykatoikìa* and more traditional Greek housing. It lacked innovation and precision and shunned any effort toward standardization (except when it came to sizes of building materials, windows, doors, and so on), despite the efficiencies allowed by reinforced concrete. Instead it relied on quasi-craft processes of construction.

High or elite modern architecture needed mass media, as Beatriz Colomina has persuasively argued. One of the places the popular Athenian version was publicized was the widespread Publishers' Lottery project. In existence since the late 1940s, the Publisher's Lottery featured simplified middle-class *polykatoikìa* buildings in nationally distributed newspapers and women's magazines in the 1950s and early 60s, and until the onset of the junta in 1967. Apartments and sometimes whole *polykatoikìa* buildings were some of the prizes given to lucky lottery winners.

In the 1960s other household goods, such as electric vacuum cleaners, refrigerators and mixers, as well as cars, also appeared alongside the images of apartments, showing the extent to which Greece had entered the postwar climate of consumption, even if belatedly. As we will discuss in more detail in the next chapter, these ads also betray the extent to which an apartment in a *polykatoikìa* was seen as a highly desirable possession—clearly at least as desirable as a car and other domestic appliances. Another interesting source of images are the renderings found in *Sygxronos Oikodomiki,* "a compendium of Architecture, Urbanism, Art and Crafts" that featured a sense of modern life in the city. Here the *polykatoikìa*, clad in colorful murals and inhabited by well-dressed people, were presented alongside glamorous American-style cars.[15]

Despite the seemingly replicable nature of the *polykatoikìa*, it is important to note that there were also some outstanding and formally innovative examples produced during the postwar period. *Sygxronos Oikodomiki* featured commercially successful architects such as Fotis Pappas, who worked with the basic format of the *polykatoikìa*.[16] Other publications, such as the journal *Architektoniki* (published by Kostas and later Antonis Kitsikis) and *Architektonika Themata/Architecture in Greece*, published by Orestis Doumanis) tried to present less commercial and more innovative projects.

Some of the architects featured in these journals whose work enriched the *polykatoikìa* as a basic urban typology include Nicos Valsamakis (Semitelou Street of 1951, Vassilissis Sofias Avenue of 1955, Kifissias Avenue of 1957–1958); Takis Zenetos and Margaritis Apostolidis (Amalias Avenue and Daidalou Street of 1959); Ioannis Liapis and Elias Skroumbellos (Papadiamantopoulou Street of 1954–1957); Thalis Argyropoulos and Constantinos Decavallas (Dinokratous Street of 1960–1962) and from the early 1970s; Suzanna and Dimitris Antonakakis (Emmanuel Benaki Street of 1972–1974).[17]

Athens street scene, ca
1950s, showing the city
under construction, or
as some newspapers
proclaimed, "the whole
city is an enormous
building site".

Local Processes: The Builders

Despite Kostas Biris's critique of city planning in the 1920s and 30s, scholars who have compared the 1929 General Building Code with that of 1955 have found it to be quite enlightened. According to most, the 1929 Building Code addressed quality of life and the new urban spaces created by the *polykatoikìa* by considering building heights and proportions in terms of geometrical relationships. In contrast, the postwar code allowed greater simplification in the official architectural vocabulary and, as mentioned above, gave a new emphasis on maximum built areas in each *polykatoikìa*. Significantly, if during the interwar period the size of each apartment was at least 100 square meters and usually took up the entire floor area, in the post-Second World War period certain other predetermined sizes became "typical". There were apartments of 35, 120, and 150 square meters, the most prevalent of which was the "three-room" 70 to 80 square-meter apartment.

As Christophoros Sakellaropoulos has pointed out, there was also a shift in the language of the new Building Code of 1955 where "articles or decrees no longer 'define', 'arrange', 'organize', and 'foresee', but rather 'limit', 'enforce', and 'prohibit', or 'disallow'."[18] At the same time, there was a new more lenient attitude towards building, despite the "authoritative and intensely forbidding tone of each article":

> The building was no longer a single volume defined from geometrical proportions in terms of adjacent public areas [...] but the sum of floors of usable surface area and volume. Therefore there was a radical shift in the perception of space: instead of a unified geometric definition of a building's proportions, from now on the final volume was defined by the density derived from [individual and constantly changing] administrative decrees.[19]

Floors could now be lower in height (as low as 2.9 meters), setbacks were reduced to 2.5 meters behind the building line of the previous floor, and the minimum ventilation area, the light well area, was reduced to a shaft as narrow as 1.2 x 1.2 meters. These measures were taken so as to increase the density of city blocks. It was calculated that by these measures alone the city's population could potentially increase by six million people.

Many of the new migrants came to Athens because of the Civil War. Unlike the refugee crisis of the 1920s, however, during the 1950s and 60s internal migrants were now incorporated "more or less automatically" into an urban working class composed of what was left of a prewar middle class, which had diminished during the war years. Peter S Allen noted an important reason for the successful assimilation of migrants: unlike other areas in Europe, "even southern Europe, [Greece had]... a tradition of small freeholding land tenure", which meant that the majority of migrants to the city "were not landless serfs, share croppers or renters, but rather [had] owned and operated small farms in an open and relatively free marketplace environment".[20] Allen adds a list of other interesting reasons, among them that migrants spoke the same language, were ethnically homogeneous and usually retained property and assets in their villages.[21]

One of the main ways in which these rural migrants found employment, however, was to work as builders in *polykatoikìa* construction. In the construction sector no one cared whether a worker had the obligatory evidence that he was not a communist (the "Certificate of Social Beliefs") that was needed to find work in the public sector. This was the Cold War; Greece was seen by England and the US as an important bulwark state against the spread of communism and there was great pressure to keep the "danger" at bay.[22]

There were two broad types of *polykatoikìa* builders. The first were the largely uneducated migrants who had come to Athens in search of work, and who often had a background in the building trades. If they prospered, they would start their own teams of builders or building contractors (it was understood that their priority would be to hire extended family members and others from the same place of origin). The other main group were the middle and upper-middle-class engineers who worked as small-scale businessmen.[23] Both groups ran small-scale operations; large corporate-style businesses were rare in this industry at the time.[24]

Builder-developers typically "economized" on hiring architects: their skills were viewed as mostly superfluous. Either an architect or an engineer was required to sign and stamp a basic set of drawings for the planning permission. Once that was issued, the builder-developers would mostly work alone to keep costs low, altering aspects of the building as they saw fit, especially in the interior, relying on their own experience and that of their teams. Engineers who worked as small-scale businessmen did not necessarily need architects at all: they were legally allowed to complete the work themselves.

As during the interwar period, the builder-developers from the private sector completed most residential *polykatoikìa* construction. In the early postwar period an important debate took place among economists as to whether housing construction was a productive or consumptive activity, and therefore whether it should be supported by the State. There were two prevailing points of view, those of Xenophon Zolotas and Kyriakos Varvaressos, both powerful economists in the Bank of Greece.[25]

Zolotas maintained that the housing sector was "not productive" and urged the government to concentrate on the creation of industry, which was still very underdeveloped in Greece at that time. Instead, in the words of sociologist Sophia Antonopoulou, Varvaressos thought that the development of the housing sector "would contribute to the creative employment of the population and the increase of the level of living of the lower classes and that therefore this was where the government should place its emphasis". The government ultimately sided with Zolotas.[26] Thus, according to statistics, State involvement in housing dropped from 5 percent between 1959–1968 to 3 percent between 1969–1972, while according to another source, between 1970–1977 the State contributed about 1.5 percent to the total housing production.[27]

There were several reasons for this. First, the small parceling of land meant that organized building with large-scale construction was difficult. Secondly, as shown in chapter 2, there was a long tradition of private residential construction dating back to the nineteenth century. During the 1920s and 30s, partly as a result of the influx of refugees, this tradition continued. It became more prevalent with individuals not only building their own housing but also, at times, creating their own neighborhoods, areas that were eventually incorporated into the city, with little involvement from the State.

Paradoxically, while the government did not give out loans or other benefits to encourage construction, this attitude only encouraged construction in the private sector. Furthermore, the State's lack of involvement gave way to a huge increase

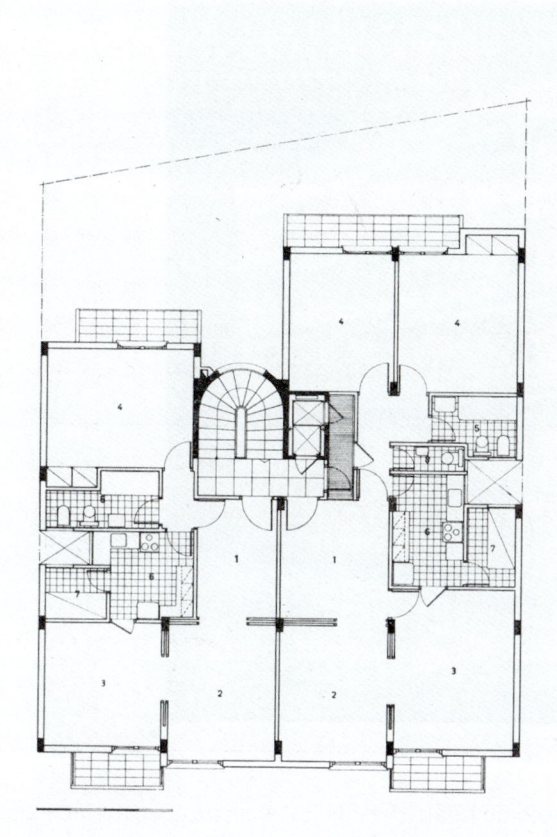

Polykatoikìa at 30 Agiou Meletiou Street, by the architect Nikolaos Siapkidis. Construction by Technical Office of Civil Engineers Bobola, Babi and Papachimona. Published in *Sygxronos Oikodomiki*, 1961.

in illegal building by the end of the 1950s. By 1967 there were an estimated 20,000 illegal buildings constructed per year, almost all of them in the city's periphery; soon the illegally built areas on the outskirts of Athens were denser than those within the lawful City Plan.[28]

Antiparochè

> The builders would set up a small desk in front of a *polykatoikìa* construction site. Clients would come and choose their apartments as they were going up. At this point, and even if plans existed, clients could make changes to fit their own needs by talking about them with the developer on the job site.[29]

This account by architect Nikos Valsamakis encapsulates a great deal of postwar Athenian development. It also describes a developer-client relationship that may seem unusual today. In postwar construction, after acquiring a basic building permit (required for buildings with more than two floors), there was much improvisation. Many non-structural issues were discussed and negotiated between the client and

"*Polykatoikía* for
E. Pantikidis, on 5
Metamorphosis Street,
Athens 1970."
Designer unknown.

"*Polykatoikía* for E. Pantikidis, on 5 Metamorphosis Street, Athens 1970." Designer unknown.

the developer, who would try to accommodate the clients' wishes, even in the midst of construction.

A similar sense of immediacy is present in the financial process most-often utilized at that time, the *antiparochè*. The *antiparochè* system "evolved" from the interwar period's "*futùra*" system, in use since the early 1930s, whereby the owner of a piece of land would give the land over to a developer in exchange for his team's contribution to the construction work. The developers did not own the land themselves; the owners often purchased and kept track of the building materials, although this was less likely as the teams became more organized. At the end, the construction teams would own most of the new building, which they would sell to finance their next job. A portion of the building would remain to the initial landowners, to live in and to rent out for additional income.

As an economic act, the *antiparochè* is not unlike bartering: a basic organizing mechanism among peoples throughout the world, or gift exchange, which in Greece dates at least as far back as the Homeric epics. In the postwar period, this financial process became more and more widespread. The landowners were no longer exclusively from the upper classes: everyone in the construction business worked with the *antiparochè*. One exchanged what one had for what one needed: a plot of land, with or without a house, was exchanged with the prospect of a new apartment, and more apartments to rent. The builder-developer exchanged his and his team's work for what he needed: apartments to sell to make a living and enough profit so as to be able to build more.

The system was such that the outcome brought about a semblance of equity (in gift-exchange, profit was taboo).[30] One's "word of honor" went far in the early postwar

Polykatoikìa from Sygxronos Oikodomiki. The caption says in English "Block Building, Valaoritou-Kriezotou St, Architect: Fotis Pappas". Undated, likely late 1950s. This rendering includes American-style cars in front of the buildings and people walking by to convey a city scene with a certain amount of sophistication if not glamor associated with polykatoikìa life.

decades amongst a large segment of those who came to the city after the war: people who were not particularly literate were used to fixing transactions through oral agreements in the countryside. Determined by equivalences, the aim was mutual benefit for the builder and the landowner. Of course there were many who abused the system, but the absence of large construction companies in Greece at that time—few if any had investors and profits to report—the scale of this process remained uniquely small and fast.

Developers advertised individual apartments, selling them often before their construction had begun, allowing new buyers to suggest changes to typical floorplans—another process of oral negotiation—so as to suit their needs and allow contractors to obtain the necessary cash to complete construction. Any existing building on-site would simply be demolished. The speed with which this process worked, combined with people's desire for housing and developers' and owners' needs for cash, meant that Athens' nineteenth-century neoclassical architecture, as well as some of the architecture of the interwar period, both elite and popular, vanished very quickly.

The main particularity of antiparochè was that unlike financing systems in the rest of Europe, it sidestepped banks completely. After all, despite Jacob L Crane's suggestion, mortgages were not given until much later. The huge demand for urban apartments gave many incentives to save: due to the dowry system, buying a new apartment was an important way of transferring funds from the countryside to the city.[31] Thus the antiparochè helped the lower and middle classes to channel their savings (previously kept "under the floorboards") directly into housing.

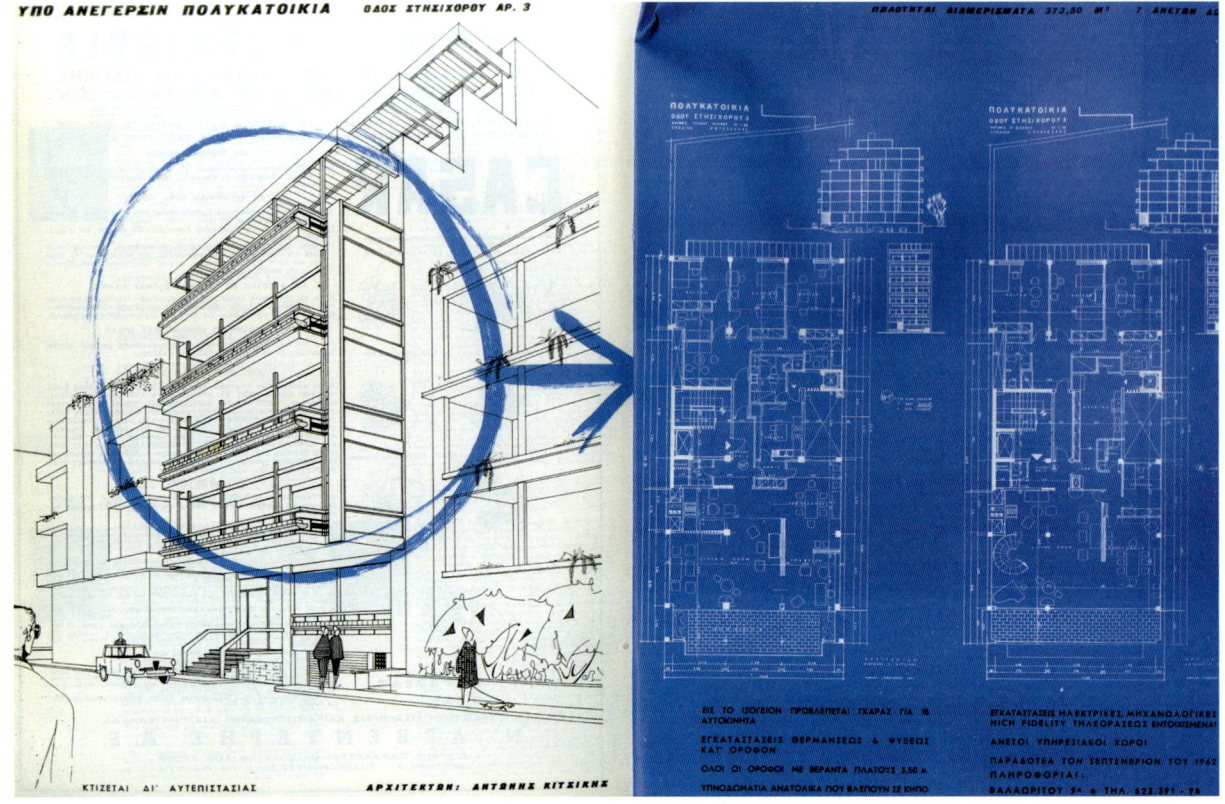

"Polykatoikia Under Construction, 3 Stissihorou Street" by Antonis Kitsikis, architect and co-publisher of *Architektonikì* magazine. This was a two-page spread in the magazine advertising apartments for sale in 1962. The caption informs us that the building was designed, constructed and supervised by the architect. On the left, a perspective drawing shows this upper-class street and the *polykatoikìa* with ample balconies (3.5 m wide), and setbacks on the upper floors covered with pergolas. On the right, we see blueprints of the building with plans, sections and elevations and notes below that mention ample parking space in the building, the newest mechanical systems, bedrooms facing east and comfortable servants rooms.

But to say that the State stayed completely outside the housing sector is not altogether true. The so-called KH' (eighteenth) vote initiated under Doxiadis's tenure in the Ministry of Housing and Reconstruction was a strong incentive to private investors in the rebuilding of Athens, exempting earnings from real estate built or bought after 1945 from tax purposes. As Doxiadis's archives suggest, this proposal and others instated during his tenure in the Ministry were calculated to appease people's fears of rent control and to encourage individual investment in housing. Historians have judged the KH' vote negatively, claiming that it ultimately encouraged urban density and the growth of the *polykatoikìa*. One must bear in mind that this incentive was counterbalanced by the aim of rebuilding the countryside, a policy intended to have the exact opposite effect.[32]

Economist Chrisafis Iordanoglou has claimed that by restricting mortgages the State actually wished to slow down the tempo of urban growth, since it was believed that a more lenient lending policy would lead to overdevelopment and an increase in prices and wages. And, for Iordanoglou, "the experience from the junta years proved that these fears were not unreasonable".[33] In fact, Iordanoglou thinks that it is possible that loan restrictions encouraged greater individual savings.

In another analysis, sociologist Sophia Antonopoulou has remarked that the *antiparochè* and the *polykatoikìa* as its closely related product "worked as a mechanism of sharing income to the benefit of the lower and middle layers of the population".[34] Antonopoulou gives us a very interesting account of class mobility in the postwar period:

There was great class movement. [...] Someone who was a farmer yesterday became a worker in the city or abroad, but he continued to also be a small landowner. Equally, someone who was a worker yesterday could potentially be self-employed today [...] Therefore often the same person combined characteristics of more than one class: small landowner, small income earner, day laborer, or office worker in the public or private sector. The fact that workers were almost always first- or second-generation farmers and therefore still had a plot of land that was theirs meant that in Greece there was no proletariat class in the strict sense of the term, but only through exceptions.[35]

With the *antiparochè* (still in existence to this day), everyone profited: the builders and small developers; the owners of old houses in urgent need for repairs; and the government that stood to gain from taxation (though not in the first postwar years) with almost no investment. The construction sector grew enormously. There was low unemployment and a concentration of savings from remittances and foreign exchange. Although construction was a "technologically retarded field", it ultimately acted as "a lever to activate the Greek economy and eventually became a whole independent production base".[36] Thus in the postwar period Greece achieved a higher owner-occupancy rate than other European countries, whereas at the same time there was almost a complete absence of State (social) housing policy.

Processes and Techniques

As previously mentioned, there was a gradual process of simplification from the relatively elite interwar *polykatoikìa* to those of the postwar years. There was also a process of adaptation of elements drawn from modernist architecture and applied to the *polykatoikìa* by the practical architects and small developers. These processes were probably more complex than a simple one-way "copy" of professional designs into humbler, ostensibly less original works, as historians have often claimed. For whereas "informal" is not the same as "vernacular", the fact is that in both instances there is much creativity and imagination involved, particularly in making the most with what is available.

In the images that follow we see groups of women builders working under a male contractor/developer on the construction of a *polykatoikìa*. This is clearly an informal group, perhaps a family. The building facade they are working on was most definitely not planned in advance—at least not in the ways architects typically work. The reinforced concrete frame is being filled up with bricks, the small cantilevered balconies are in place, but the openings of doors and windows seem randomly positioned, some slightly larger, others slightly wider with no apparent order or logic. How did these groups begin to produce these designs themselves?

If during the 1930s a simplified modernist language became part of popular architecture, it is reasonable to argue that a similar process took place in the 1950s and 60s, this time with a different formal vocabulary. But how does this process work? The term "local knowledge", coined by anthropologist Clifford Geertz, refers to the idea of a collective expression or sensibility that appears in various art forms. Thinking of artifacts like the *polykatoikìa* as representing a collective sensibility does not preclude other factors that we usually study when we study architecture, such as the relationship of form to economy, climate, materials, and so on. In fact, it enriches our understanding of the ways in which artifacts are connected to the society and time in which they emerged. Geertz claims that all art has to be seen in this way.

Bringing up Michael Baxandall's work on fifteenth-century painting, Geertz suggests a different kind of analysis and appreciation of how artifacts become incorporated "into the texture of a particular pattern of life".[37] This analysis is particularly useful in starting to suggest ways to study buildings produced by non-architects, drawing as they do from many different sources directly related to the culture from which they spring. The elusive knowledge shared by informal builders was clearly rooted in everyday life. Rather than copying more elite works, I suggest that their processes had to do with ways of understanding and operating in the pre-industrial rural culture that they brought with them to the city, especially in terms of construction techniques and in ways of working with materials. After all, as we have already seen, at this time the village literally came into the city.

The "unschooled" strata of the construction industry, arriving from the provinces with little or no formal education, quickly (in the architects' view) "stole" the work away from "real" professionals. Even if the generic postwar building techniques were not identical to "traditional" stone building, it was an updated version of it. Construction methods were relatively simple, equipment minimal. Building primarily with wood and concrete—mixed on site and carried up thin ladders in modified rectangular tin containers that previously held olive oil or feta cheese—this work was easily learned, with few changes for the first postwar decades.

The most extreme or literal example of the continuity between rural and urban worlds of the "builders" had taken place during the nineteenth century when builders from Anafi, a small Cycladic island, arrived in Athens to work on the construction of Otto's palace (1836–1840) and decided to build houses for themselves on the northern side of the Acropolis Hill. The resulting neighborhood, Anafiotika, was Athens' first informal and truly illegal development. Built during the night to avoid being seen by authorities that had prohibited any new building on the Acropolis Hill, these builders succeeded in constructing a small Cycladic village of whitewashed flat-roofed houses, and a tiny whitewashed church, just below the ancient temples. Many subsequent attempts to demolish the settlement have never succeeded—and today this village has become part of the tourist routes on the way to the Parthenon.[38]

Whereas the Cycladic builders literally "brought" their village of origin to the Acropolis Hill, in the postwar years the rural world started becoming present in Athens gradually in a less literal sense. For instance, at least up until the postwar period, specific regions produced construction crews who specialized in particular building tasks. Echoing or continuing these traditions, builders in the postwar city were never more than loosely composed groups of varying specialties, such as marble workers (marmarádes), concrete workers (betatzìdes), plasterers (sovatzìdes), terrazzo makers (mosaikoì), floor workers (patomatzìdes) and ethnic Armenians, known for iron reinforcement work.

Anthropologist Alki Kyriakidou-Nestoros has discussed the shift from the pre-industrial to industrial popular civilization in a fascinating way, speaking to the broader concept of collective sensibility and local knowledge, even if on a different scale. Kyriakidou-Nestoros observed an intriguing shift between old handmade domestic utensils and plastic utensils produced in the postwar years. She realized that despite being made of different materials and being brightly colored rather than in straw or tin and brass, these objects retained their shapes, types and even names. Housewives "need no new linguistic effort to ask for 'dishes', 'cups', 'raki glasses' [...] 'buckets', 'water-jugs', 'baskets', 'brushes', 'clothespins' in this modern material".[39]

Housewives recognized these objects easily and felt a sense of familiarity, especially since they mimicked the older objects rather than being shaped in a way that would make more sense for the new materials. We might feel that on the one hand these plastic domestic objects were a parody of the older ones—attempts at imitation so poor that they might seem ridiculous. On the other hand, these plastic objects were not necessarily less "authentic". They were indicative of a newer popular urban civilization.

Writing in 1935, architect Dimitris Pikionis also suggested that the traditional civilization of pre-industrial times may one day transform into equally fascinating contemporary urban forms. In an article about toys being sold in Aiolou Street, an area of Athens near the central city market lined with inexpensive shops and street peddlers, Pikionis found spinning tops, tin animals and more traditional shadow theatre characters, and noted the "creative contrasts" through which "new authentic art forms are born".[40]

The postwar Athenian *polykatoikìa* exemplified such a creative contrast, a transposition from the rural world to the city that somehow represented or signified another kind of adaptation, one that enriches our understanding of the simple movement between "high" elite works to "low" informal building.[41] Like the plastic cups and Pikionis's toys, the *polykatoikìa* worked as an updated version of processes and techniques that had existed in rural life for centuries. This helped render the *polykatoikìa* less alienating to the average person than modernist housing produced by architects elsewhere; instead it was widely accepted and easily assimilated into postwar domestic culture, both formal and informal.

The adaptation between rural and urban worlds and the work of uneducated builders was to some extent imaginative, for it had something to do with a process of interpretation, no matter how unconscious. This interpretation was formed collectively; it produced something new and represented something important about the context from which it grew, no matter how aesthetically displeasing it might still be for most observers and critics to this day. The fact that this creativity could not be pinned on a single "author" or creator, that it did not belong to someone in particular, illustrates Geertz's concept of collective or group creativity. There were always small variations in the *polykatoikìa*, but over time a new basic form emerged that was adopted and used widely.

Mêtis: The Art of the Weak

There is no doubt that *mêtis* is a type of intelligence and of thought, a way of knowing; it implies a complex but very coherent body of mental attitudes and intellectual behavior which combine flair, wisdom, forethought, subtlety of mind, deception, resourcefulness, vigilance, opportunism, various skills, and experience acquired over the years. It is applied to situations which are transient, shifting, disconcerting and ambiguous, situations which do not lend themselves to precise measurement, exact calculation or rigorous logic.[42]

Women builders supervised by a male contractor/developer building a *polykatoikìa* somewhere in Athens in the early 1950s. Women, too, worked in the construction business even though we do not have information on the percentages of women in the building trades. Note the unevenness of the openings of this *polykatoikìa*: this is clearly work that relies on an almost traditional way of production.

Another particularity of postwar Athenian development was that there was an ongoing distrust of authorities. People were continually trying to find ways to "get away" with things, to skillfully and craftily find new ways around certain situations. In fact it is generally acknowledged that everyone who wanted to build in Athens during the postwar period utilized some ruse—*mêtis*, as described by classical scholars Vernant and Detienne above—in order to overcome government-imposed restrictions and bureaucracy. From the small builder-developer who may have cheated in declaring the amount of iron he used as reinforcement for concrete, to the one who may have sold apartments to unsuspecting customers without really owning the land they were built on, in a sense, it is as if the whole system—especially the financial process of *antiparochè*—encouraged, almost institutionalized, a certain type of character, or way of doing things.

But it was not only the less privileged who resorted to craftiness, but also those in positions of power. One example of this attitude is the practice of "amendments" to a given plan or building permit issued by the Municipality. In practice, this meant that illegal buildings or parts of buildings would eventually, inevitably—and especially in times of election—become "legalized". As a process, "amendments" existed since the beginning of the modern State. In 1924 amendments were instituted into the General Building Code.[43] At that time, the building code included articles about adequate ventilation and sunlight, which never took effect—instead there were repeated "exemptions" in all areas of central Athens, renewed every two months up to the Axis occupation, from which point there was an "indefinite suspension" (*ep aoriston anastoli*) until 1955.[44]

The 1955 Building Code in turn allowed even more such amendments. In fact it allowed for deviations [*parekliseis*] in up to 10 percent of the anticipated surface area in central Athens and 5 percent in areas surrounding the center, essentially making central areas more vulnerable to so-called urban anarchy. Put differently, the postwar building code allowed or even encouraged a certain degree of craftiness, if not lawlessness, that was instituted in the legal procedures themselves. This same building code "legalized" all illegal construction up to that point, a populist move that was repeated later on by the junta government. Since it was common knowledge that authorities were as prone to "amendments" as any citizen trying to obtain a permit to build, the very idea of authority also remained unclear and undefined, if not questionable. One has the sense that people's persistent distrust of authority drove them into a continual search for new ways to get away with things; it fueled their craftiness.[45]

So strong was the opposition and resistance to organized authority in general that historians like Constantinos Tsoukalas have used the term "para-State" (*parakràtos*), and "para-Constitution"(*parasyntagma*) to talk about the parallel worlds that existed during the early decades following the Civil War, which didn't necessarily meet. Those on the Left accused the Right of having put into place (an illegal) "para-State" in order to police citizens, populated by the right-wing extremists. Others used "para-State" to refer to all the semi-legal or outright illegal ways in which people got away with doing what they wanted, in politics and elsewhere. The "para-Constitution" referred to sudden changes in electoral law, apparently dictated by the US and followed through by the Greek State. Tsoukalas has talked about the "para-administration", referring to the ways in which citizens approached "the deadened and incompetent public services" of the post-Civil War State. At the same time, Tsoukalas admits that since the economic system could not absorb the workers in sectors such as large-scale industry, these workers had to look after themselves: "the inventive Mediterranean mind 'discovered' new products, new technologies, new services and new professions".[46]

In fact the small developer-builder of the *polykatoikìa* was exactly such a "new profession". The Mediterranean "invention" of new professions points to the idea of *mêtis,* with examples from Karagiozis shadow-puppet theater, to Vernant and de Certeau, as another kind of intelligence at play. For Tsoukalas, rather than being in the minority, these "new professions" were quite successful and predominated at least until the late 1950s and early 1960s. From that point on there was a more clearly defined middle class made up of a "new layer of technical experts, higher administrators, independent practitioners and intellectuals" that eventually brought the government of the Center Union Party back to power in 1963.

Perhaps inspired by Tsoukalas, architectural historian Dimitris Philippidis coined the term "para-urbanism" (*parapoleodomìa*) to express a similar set of illegal or marginally legal processes in architecture:

> That which we consider as "official" urban planning, represents an ideological representation of Greek society which is not related to reality. Moreover, we could say that all these so-called "marginal" phenomena of an urban practice 'outside' the 'official' one, is in fact the main nucleus of Greek urbanism.[47]

According to Philippidis there were three important categories of para-urbanism: "land-trafficking" (*oikopedembòrio*); the construction of totally illegal buildings; and sidestepping the law—with "alterations" of city plans, for example. This para-urbanism existed not only in parallel with official urbanism, but also, for Philippidis, the two worked symbiotically, each side satisfying specific and complementary interests. He has shown that it was not uncommon for government officials to submit "addendums" to the building codes in order to accommodate their relatives, friends or electorate. In another example, whereas after 1923 no one was legally allowed to parcel up agricultural land and sell it as buildable urban land, "between 1957 and 1977 about 1.5 million of these pieces of previously classified agricultural land, were sold as urban plots, with the State's tacit approval".[48]

Philippidis's research suggests an ongoing game between those involved in construction and those who issued State regulations. It is important to realize that it was not only the poor rural migrants who built illegally or semi-legally, but also often the middle classes, particularly businessmen who could "extract a suitable law in order to build upon a public square".[49] The upper classes had more choices available to them and could do very much as they pleased. The whole game between the State and prospective builders intensified during the junta period, when according to Philippidis, the ambiguity over what was legal and what was para-urbanism became greater.

The extent to which both the State and private individuals were implicated in producing illegal or marginally legal buildings is hard to gauge with complete precision. Philippidis saw this whole process as a "cycle" that consisted of "tolerance, awakening of the administration, pursuit, reaction by interested parties, tactical surrender, tolerance".

The result was always the same, namely "the autonomous production of shelter with the blessing of a system that sees to it that there will be enough favorable conditions for the cycle to take place again".[50] Whether a "cycle" or an ongoing game, this kind of activity once again puts into question the categories of legal and illegal, for they were constantly and intentionally in flux.

The General Building Code itself was extremely complex and full of ambiguity and contradiction, almost as if to open itself up for "interpretation" by interested parties. Foreigners who had no access to the details of this game were endlessly fascinated with the Athenians' apparent disregard of municipal law and unusual ways of addressing construction. As travel writer Kevin Andrews exclaimed in 1967,

> Squatter's rights are confirmed if a house is roofed during the night: 30,000 such sprang up during a few weeks of 1963 while the police were anticipating the *coup d'etat* that hangs over every general election. If one is highly placed or well enough connected, it is quite easy, up on Lycabettus where the limit is two stories out of respect for one of the world's rare views, to build a broad-beamed skyscraper with ritzy penthouses and then get somebody in Parliament to change the law.[51]

Instead, for postwar Athenians the need to utilize some ruse in order to get around certain institutions was clearly part of local knowledge. The comedy in some of these cat-and-mouse acts, and the official and non-official language used to describe them, evokes the shadow theater character Karagiozis once again. The popular ironic use in the press and elsewhere of such terms as *oikopedofagos* (land-eater or land-stealer, encroacher), *mneimeiofàgos* (monument-eater), *oikopedembòrio* (land-trafficking), *polykatoikiàs* (*polykatoikìa*-maker), *antiparochitzìs* (part-exchanger), *emporospitàs* (house-trader), recall Karagiozis's insatiable hunger and crafty sleights of hand. For those who can understand them, these terms vividly evoke the cultural and social specificity of Athens in the postwar period.

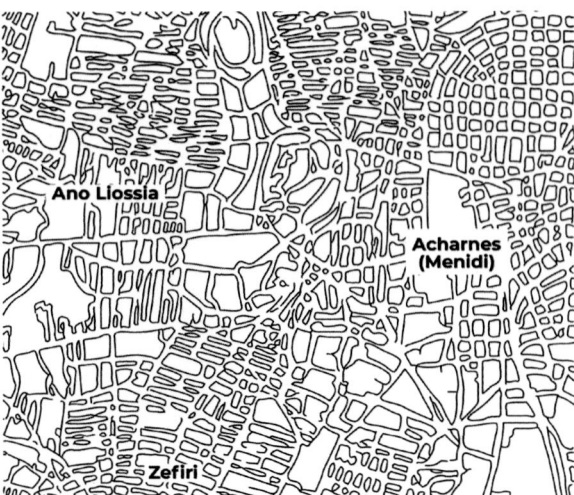

Left: A typical street grid, showing an area of informal, "atypical" development, in this case Nea Liossia and Peristeri, below.

Right: A typical street grid, showing the mix between an older settlement in the periphery and a newer informal one, Zefiri on the left, Acharnes (Menidi) on the right.

Polykatoikìa as Local Language

The ambiguous legality of building in postwar Athens is one way to consider postwar *polykatoikìa* urbanism in the context of Greek culture. By the mid- to late 1950s, the expansion of *polykatoikìa* housing signaled that modernization processes had become a common local language, successfully negotiating the oppositions between modernization and tradition *and* modern architecture and popular civilization.

But how did this complex achievement come about? Inspired by the study of Karagiozis theater, I would like to propose the idea of an urban performance as an interpretative tool: Karagiozis's struggle to survive opens up interesting questions about Greek postwar building culture. Articulating the opposition between feast and famine, the shadow-puppet theater is especially fitting in exploring a similar opposition in practices that seemed to oscillate between great restrictions on the one hand, and large financial and social profit and achievement on the other.

In fact, the opening scene of every traditional Karagiozis performance is framed by two buildings: on the left, the Greek hero's hut, and on the right, the Ottoman ruler's palace. The hut is always tilting, unstable, supported by some old tree trunk, with holes in the roof, while the ruler's palace is large, splendid and beautifully maintained. Beyond the opposition between the Greek (oppressed) and the Turk (oppressor), these two representations succinctly encapsulate one of the most fundamental aspects of modern Greek society of that period: the split between "official" and "unofficial" culture, "high" and "low", or what some anthropologists have termed the "Romeic" (inward-looking, retaining continuities with Ottoman times) and the "Hellenic" (outward-looking, trying to relate to the West and to express continuities with an idealized ancient world).[52]

What might this urban (anti-) hero and his techniques for survival have to do with informal housing development in postwar Athens? To propose that these images may help us think about Athenian postwar architecture and urbanism is not to suggest they have any apparent similarities. Rather, in very different ways, they allow us to understand some important aspects of Greek modernity. The kinds of building

A 1930s house or small apartment building extended upwards into a five-story *polykatoikìa*. Notice the bullet holes in the adjacent building: evidence of the Axis occupation and the Civil War. The label on the scaffolding names a Vassilis X Paptzimas as responsible for this construction.

Panosikoma, or vertical addition technique, practiced in this case by an engineer, Nikos Chatzipantagiotis, in Pagrati, Athens, 1956–1960, in order to turn a single-story dwelling into a small three-story *polykatoikìa*.

practices or modes of performance of those involved in construction during the postwar period, like Karagiozis theater, relied on a very specific set of actions, modified opportunistically according to particular circumstances, identified here as the ruse, the status reversal and parody.

The *antiparochè* was close to being a ruse in and of itself. Dependent on negotiation as it was, it was a shifting, unfixed way of operating that left a lot of room for cunning if not outright deviousness, since the more adept one was at negotiating, the more apartments one was able to gain in return for a plot of land. The elasticity of State policy and the success of the *antiparochè* led to the State tolerating more lenient conditions in terms of laws for housing that then encouraged the private sector more and more. Economist Chrisafis Iordanoglou has poignantly called this a "therapy", adding that "the whole thing had something of the bargaining of Dr. Faustus with Mephistopheles".[53] The confusion between who was legally able to design and to build and who was not remained consistently in an ambiguous state.

The theme of undermining professional/non-professional roles is parodied in the popular 1960 film *Ta Dervisopaida*.[54] Like Karagiozis, the protagonists in this film are two men just in from the provinces who claim proficiency in every conceivable building trade. They even call themselves "master builders". But as the audience soon discovers, neither of them know how to put two bricks together. Causing chaos on the *polykatoikìa* building site, they are soon chased away by the head supervisor, causing hilarious small accidents while on the run. But the trickery does not stop there: whereas the two protagonists try to fool the developer into thinking that they are expert builders, he in turn tries to fool his clients that the new neighborhood is to have many non-existent amenities—a practice that was not uncommon at that time. Stories about this kind of practice appeared in the press, and were often parodied in early comic films, as if in a kind of modern-day update or continuity of Karagiozis theater.[55]

Parody, or the Type and Stereotype

Having discussed ruse and status reversal as interpretative tools, the last such urban performance I wish to point out, is parody, or the type and the stereotype. I suggest that it is the relationship between improvisation and stereotyping that forms a basis to enrich our study of the Athenian *polykatoikìa* further—and perhaps other cities that grew in similar ways. For *polykatoikìa* construction was not wholly improvised or spontaneous. Instead, like in Karagiozis's theater, certain parts were stereotypically conceived—standardized without innovation—and others had small, improvised variations. For instance, the *polykatoikìa* facades may have always been white and without ornament, but there were infinite versions and combinations of balconies possible; some wider, some narrower, some with glass partitions while others were more open. There were variations in the lobbies, in the amount of window openings, the height of the building, and so on.

Overall, the postwar *polykatoikìa* is an extremely simplistic version of modern architecture. If modern architecture was about the notion of "type", the *polykatoikìa* was reduced to a stereotype. Thus the *polykatoikìa* came to use things for purposes other than they were originally intended, in ways that have popular appeal. But stereotypes can sometimes be enabling. In a literary example, Rey Chow's discussion of Jacques Derrida's misunderstanding of Chinese writing helps us to see how stereotypes can be enabling, and not necessarily only "forms of entrapment and victimization".[56] Postwar *polykatoikìa* development enabled the transformation of rural migrants into urban dwellers with urban aspirations and a modern way of life. It helped people feel empowered by being (almost legally) unregulated. It therefore contributed to the modernization of Greek society, and should be celebrated for its contributions. Like the typical postwar American suburban home, the *polykatoikìa* was also successful at the level of popular symbolism, both representing and expanding access to "the good life", as well as progress and optimism.

Rather than thinking of the phenomenon of the Athenian *polykatoikìa* as a local appropriation of the Corbusian Dom-ino, we might think of it in similar terms as the performative processes that create a Karagiozis play. In those performances, certain cultural codes familiar to the audience are combined in various ways in each performance: "each time, the play would be enriched by new 'contents—like in language—that eventually transformed its own stereotypical format'".[57] The popular postwar *polykatoikìa* "emerged" from similar performative processes over time.

It was theater critic and Karagiozis scholar Yiannis Kiourtsakis who touched upon the way in which Greek building culture developed throughout the pre-Independence period despite the lack of professional schools, and the similarities with other aspects of Greek culture of the time. Kiourtsakis pointed out that the ("*naïf*") frescoes of wealthy late eighteenth-century domestic buildings created by itinerant builders and craftsmen were in fact closer to demotic songs than to the paintings' "direct European prototypes".[58] The question of the relationship of a largely non-literate, oral culture to art and architecture is key in understanding building culture in Greece, for a non-literate oral tradition has existed for centuries, partly as a result of subjugation to a foreign power.

As mentioned in chapter 3, throughout the twentieth century and certainly also during the early postwar decades, there was a complicated cultural chasm between the worlds of those with and without formal education. In the eyes of the public, the latter were often preferred because they were seen as being more in tune with everyday life. Those with formal education tried to claim that they too knew about "life", as if to say that they had not lost their ability for immediacy just because they could also think rationally. In a letter from 1965, in one of the many efforts to end the "interference" of those with practical training in the building professions, the head of the Association of Architects and Civil Engineers wrote:

> We are specialists not because we took a degree from a university but because we have *lived* and continue to *live* with technical matters and education every day of our lives. [...] We have the responsibility for the technical progress of this sector [...].[59]

Another way to read this letter is to say that the oral/written debate at the center of Greek cultural life was inscribed or embedded into architects' worlds as well.[60] As we have seen, architects (Doxiadis, Konstantinidis) and laographers (Megas, Hatzimihali), tried to document and inscribe the orally transmitted building culture, particularly from rural areas, as others were documenting demotic songs. By this process they were also formalizing it, trying to fit it into "types"—particularly Megas—rather than recognizing that there are actually unique characteristics at play in this tradition.

To pursue the analogy between the processes of *polykatoikìa* production and those of oral literature further, we might add that literary scholars who have studied oral literature suggest that it possesses certain important characteristics, very different from written works: additive structures, repetition, redundancy and accumulation rather than composition. Taking one example, "additive structure", which is accumulative rather than compositive, is self-evident in popular building processes. Common builders in the countryside always start building a house by making one small room, and as their family expands, they add more rooms and expand the house horizontally. In fact, it has been documented that addition was one of the ways in which the postwar *polykatoikìa* also expanded, particularly in the outskirts of a city. Addition and repetition took many other forms in building. One involved the vertical addition of one or more stories above existing small buildings to turn them into *polykatoikìa* housing. This so-called *panosikoma* (literally meaning "up-lifting") technique was very common, used in a variety of contexts, particularly for small-scale projects (one to two floors), where no permit was required. "Up-lifting" is still practiced today.[61]

These overwhelmingly self-built dwellings in the outskirts of Athens, primarily populated by the working classes, would often begin as one- or two-room structures utilizing traditional techniques and materials. With the "up-lifting" technique, as the owners became more affluent these dwellings gradually became small *polykatoikìa* buildings, increasing in value and improving the lives and livelihood of their inhabitants. This was an easier task where the initial dwellings were built utilizing a concrete frame

Tourkovounia area ca 1957, an area that at the time was on the outskirts of Athens. This image shows illegal expansion outside the city plan that starts from a simple one-room dwelling (nucleus) and expands by addition, developing into small *polykatoikìa* units (towards the back of the photograph), using *panosìkoma* and other such additive processes. This area is now one of the most densely populated in the whole city.

(a version of the *pilotis*), that allowed for a gradual "filling in" of parts according to when the owners had the money or when the police would "turn a blind eye" during elections, to proceed with construction. Thus the so-called "waiting" reinforcement rods (*anamonès*) that stick out on so many terraces of Greek buildings are exactly there to "wait" for another, often illegal, addition.

Historian and urban planner Maria Mantouvalou writes that such areas just outside the city limits inhabited "by those who acquired land by chance—farmers and shepherds, ethnic Greeks originally from Albania [Arvanites], that is, people with neither financial nor political means, nor negotiating ability", were later "legalized", whereupon

the initial self-built [illegal] building in Peristeri, Petroupoli, Liosia, Brahami, etc, after 15–20 years became a 3-floor *polykatoikìa* with *antiparochè*, and the family had both shelter and a small fortune with income from rent. Through this process, the areas around Athens that were initially inhabited with self-built housing, eventually were transformed to veritable 'new towns' with centers that are equivalent to middle-class consuming prototypes."[62]

Mantouvalou's comments about the ease of the social shift between the one-room buildings and the three-floor *polykatoikìa* are extremely illuminating. They show that these one-room dwellings were, as she puts it, "a promise" for the rise of these "outsiders" into the urban middle class. This factor alone makes the *polykatoikìa* a more structurally permanent, less temporary form of illegal or semi-legal building, different from other such buildings around the world. The so-called shanty towns on the margins of major cities, particularly in the Global South, tend to remain as shacks, temporary and unstable, whose inhabitants are much less likely to move up to the middle class.

Although based on a capitalist mode of production, *polykatoikìa* construction operated in very specific ways (no large firms, no capital in advance, almost no involvement from banks or other lending institutions) that were unique. Paradoxically, this informal financing structure seemed to actually encourage class mobility, an unusual quality under capitalism. It allowed for possibilities of a better life for rural migrants and thus offers us a powerful example of architecture's transformative power.

All of these processes together created the sense of the *polykatoikìa* as local language. Put another way, the postwar *polykatoikìa* succeeded as a local language by drawing and adapting material from different sources, new and old, formal and informal, local and foreign, and utilizing very old processes and techniques. With such great social mobility, if one could make it into a *polykatoikìa*, one was more or less certain of middle-class status. A large middle class was something that was politically very desirable for Greece, especially during the Cold War. It makes sense that it was at that time that the *polykatoikìa* became so successful both as concept and as object, for it worked like a machine for equalizing or reconciling social, political and economic differences, helping heal the rifts between the political Left and Right.

In its proverbial homogeneity, the *polykatoikìa* is a good synechdochical image of the historical form of modern Greek society, with the blurry distinctions between its classes. The *polykatoikìa,* while not erasing class distinctions, served as a formal type that crossed social layers, canceling strict dichotomies. As I have tried to show, this homogeneity is not uninteresting—though it may still be hard for some to live with. The *polykatoikìa* was successful in blurring or uniting realms that were previously kept separate: informal/formal, local/foreign, traditional/modern. And like the shadow-puppet theater protagonist himself, the *polykatoikìa* embodied the negotiability of Greek society, where some things can so easily be turned around, yet others always remain the same.

1   Crane, Jacob L, "Ethniki Stegastiki Politiki en Elladi" ("National Housing Policy in Greece"), *Technika Chronika*, Athens, 1–15 May 1956, collection of the Library of the Technical Chamber of Greece, Athens, pp 51–52.

2   Antonopoulou, Sophia, *O Metapolemikos Metasximatismos tis Ellinikis oikonomias kai to oikistiko phenomeno 1950–1980* (*The Postwar Reconstruction of the Greek Economy and the Housing Phenomenon 1950–1980*), Athens: Papazisis Publications, 1991, p 261.

3   In power from 1955 to 1963, Konstantinos Karamanlis left Greece after losing the elections to the Center Union Party of Georgios Papandreou. After the fall of the military junta, he returned to become Prime Minister again, 1974–1980, then President of the Republic, 1980–1985, and again in 1990–1995, leaving active political life only three years before his death in 1998.

4   Between 1958 and 1961 alone, spending in large infrastructural works increased per annum by 21 percent. Constantinos Tsoukalas writes that this policy was "the most serious and with historic consequences of the Karamanlis government". *I Elliniki Tragodia: Apo tin apeleutherwsi ws tous syntagmatarxes* (*The Greek Tragedy: From Independence to the Colonels*), Athens: Nea Synora/Livani, 1981 (written in 1968), p 122.

5   On the landscaping of the Acropolis and Philopappou hills, see Kenneth Frampton, "A Sentimental Topography", *Dimitris Pikionis, Architect 1887–1968*, London: Architectural Association, 1989, illustrated with exquisite photographs by Hélène Binet.

6   The EEC gave Greece a 21-year period for "adjustment" toward full membership.

7   Nikolakopoulos, Elias, "*Elegxomeni Dimokratia: Apo to telos tou emfyliou ews ti diktatoria*" ("Controlled Democracy: From the End of the Civil War to the Start of Dictatorship") *Istoria tou Neou ellinismou - 1770–2000. Nikites kai Itiimenoi 1949–1974. Neoi Ellinikoi Prosanatolismoi: anasygkrotisi kai anaptyxi* (*History of Modern Greece 1770–2000. Winners and Losers, 1949–74. New Orientations: Reconstruction and Development*), Athens: Nea/Ellinika Grammata, 2003, vol 9, p 60.

8   Allen, Peter S, "Positive Aspects of Greek Urbanization: The Case of Athens by 1980", *Ekistics*, vol 53, no 318–319, 1986, p 190.

9   "Between 1951 and 1971 the proportions of the urban and rural populations were reversed, from 38 and 48 percent respectively to 53 and 35 percent. The rest were categorized as semi-urban. Between 1961 and 1971 the population of Greater Athens increased by 37 percent and, during the following decade, by a further 19 percent." Clogg, Richard, *A Concise History of Modern Greece*, Cambridge: Cambridge University Press, 1992, pp 148–149.

10 My thanks to Jean-Louis Cohen for his input on this point.

11 As we saw in chapter 3, the first reinforced concrete building in Athens was constructed in 1906.

12 Stamatiadis, Thucydides, "*I istoria tis polykatoikìas stas Athinas*", "The History of the *Polykatoikìa* in Athens", *Architektoniki*, no 3, May–June 1957, p 50.

13 Conceptually, this social stratification is not dissimilar to Haussmann's Paris from the mid-to late nineteenth century, one difference being that in Paris the top floors and attics were less desirable and were allocated to poorer tenants or to the servants of those who lived below.

14 The Greek terms, still very much in use today, are *fotagogos* (light well) and *akalyptos* (uncovered or left-over space). See Memos Philippidis, "The Fears of Inter-war Architecture before the 'Face' of Uncovered Space", *Urban Housing of the 30s: Modern Architecture in Pre-War Athens*, Dimitris Philippidis ed, Athens: Nereus Editions, 1998, p 53.

15 *Sygxronos Oikodomiki: Poleodomia, Architektoniki, Techni kai Techniki* (*Contemporary Building Science: Planning, Architecture, Art and Technology*), Athens: ChG Cornaros and Co, 1961. Although the title of this catalog implied that the contents would be about "buildings"—not "architecture"—it in fact tried to present the most current artistic and technical achievements of its day.

16 The work of Pappas and others would also eventually become copied and modified.

17 For a discussion of these architects' work see Dimitris Philippidis, *Neoelliniki Architektoniki* (*Modern Greek Architecture*), Athens: Melissa Publications, 1984, pp 283–295; *20th-Century Architecture: Greece*, Wilfried Wang and Savas Condaratos eds, London: Prestel Publications, 1999; *Landscapes of Modernization: Greek Architecture, 1960s and 1990s*, Yannis Aesopos and Yorgos Simeoforidis eds, Athens: Metapolis Press, 1999.

18 For a detailed study of these two building codes that includes all articles and a comparison between them, see Christophoros P Sakellaropoulos, "Modern Architecture and the Politics of Urban Reconstruction, Athens 1945–60", PhD dissertation, National Polytechnic University (EMP), Athens, 1993, pp 200, 247.

19 Kotzamanis, Vassilis, and Thomas Maloutas, "*I kratiki epemvasi ston tomea tis ergatikis-laikis katoikias*" ("The State Intervention in the Working-Class House"), *The Greek Review of Social Research*, no 56, Athens: EKKE, 1985; and Dimitris Philippidis, *Gia tin elliniki poli. Metapolemiki poreia kai mellontikes prooptikes* (*About the Greek City: Postwar Paths and Future Possibilities*), Athens: Themelio, 1990, p 132.

20 Allen, Peter S, "Positive Aspects of Greek Urbanization", p 191.

21 Another important factor was that a large number of the more needy people emigrated abroad (primarily to Australia and the US) and sent billions in remittances in foreign currency. We may gauge that they were less traumatized by moving to the city, Allen says, by the fact that in postwar Athens we find hundreds of regional associations concerned with villages left behind rather than aid organizations for migrants, as we see in other rapidly developing countries at the time.

22 Tsoukalas writes: "The Communist Party was outlawed. [...] thousands of people continued to be held in camps in remote Aegean islands, such as Agios Efstratios and Gavros until almost the end of the Karamanlis period. [...] the 'certificate of social beliefs' was necessary for all activities that needed permission from the administration for public servants and for all white collar workers; to obtain a passport or driver's license, entry into University, hunting or fishing permits, etc." Tsoukalas, *The Greek Tragedy: From Independence to the Colonels*, pp 133–134.

23 The Greek term for "developer" (*ergolavos*, from *ergo*, "work", and *lamvano*, "to receive" or "take responsibility") denotes "small builder" or "head of small construction team". In America, the equivalent term would be "contractor", since "developer", especially since the 1950s, signifies someone who works with large-scale land and building projects. As mentioned in chapter 3, the term "engineer" encompasses all kinds of engineering specialties, a fact that architects have consistently fought against, without much success.

24 As we have seen, the tradition of small construction firms already existed in the nineteenth century, and went hand in hand with the prevalent system of small-scale private land ownership.

25 Zolotas had also had a public disagreement with Doxiadis about the latter's "Survival Plan". See Andreas Kakridis, "Rebuilding the Future: C. A. Doxiadis and the Greek Reconstruction Effort, 1945–1950", *The Historical Review/ La Revue Historique*, Section of Neohellenic Research/Institute of Historical Research, vol 10, 2013, pp 135–160.

26 For an analysis of this argument, see Antonopoulou, *The Postwar Reconstruction of the Greek Economy*, pp 133–134, 137.

27 Antonopoulou, *The Postwar Reconstruction of the Greek Economy*, pp 127–128.

28 Lefas, Pavlos, *Athina. Mia Proteuousa tis Europis* (*Athens: A European Capital. A Brief History of its Development from becoming a Capital City to Our Day*), [Athens], 1985, p 128. Lefas adds that the "legalization" of these illegal areas during the military junta in the late 1960s and later, "solved a social problem but perpetuated an urban one."

29 Excerpt from the author's conversation with Nikos Valsamakis, Athens, 2000. Valsamakis, one of the foremost architects working in postwar Athens, designed highly innovative *polykatoikìa* buildings, among his many built works that have been amply documented by architectural historians.

30 For more on this fascinating topic see Moses I Finlay, *The World of Odysseus*, New York: New York Review of Books, 2002, first published 1954.

31 The dowry was officially abandoned as late as 1983, although it still exists in rural areas as a customary, not an official, negotiation.

32 Those who have written negatively about the KH' vote might not be adequately familiar with Doxiadis's work for the reconstruction of the Greek countryside, since this material has remained largely unknown in Greek historiography up to very recently. For a discussion about Doxiadis and the KH' vote, see Dina Vaiou, Maria Mantouvalou and Maria Mavridou, "Planning in Greece 1949–1974", Second Conference of the Greek Society for Urban History and Planning, *Postwar Greek Planning Between Theory and Chance*, Volos: University of Thessaly Press, 2000.

33 Iordanoglou, Chrisafis, "I oikonomioa 1949–1974. Anaptyxi kai Nomismatiki statherotita: episkopisi: anoikodomisi-katoikies, 1953–1973" ("Economy 1949–1974. Development and Monetary Stability: Review: Reconstruction and Housing, 1953–1973"), *Istoria tou Neou Ellinismou 1770–2000* (*History of Modern Greece 1770–2000*), Vassilis Panagiotopoulos ed, Athens: Nea/Ellinika Grammata, 2003, p 80.

34 Antonopoulou, *The Postwar Reconstruction of the Greek Economy*, p 20.

35 Antonopoulou, *The Postwar Reconstruction of the Greek Economy*, p 26.

36 Antonopoulou, *The Postwar Reconstruction of the Greek Economy*, p 261. Maria Mantouvalou notes another important factor in the growth of the construction industry:

the successful unionization of the builders. From "*I oikodomi stin Athina: Oikonomikes kai koinwnikes apopseis mias eukairiakis anaptyxis*" ("Building Construction in Athens. Social and Economic Aspects of Speculative Growth") in *I Athina ston 20o aiwna. I Athina opws (den) fainetai 1940–1985* (*Athens in the 20th Century. Athens as it Can (Not) Be Seen*), Athens: Ministry of Culture/DAS Architects' Association, 1985, p 39.

37 Through his analysis on *gauging*, ("as a man gauged a bale, the painter surveyed a figure"), art historian Michael Baxandall came up with the term "the period eye" by which he meant "the equipment that a fifteenth century painter's public brought to the complex visual stimulations like pictures". Geertz uses this as an example to talk about how a critic has to learn to "read" artifacts as products of a very specific cultural, social and intellectual context. Geertz citing Baxandall, *Painting and Experience in Fifteenth Century Italy*, Oxford: Clarendon Press, 1972, p 107.

38 On the settlement of Anafiotika, see anthropologist's Roxani Kaftanzoglou's book *Sti Skia tou Ierou Vraxou: Topos kai Mnimi sta Anafiotika* (*On the Shadow of the Sacred Rock: Topos and Memory in Anafiotika*), Athens: Ethniko Kendro Koikonikon Erevnon-Ellinika Grammata, 2001.

39 Kyriakidou-Nestoros cites the work of Dimitris Loukatos, *Folklorica Contemporanea* (*Sygxrona Laografika*), Athens: Filippotis, 2003, first published 1963, pp 55–56 as an influence in the development of her ideas about this shift from old to new utensils. Kyriakidou-Nestoros, Alki, "Greek Laography in Contemporary Perspective", *Laographika Meletimata* (*Folk Studies*), Athens: Etairia Ellinikou Logotexnikou kai Istorikou Archeiou, 1989, pp 90–91.

40 Pikionis, Dimitris, "Ta paichnidia tis Odou Aiolou" ("The Toys of Aiolou Street"), *Dimitris Pikionis Keimena* (*Dimitris Pikionis: Texts*), Athens: Morfotiko Idryma Ethnikis Trapezis, 1985. This text was originally published in the first issue of *The Third Eye* (October 1935), an important literary and artistic magazine that Pikionis co-edited.

41 I use the term "transposition", which in Greek would be *metaforà* or *metatòpisis* and denotes a literal process of movement from one place (*topos*) to another, rather than "translation", which would be *metàphrasi* and would be more specific to a literary process.

42 Detienne, Marcel, and Jean-Pierre Vernant, *Cunning Intelligence in Greek Culture and Society*, Janet Lloyd trans, Chicago: University of Chicago Press, 1991, p 4. See also Michel de Certeau: "The Greeks called these 'ways of operating' *mêtis*. But they go much further back, to the immemorial

intelligence displayed in the tricks and imitations of plants and fishes. From the depths of the ocean to the streets of modern megalopolises, there is a continuity and permanence in these tactics." *The Practice of Everyday Life*, Berkeley, CA: University of California Press, pp xix–xx.

43 Predating the Horizontal Ownership code legislating the *polykatoikìa*, which was incorporated into the General Building Code in 1929.

44 Details from Sakellaropoulos, pp 230, 241.

45 There is evidence that while Minister of Reconstruction, Doxiadis tried very hard to put an end to the unruly procedures associated with planning and amendments: in one of the booklets published through his Ministry in 1948 called "Instructions for the Implementation of Urban Plans and Regulations" ("*Odigiai dia tin efarmogin ton poleodomikon sxedion kai kanonismon*"), Doxiadis specifically wrote that there was to be no legalization of illegal buildings after the fact. The policy was to organize the demolition of any illegal buildings and moreover the owner would bear the expense of demolition, not the State, and there would be no "private plans" by individuals for the extension of City Limits. See "Series of publications from the Ministry of Reconstruction", booklet no 30, Athens, 1948, especially pp 34–42.

46 Tsoukalas talks about the creation of a "parasitic" middle class who supported this "para-State" and its administration and he names "small businesses, artisanal craft, private services of all kinds and various mediating activities... [that] absorbed hundreds of thousands of people. With the passage of time, this way of life became stabilized [...]." Tsoukalas, *The Greek Tragedy*, p 118.

47 Philippidis, *About the Greek City*, p 25. For the concept of "para-urbanism" see chapter 6 in the book, pp 192–214.

48 Philippidis, *About the Greek City*, p 192. Philippidis has written a lot about this particularity of Athenian development. See also his essay in *Athens 2002: Absolute Realism*, Takis Koubis et al eds, Athens: Futura, 2002.

49 Philippidis, *About the Greek City*, p 200.

50 Philippidis, *About the Greek City*, p 203.

51 Andrews, Kevin, *Cities of the World: Athens*, London: Phoenix House, 1967, p 13.

52 Herzfeld, Michael, "Within and Without: The Category of 'Female' in the Ethnography of Modern Greece", *Gender and Power in Rural*

Greece, Jill Dubisch ed, New Jersey: Princeton University Press, 1986, pp 217–218. Although the Ottoman and Hellenic are obviously not the same, they function in the same way in this example, as a foreign "other" culture.

53 Iordanoglou, "Economy 1949–1974. Development and Monetary Stability", p 80.

54 The film *Ta Dervisopaida,* directed by Stelios Tatasopoulos, refers to the Turkish word *dervish* and means "somebody who behaves very energetically". The film opens with a *polykatoikìa* under construction. A voice-over declares: "Athens is changing. The old picturesque houses are torn down and in their place rises massive modern *polykatoikìa* housing. Everywhere you look there are cranes, shovels, machines and people working for reconstruction. Athens is changing. A new city is being created."

55 One such well-known comedy was *Enas Veggos gia oles tis doulies* (Dinos Katsouridis, 1970) where the protagonist Thanasis Vengos plays a bogus realtor in 1950s Athens luring clients into mountainous and inaccessible plots of land promising them amenities that clearly did not exist.

56 See Rey Chow: "without the cliché of Chinese as an ideographic language, as a writing made up of silent little pictures, the radical epistemic rupture known as deconstruction could perhaps not have come into being in the manner it did". "How (the) Inscrutable Chinese Led to Globalized Theory", *PMLA,* January 2001, vol 116, no 1, pp 70–71.

57 Kiourtsakis, Yannis, *Proforiki Paradosi kai Omadiki dimiourgia. To paradeigma tou Karagiozi (Oral Tradition and Group Creativity. The Example of Karagiozis),* Athens: Kedros, 1983, p 143.

58 Kiourtsakis, *Oral Tradition and Group Creativity,* p 89.

59 Letter from IO Christodoulidis, Chairman of the Association of Civil Engineers, 6 February 1965, Archives of the Technical Chamber of Greece, Athens.

60 According to literary scholar Dimitris Tziovas: "One of the main characteristics of Greek intellectual life in the last two centuries has been the conflict between orality and textuality. The language controversy is one of the most important manifestations of this conflict. [...] Approaching Greek literature and culture in terms of a duality is not to adopt either a structuralist perspective or to discuss the problem of Greek identity in terms of binary oppositions [...] Rather [...] this study shows that the conflict between orality and textuality is far-reaching in its implications, permeating many cultural phenomena and intellectual practices". Tziovas, Dimitris,

"Residual Orality and Belated Textuality in Greek Literature and Culture", *Journal of Modern Greek Studies,* vol 7, no 2, October 1989, p 321. Tziovas also points out that the term for "literature" in Greek (*logotechnia*) is etymologically closer to the spoken word (*logos*), rather than the Latin term *literature* (from *litera,* meaning "letter"). Similarly the word for "writer" in Greek is *syggrafeas,* which "is based on the verb *rapto* and means 'he who stitches songs together', as in an epic oral narrative."

61 This practice of vertical addition was legally instituted by the junta government when Brigadier Patakos suddenly allowed an additional floor on existing buildings. Dimitris Philippidis sees the "up-lifting" process at work when architects work in small installments or "revisit" their old work adding parts, or even common people adding on top of architects' work, at times by so doing "cancel the monumentality of the original". Philippidis, Dimitris, "Eponymi kai maziki architektoniki (1930–1970)" ("Formal and mass architecture 1930–1970"), *Moderna architektoniki stin Ellada (Modern Architecture in Greece),* Athens: Melissa Publications, 2001, p 72.

62 Mantouvalou, "Building Construction in Athens", p 40.

A view of the expanding
city from Lycabettus Hill,
early 1960s.

Chapter 6: The Polykatoikìa Interior
Housewives and Modern Life

When I was a child I often heard the story of how one day, while my grandfather was away, my mother and grandmother used white paint to cover the ceiling decorations in their neoclassical house in Crete. From the way my mother recounted the story, I always felt that the whitening act was a great thrill for the female side of the family, something that gave them a sense of achievement and satisfaction. They had cunningly managed to make the changes they wanted and caught my grandfather by surprise, utilizing their female *ponirià* (*mêtis*, "craftiness", "guile"). It seemed like a defiant, emancipatory act but at the same time it was an act of erasure that left me with a sense of unease every time I heard it.

Why white paint, the "unspoken obsession" of modern architecture?[1] Were these women obeying Le Corbusier's "Law of Ripolin" that suggested that "inner cleanness" can come only after whitewashing one's walls?[2] Or were they trying to turn their well-to-do, architect-designed house into a humble dwelling from an Aegean village? Were my mother and grandmother hoping to dissociate themselves from decoration, which after all, was what (male) modernist architects famously rejected? Were they somehow aware that to be modern one has to be unornamented, stripped from the primitive urge to decorate? And how might that fit with traditional conceptions of women's work in the interior? It is more as though whitening the ceiling fused a traditional model of cleanliness with a new idea in the air, that of modernity. Indeed, the crucial next step in my family narrative involved my mother's move into an urban *polykatoikìa* apartment in Athens, a housing type that exemplified this fusion.

This story raises important questions. Why should the tropes of erasure and modernity be linked to housewives in the postwar era? What can we learn about urbanization by paying attention to the domestic environment? And how can we gain a more complex understanding of domestic space as a central aspect of modernity? In this chapter I want to extricate my sense of unease about my own family's liberating act by connecting themes of modern architecture, Greek modernity and tradition with questions of gender and the interior.

In order to open up the theme of women and interiors, let us first turn to anthropology. In a fascinating article from 1986, Michael Herzfeld gave us an anthropological interpretation of the close relationship of women to interiors in rural Greece. After establishing that "women exercise more authority in intimate settings"—ie the interior of their homes—Herzfeld argues that female modesty in rural Greece can be seen as "a public reversal of domestic power relations".[3] Was my mother's act of cunning then, to some extent, calculated to reinforce her and her mother's (private) influence over the (public) supremacy of the men of their household?

Whereas the outcome and details of that episode will remain forever lost in family lore, the idea that in the twentieth century women's decisions somehow reflected a desire to embrace modernity in their own terms is gaining more attention from architectural historians. For instance, Hilde Heynen argues that "far from being an antidote to modernity, for most [...] women the home was indeed the place where modernity was enacted".[4] Going against previous scholarship that tended to suggest that modernity and domesticity were primarily oppositional, Heynen urges us to broaden the "scope of investigation more widely" so as to see that "there is also a certain complicity between modernity and domesticity".[5]

This chapter shows how some of these issues played themselves out in the context of postwar Athens. Studying the history of the domestic interior presents major challenges due to its ephemeral nature and the lack of documents and sources that deny us direct access to interior spaces and ways of inhabiting them, as well as the general scarcity of scholarship about modern Greece in particular. To address these challenges, we will try and construe, in Charles Rice's words, "a kind of imagined association" rather than attempt complete transparency and objectivity of the visual evidence.[6]

Angeliki Hatzimihali and the Search for the Material Culture of The Hellenic House

We owe a large part of the history of domestic space in Greece to the artist and laographer Angeliki Hatzimihali (1895–1965).[7] Hatzimihali began recording domestic life in rural Greece in the early 1920s. Her first book, *Skyros* (begun 1922, published 1925), contained black-and-white photographs, sketches and detailed explanatory texts of domestic life in this Aegean island. During the 1930s she was a member of a group called *Syllogos Elliniki Laiki Techni* (Hellenic Popular Art Association) whose members included notable architects such as Pikionis and Doxiadis, and artists such as Yannis Tsarouchis and Nikos Engonopoulos, all of whom were involved in trying to document buildings that for them were important parts of Hellenic heritage.[8] During the Second World War and the Axis occupation of Athens, Hatzimihali was involved in active resistance by organizing help for Greek soldiers fighting at the front and taking part in Doxiadis's Circle discussions.[9]

The rural dwellings Hatzimihali sketched and wrote about seemed to have been unchanged for centuries. Her documentation of the typical Skyros island house— particularly its interior—and her ideas about what constitutes a "Hellenic Popular House" were updated by the time of her *Chorotaxìa* contributions in 1942, 1949 and 1955. In these texts Hatzimihali praised the wisdom of rural houses and showed how even with minimal means, they displayed a wealth of artistic expression.

Hatzimihali's book on Skyros provides us a point of comparison with Aris Konstantinidis's *The Old Athenian Houses*, 1950, analyzed in chapter 2. For in some respects, Konstantinidis's work presented an idealized and abstract image of pre-Independence domestic Athenian architecture: there were no people in his photos and drawings, and there was certainly no mention of women's lives inside these houses.[10] In contrast, Hatzimihali's research shows us how people lived in rural dwellings, their tools and domestic utensils or equipment, and includes figures showing them inhabiting their space.

Angeliki Hatzimihali (1895–1965). Born to an upper-middle-class family of intellectuals and art collectors, her father a university professor and her grandfather a prominent lawyer, Hatzimihali was encouraged to become an artist, although as a woman she was not allowed by her father to go to university. She began collecting objects of decorative art already in the first years of the twentieth century. By 1920 she had decided that this was going to be her particular calling in life—even above her own family and her work as a painter. Hatzimihali was well known among Greek intellectuals especially in relation to her humanitarian work during the war, her involvement in the Lykeion Ellinidon (Institution of Greek Women) her work on the Sarakatsan nomadic populations and her book on Skyros.

Being an Aegean *megaron*-type building, the typical Skyros house comprised a long and narrow room, with a door and windows in the front facade and perhaps smaller windows to one side. All household activities took place within this space: the preparation of food, sleeping, resting and social life. Hatzimihali noted that the separation of spaces was less about the difference between public and private areas within the house than it was between different activities that take place at different times of the day or night. She showed the structural components such as the fireplace to one side and the cooking area, and discussed how inhabitants lived in the house, indicating their woven tablecloths, embroideries decorating the fireplace, the hand-painted ceramic plates and the intricate woodwork.

On its long and narrow rectangular plan, there were few openings on the side walls, and none at the back, the sleeping area. One would have to climb up a small narrow ladder to reach the bed, which was on top of a raised timber structure, with storage and other functions underneath. The bed was wide and often accommodated several members of the family. The roof was flat, covered with naturally insulating material, and could be accessed by external stone steps set against a side wall; the kind that is found all over the Aegean islands and that Le Corbusier admired on his visit to the Aegean during the CIAM IV symposium.

Unlike the architectural historians Aristotelis Zachos and Anastasios Orlandos who both studied the "noble" Greek house during the 1920s, Hatzimihali's main area of interest was the popular house, the house of peasants and farmers.[11] Hatzimihali

Angeliki Hatzimihali, "Skyros House Interior", photograph, from her book on Skyros, 1925. A woman dressed in black is sitting on the attic with a timber wall partition underneath in this sparse interior. Coats and hats are hanging on hooks, and decorative objects, such as ceramic plates and copper cooking utensils, are part of the design of the interior.

believed that such a typical rural house, no matter how humble it may be, could give us important clues as to how to develop a new and relevant Greek architecture. And in contrast to the academic laographer Georgios Megas, discussed in chapter 4, Hatzimihali sought to find ways to demonstrate the value of these sparse interiors without resorting to rigid typological analyses, and tried to suggest how they may be relevant to contemporary urban life.

If it were possible to demonstrate the creative value of the individual artifacts and interiors based on studying the peasant house, Hatzimihali believed that it would become clear that there could be a modern "Hellenic" house.[12] In 1921, at the age of 26, Hatzimihali began organizing exhibitions of women's work—such as woven textiles, fabrics, ceramics, needlework and other handmade objects for domestic use—from different rural areas, as a member of *Lykeion Ellinidon* (Institution of Greek Women), an organization that still exists. This well-received exhibition enabled her to found *To spiti tou koritsiou* (The Young Woman's House) in 1923, to help women refugees from Asia Minor; these women were taught how to craft such domestic objects, following traditional prototypes that she had been researching, collecting and preserving. The work these young women produced was very successful and was shown in the Greek Pavilion at the International Exhibition of Modern Decorative and Industrial Arts in Paris in 1925, where they won two prizes: in 1928 in Thessaloniki's International Exhibition; and at the Delphic Celebrations of 1927 and 1930. In 1938 The Young Woman's House became an official trade school, "The Hellenic House: Domestic, Craft, Trade School" (*Oikokyriki, Viotechniki, Epaggelmatiki Scholi: To Elliniko Spiti*). This became known as "Hatzimihali's School", and Hatzimihali celebrated 20 years of its operation in 1957 with an exhibition called The Hellenic House, re-shown in 1962.[13]

Like others engaged in ethnographic work at this time, Hatzimihali realized that the home and its contents was an important place for the expression of the identities and world views of its inhabitants. She studied evidence of everyday life in rural interiors and also collected the language and specific terms that were used to describe these interiors, much like Megas had done in his research on northern Greece. She indicated the importance of this work in her 1925 book on Skyros, saying: "the popular house is to the architecture of a country as the legend [*thrylos*] is for literature or popular song for music".

Hatzimihali drew connections between popular art, the art of humble people who inhabited the countryside and architecture. In fact she included architecture in her category of "popular artifacts", thus linking the "high" art of architectural design with the "low" (women's) work of household decoration; an important link, one that she made because of her attention to women's work. In her views about traditional art and crafts, Hatzimihali may be considered an early scholar of material culture, reading a culture's beliefs, traditions, attitudes and values in its cultural artifacts. She remarked on the origins of important names and terms, told stories, recounted important customs for feasts and other celebratory occasions, discussed local beliefs and often spent weeks and months staying with her subjects of study, doing what today we might recognize as fieldwork, but was perceived as more than slightly eccentric behavior at the time.

Paying attention to women's work in the domestic setting was important in another sense: in Greece, as elsewhere in the southern Mediterranean, housekeeping is exclusively women's work. The word in Greek is *noikokyriò*, from *oìkos* and *kyrios*, roughly meaning "mastering" or "ordering the interior of the house". The female inhabitant is the *noikokyrà*, the housemistress, a term of distinction.[14] As anthropologist Jill Dubisch suggests, "even when she does not actually own her dwelling, a woman is viewed in terms of the house and the house is viewed in relation to the woman. It is still a high compliment to say of a woman (but not of a man) that she is *tou spitiou*, or 'of the house', that is, that her time and attention are devoted to the house and family and their care."[15]

In most parts of Greece, women were (and still are) the ones to inherit houses as part of their dowry. But even when a woman's family could not afford to build her a house, a woman was responsible for at least owning her own domestic equipment. Growing up in rural Greece meant that the production of this equipment as part of a woman's dowry was both her main focus as well as her main form of education. A dowry, as we learn from Hatzimihali's work, included providing the material to "dress" and to display the interior primarily with items weaved on the loom, such as bedding, clothing, tablecloths, curtains and other such handmade domestic items.

The display of women's work and dowry items was central to the rural interior. There were items that were displayed daily and those that were shown only on special occasions, such as a religious feast or a wedding ceremony. There were specific places in the house where decorative items were placed (in the image on the previous page, for instance, we see decorative plates arranged linearly on a special shelf that spanned the length of the entire room). Women individually designed every item, and they were proud of their work and that of their ancestors (dowry items are still handed down to each generation). We sense that a woman's identity was bound up with the identity or design of her interior, not least because her future husband was expected to be adept at reading her interior to recognize and judge her skills. As another anthropologist, Lucy Rushton, commented, "there is a strong sense that it is more than [a woman's] skill that is being displayed. She [lays] out her virtue before [her guests.]"[16]

The Contemporary Housewife and Life in the Polykatoikìa Interior

These very qualities of the traditional interior that Hatzimihali and other laographers appreciated also point to the vast difference between how people—especially women—experienced everyday life in rural prewar and urban postwar Greek homes. Even though there were in fact many remarkable things about rural houses, they were also very inadequate, even primitive, primarily on the level of household technology, a fact that was not pointed out by anyone, perhaps because it was widely understood. They had almost no amenities: no running water, no bathroom inside the house, and no appliances. Daily household tasks were remarkably difficult, arduous and tiring for women in these rural settings.

In fact, following the war there was a vast and increasing disparity between the apparent ease of life in the city, and the harshness of life in the countryside. Even in urban areas, there were big differences between how ordinary people lived before the war and the promise of life in the new *polykatoikìa* apartments. For women in particular, *polykatoikìa* apartments represented a sense of modern life, something that was intensely desirable at a time. Unlike northern European and American contexts where a woman's role was stereotypically seen as "applying the brakes [...] to the frenzied pace of technological progress",[17] in Greece women were actually the ones who seemed more eager to move forward to a modernized domestic interior.

This fact was expressed in very touching ways in the popular 1965 film *I de gyni na fovatia ton andra* (*Woman Shall Fear Man*).[18] With the city of Athens as a background, noisy scenes show crowds crossing busy intersections and brand new white *polykatoikìa* buildings. The story of this film is about a man and a woman and their struggle to overcome the anxiety of the city's transformations and agree as to what constitutes a "proper" domestic setting. Whereas the man laments change, the woman is longing to see it. Going to his office job in the center of Athens every day, the man grieves what he sees around him, mainly more "*polykatoikìa* buildings that are suffocating us". He wishes to remain in what could easily have been one of Konstantinidis's "old" Athenian houses: a tiny part of a courtyard house that feels like "home" to him, but has no running water and heating, not to mention noisy neighbors.

His wife, who after all, spends her whole day in the house, has different views. As soon as he is promoted, her girlfriends help her realize that she simply must move: "your husband has to buy you an apartment [in a *polykatoikìa*] with all modern amenities". Like a chorus in an ancient tragedy, they then turn and tell the husband: "socially it is demanded of you to change your domestic situation", and "you must buy an apartment in a *polykatoikìa* and furnish it". Resisting this pressure, the husband walks out on his wife, just as their house is plainly starting to fall apart.

The domestic interior and their marital relationship are identified in their minds and ours. But as in many films of that time, there is a happy ending: after moving on, husband and wife individually go to visit their old house one more time, emerging together from the dust. Demolition crews have moved in, behind them the often-cited

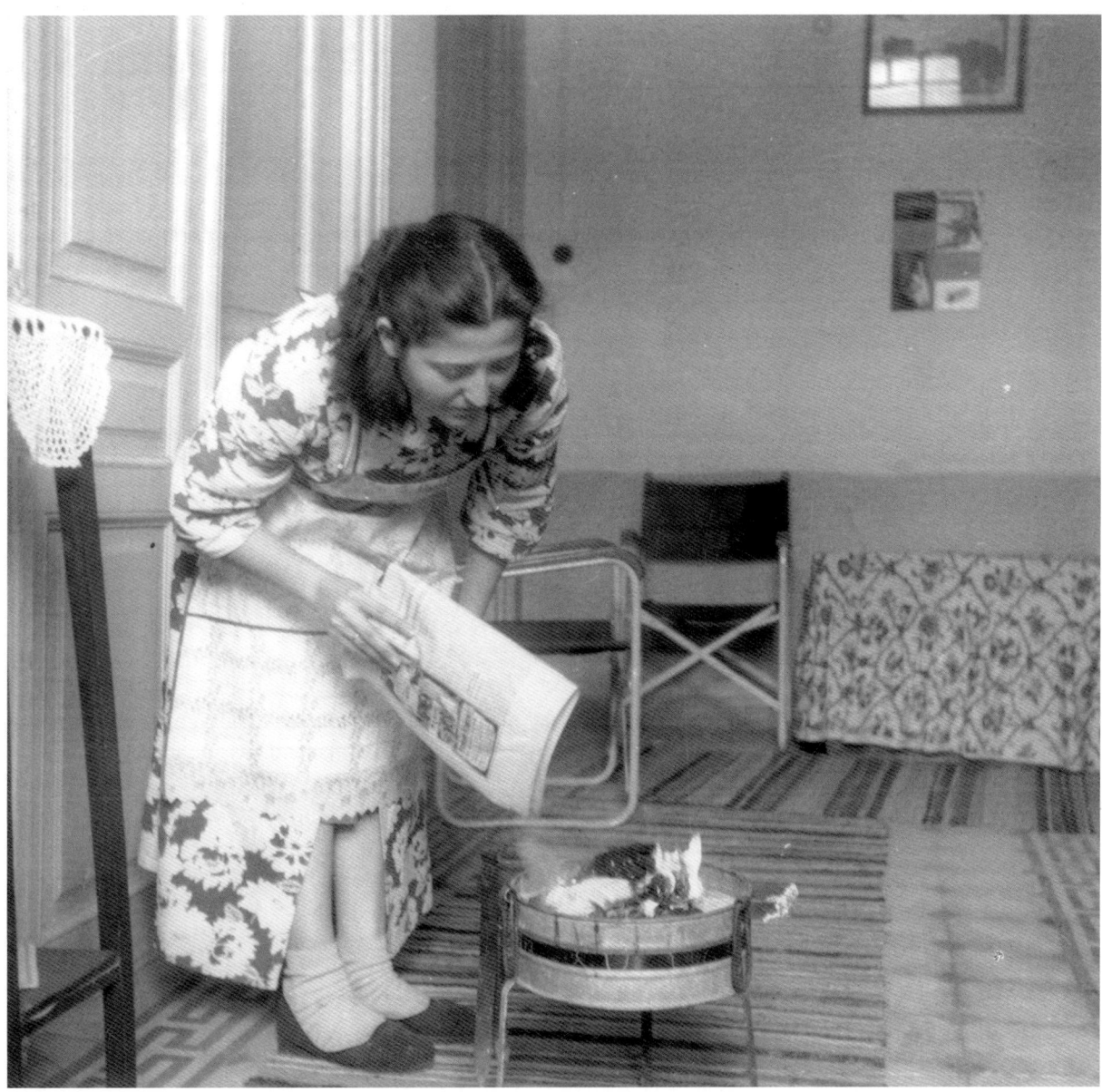

Urban life in prewar dwellings still existing during the 1950s and perhaps even 1960s: a woman lighting a fire on a small tin tray a few inches above the floor to keep warm in her interior. The high ceilings, floor tiles and generously proportioned doors suggest that this was a neoclassical house interior. January 1957.

handwritten sign advertising "old building materials for sale". The sign is misspelled, indicating the builders' lack of basic education. The husband has apparently reformed, telling his wife a phrase with intended double meaning: "don't look back, only look ahead" as the two leave the narrow street of their old house and start walking toward the wider city streets and *polykatoikìa* buildings in the distance.

Another example of an optimistic female view of impending modernization in the Greek context was Anna Kasfiki's book *Contemporary Housekeeping,* incidentally published in the same year as one of the exhibitions organized by Angeliki Hatzimihali for The Hellenic House, 1958. Echoing other such manuals published in Europe and the US around this time, author and "professor of housekeeping" (*oikokyrikì*) Anna Kasfiki was interested in studying women's work and the domestic interior and offering practical advice for the improvement of daily tasks. Organized as a dictionary of issues related to women and the house, Kasfiki's work might also be considered as a female counterpoint to Tzartzanos's (male) dictionary of building terms, which offered ways to "translate" older terms and an older way of life into a newer, modern time. To this end, *Contemporary Housekeeping* offered information and advice on both old traditional ways of doing things and newer modern ones.

Contemporary Housekeeping was clearly addressed to middle-class urban women who had by then already begun to move into their brand new *polykatoikìa* apartments. Kasfiki's guide shows that, despite the *polykatoikìa*'s modern appearance, plenty of remnants of the rural world or of an older way of life still persisted: the dowry, domestic rituals and customs. The continuity showed especially in the ways of accomplishing domestic chores that ranged from learning to use novel electric utensils, such as stoves and irons, to explaining the best ways to paint and whitewash ("when we are to paint

Cover of *Contemporary Housekeeping* handbook and a page from the housework dictionary at the back, by Anna Kasfiki, Professor of Household Science, 1958.

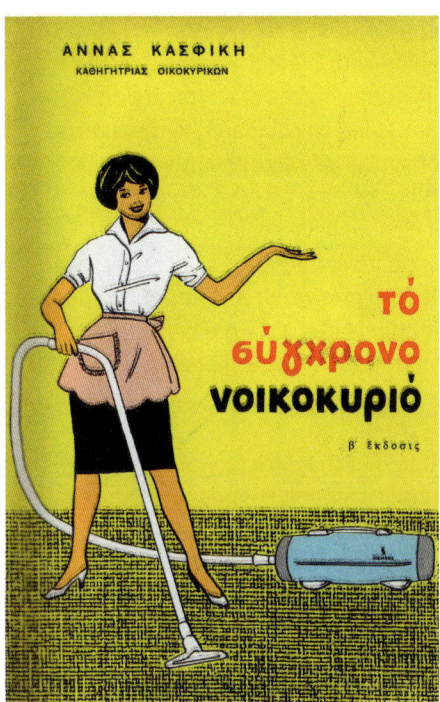

walls, doors, and so on, we mix some bay leaf oil in the paint because it drives insects away"), to cleaning aluminum kitchen pots ("with petrol" or by boiling them "with water and potatoes, milk, tomatoes or spinach")—none of which of course sound particularly modern to today's reader.

The book was arranged in two parts: the first was a general step-by-step account of the different areas in the house and how best to look after them. The second, an eclectic dictionary, was subtitled "2000 Small Secrets for Housekeeping". This section included an intriguing mix of things. For instance, under the letter "m" there are instructions on spaghetti, softeners, hair, wool clothes, pearls, marble and white paint (*Makaronia, malaktika, mallia, mallina, margaritaria, marmara... mpogia aspri*); under the letter "f", "feathers" (*ftera*) and how to pluck a chicken and prepare its feathers to stuff a pillow.

Perhaps it's not all that surprising to hear that Athenian housewives in the late 1950s were still expected to know how to pluck a chicken when we realize that often there were in fact chicken coops on the roofs of lower-middle-class urban buildings— and Kasfiki also gave instructions on how to look after a chicken coop! Greek cinema would record the coops with amusement in such films as *Oikogeneia Papadopoulou* (*The Papadopoulos Family*) (Roviros Manthoulis, 1960), and *I Roda* (*The Wheel*) (Theodoros Adamopoulos, 1961).

Even though Kasfiki discussed many traditional ways of doing things, she also showed that there were some totally new aspects to running a modern *polykatoikìa* household. One of the main advantages of the *polykatoikìa* was that it provided new household amenities. Kasfiki's book cover showed a smiling housewife sporting a vacuum cleaner, and had a whole section called "Our Electricity-Powered Household" ("*To Electrokinito Noikokyrio mas*"). In this section, somewhat reminiscent of northern

European and American domestic reformers' work, Kasfiki offered design advice for efficient housekeeping with Siemens appliances.[19]

But what of the individual spaces of a typical *polykatoikìa* apartment outlined in the first part of Kasfiki's book? Clearly, compared to the rural prewar house, the structure and organization of interior space was significantly different. Some important changes had already taken place within the neoclassical urban house, also found in many small towns outside of Athens, which as we have seen were closer to European bourgeois prototypes.

In studying various postwar magazines directed towards women such as *Gynaika kai Spiti* (*Woman and Home*), *Moderno Spiti* (*Modern House*) and *Ellinida* (*Greek Woman*), we can see that they routinely blurred what was real and existed in Athens, versus what was imagined or taken from somewhere else in the world. There are no details in the captions; we can almost never tell with certainty where the images illustrating articles in most magazines come from.[20]

Troubled, even irritated at the difficulty of locating evidence about "real" historical interiors from this period, I gradually began to accept that perhaps there is something interesting in this vague, unspecific way in which the press presented and discussed them. Perhaps these magazines aimed less at illustrating existing spaces than helping their readers daydream about possible ones they might one day achieve. In this sense, these magazine articles and illustrations worked wholly like advertisements. They promoted an illusive idea of modern life, so desirable by all layers of society, especially by women, and were "devoid of all negativity", showing only "an imaginary potentiality".[21]

Penny Sparke has noted another positive way in which to consider advertisements: in the Anglo-Saxon context they were "one way through which the idea of modernity was communicated to a mass audience, largely to women" and "formed a bridge between masculine culture that had engendered them and the feminine culture at which they were directed".[22] In our case, these unreal "imaginary" images were there to show what is "modern", a term repeated constantly, and their objective was to help readers realize and attain this goal, whether illustrating "a modern living room" (*living room*), "a modern hall" (*hol*), how to become a "modern couple", or own a "modern refrigerator". Like in my family story, magazines tried to convince women that they too could become "modern" through either transforming their old interiors or choosing the right new appliances.

Housewives and Domestic Objects

One recurrent idea in these advertisements and magazine articles was the identification of women with the domestic interior. This idea has a long history. One finds it in various guises in Victorian England and America in the ways in which people discussed the house, especially in relation to the so-called "cult of domesticity".[23] At that point women started to be seen as "beautifiers" and not only through their actions—decorating the interior—but also by their presence:

A chandelier could be described as 'delicate', an epithet long associated with femininity and the female body. [...] for the Victorians, these feminine attributes were considered to be 'natural' features of the female sex [...] Beauty, it was generally

agreed, was a fundamental attribute of women and, therefore women, rather than men, were ideally qualified to infect it into the domestic setting.[24]

In the twentieth century this idea lived on, especially revived in popular media and advertisements in the 1950s and 60s, which never seemed to tire of constructing incongruous visual images linking women with all kinds of domestic equipment and appliances—down to bathroom fittings. Greek postwar magazines about the interior adopted and adapted some of these same European and American tendencies and therefore perpetuated some of the same constructions:

> For You and Your Armchairs! The silk-cotton fabric is very much in fashion this year. There is no end to what we can make with it: dresses, skirts, ties, trousers, tablecloths, even armchair covers. Yes, yes. It shouldn't seem strange.... It's a very modern idea.... It is really very simple to dress an armchair as you can see in these photographs as long as you use your skill (or craftiness!)[25]

When not spelled out directly, as in the examples above where women "match" their furniture, kitchen appliances and toilet seats, it appears in a subliminal way, for after a while one realizes that the same coaxing, persuasive—or is it patronizing?—tone used to describe a dress or *oikostolì* (house-uniform) is also deployed in discussions of the "little living area" (*salonàki*) and the various "corners" of the interior.[26] The fact that women were still expected to do the majority of housework, of course, was not discussed. Instead, the editors seemed to suggest that if only a woman wore a modern apron, all work would happen by itself. Today we may read these double meanings more clearly, especially in such illustrations shown here and their captions: "A Tasty Kitchen and a Modern Home" is illustrated by a beautiful young woman with a short mini-skirt leaping in joy. Clearly this image is as much about the tasty girl and the modern kitchen as it is about the virtues of the modern home.

Film still, *Laòs kai Kolonaki*, (*The People and Kolonaki*), 1959, Yannis Dalianidis. Actor Costas Hatzichristos talks about a desirable blonde, comparing her to a *polykatoikìa*. This film is about a recent immigrant to Athens, pictured here, who owns a fresh dairy shop in a very expensive neighborhood, Kolonaki. He falls in love with the upper-class snobbish tall blonde who comes into his store but she pays no attention to him—until he wins the lottery. This comedy commented on the ways in which the upper classes looked down on the recent immigrants yet they had much more *filòtimo* (honor, pride) and kindness than the disaffected rich.

Popular films, too, indulged the conception that women and houses are intimately linked: one particular 1959 film likens a desirable sexy blonde to a whole *polykatoikìa*. In this film, the comic actor Costas Hatzichristos capitalizes on the feminine gender of the word *polykatoikìa* to deliver the following lines with gestures full of sexual innuendos: "I want a woman to be like a *polykatoikìa*. To have many floors. To be substantial. In length, height and width. With verandas, attics, basements... I want to look at her and my whole field of vision to be full of... floors!"[27] Hatzichristos not only articulates the link between women and houses, but also reinforces the fact that an apartment in a postwar *polykatoikìa* was—like a sexy blonde—also every man's desire.

The Polykatoikìa Interior and New Subjectivities

Despite their comic or dramatic plots, popular films were successful in portraying the new middle class and aspiring middle class. In postwar popular films the new urban dweller, who was—with rare exceptions—an Athenian, was not so much a *flâneur* lost observing the crowd, but a cheeky, crafty, outsmarting peasant, who wanted to be in the city and pretended to be comfortable there even when he or she might, in truth, be a little lost. After all, as historian Constantinos Tsoukalas has noted, Athens had a very privileged position in respect to other geographic areas of Greece at that time: it absorbed more workers, received more imports and contributed more taxes. It also had the highest number of hospital beds and medical specialists, and income above the national average.[28]

Interior of a *polykatoikìa* lobby. In the film *O Papatrehas*, 1966, Thanasis Vengos's manic doorman character, is always in motion: sweeping the lobby, mopping the marble floors as we see him doing here, running to do errands for the residents of the *polykatoikìa* apartments. When the elevator breaks down, he picks up the old ladies and all their shopping and carries them all the way to their floors.

Drama on a *polykatoikìa* facade: actor Thanasis Vengos playing the busy doorman of a *polykatoikìa* tries to help a woman from committing suicide; instead he loses his balance and falls down the flat roof of the building but escapes by holding on to a rope and getting help from the fire department. *O Papatrehas*, 1966.

Unlike rapidly urbanized areas in other countries, Athens was not a totally alien space to rural migrants. Instead, they felt the city was theirs and they wanted to be part of it. At least in popular culture, they were not portrayed as romanticizing or reminiscing about the countryside they left behind. In addition, initially migrants from particular locations settled into distinct areas in Athens (the Cyclades in Kypseli, Naxians in Thesion and Psyri, other island people in Pireaus, where traces of this regional clustering are still visible today, especially in names of streets). Thus there was a strong sense of neighborhood community that in a way recreated the kinship of village life.

Popular cinema, such as the films discussed above, gives us many clues about life in the early postwar *polykatoikìa* neighborhoods and evidence of household interiors. As film historian Eliza-Anna Delveroudi has commented, "despite the inevitable repetition of plots, social developments are gradually outlined in the stories, characters and attitudes of these films".[29] Delveroudi has noted that up until the end of the 1950s at least, popular films symbolically linked the quality of housing to a character's socio-economic situation. Thus "rich people live in newly built *polykatoikìes* with modern furniture; the middle layers in single-family homes with prewar furniture; the unemployed and all those who work for daily wages shared a room with friends, equipped with minimal furniture".[30] For instance, in *Oikogeneia Papadopoulou* (Roviros Manthoulis, 1960) we see a family who lives in a *polykatoikìa* looking down on a family living in a prewar neoclassical style single-family house with its bulky, darkly stained furniture.

Other popular films about urban life at this time placed an emphasis on the middle and upper-middle-class woman, her daughters and maids. This new middle-class woman was the "lady of the house" (*i kyria tou spitiou*). Her areas in the *polykatoikìa* apartment included the "modern" living room where she would play cards with her women friends and entertain, and the master bedroom. Even middle—as opposed to upper-middle-class—women also emerged as "ladies" in their houses (*kyrìes*).

Their young maids were another new female type who populated Athens in this period. Almost always having just arrived to Athens from her village, the very young, unmarried maid was usually portrayed as being illiterate, slightly awkward, if not outright delinquent as she attempted to adjust to the new ways of life in the city. Her province in the apartment included the kitchen, the service entry and staircase (if there was one), the pantry (or so-called *office* in upper-class apartments), and of course, invariably a tiny bedroom for herself, often badly lit and poorly ventilated.[31]

In *Prosopo me prosopo* (*Face to Face*, Roviros Manthoulis, 1966) the young maid reads photo-romances in her free time. The remarkable director of this film (which was never destined to be a commercial success), parodied women's journals and their efforts to guide and instruct women in how to dress, how to sit properly, how to cross their legs, and so on by showing the maid listening religiously to advice for women on her little radio. Clearly young maids had social aspirations and they, too, shared every woman's desire of that period, which was to find a good husband and to raise a family in a modern *polykatoikìa* apartment.

The husband was to have his own space in the *polykatoikìa* as well. Perhaps the "masculine corner" featured in some magazines was also transposed from Europe—at least the way in which it appeared in a magazine article which discussed "comfort"—again, a term with specific background in industrial Europe and America. In the Greek way of life, one imagines a man sitting in an armchair expecting his wife to serve him coffee as well as fetch his newspaper and slippers. This particular article rendered the "masculine corner" more sexy with leather upholstered furniture and sensuous paintings hanging on the walls:

The Masculine Corner: It is true my friends that all of us, more or less, have created our own corner, our own totally private space that could be an armchair or a whole room. In this space you feel absolutely comfortable—it is the same feeling as you have wearing your old comfortable shoes. [...] Well, my friends, my intention is to convince all of you who might still have objections about the necessity of this [masculine] corner and to help you make one that will be as comfortable as possible and at the same time in the spirit of modern decoration.[32]

In addition to the modern husband, the doorman was the most ubiquitous of the new male postwar types fashioned by the *polykatoikìa*. Energetic comic actor Thanasis Vengos portrayed a tireless doorman in *O Papatrehas* (Errikos Thalassinos, 1966) who was a man for all odd jobs: from cleaning and mopping the marble lobby and stairs of the *polykatoikìa* daily, to caring for inhabitants' pets, plants, laundry, even carrying the residents themselves up the stairs when the elevator broke down.[33]

Like the maid, the doorman would typically be a new migrant from rural Greece. For the perceived security of an urban job and a tiny *polykatoikìa* apartment, doormen would typically sell large plots of land and other property in (what are today considered) idyllic rural locations.[34] Another fascinating social category that sprung up together with the development of the *polykatoikìa* was the single man—as well as, to a lesser degree, the single woman. In many of these films we hear the terms "bachelor" (*ergenis*) as well as the intriguing term possibly translated as "youthful-old-man" (*gerontopalikaro*). They, too, were among the relatively new social types of postwar Greek society, since previously, especially in rural areas, people lived in larger extended family groups and almost never alone. Both in films and in reality, these single men typically inhabited a one-room or studio apartment in the newly built urban *polykatoikìa*, the wealthier ones in a penthouse at the top.

Single women, on the other hand, rarely lived alone—unless they were wealthy widows or not altogether respectable, as parodied in *Triti kai Dekatreis* (*Tuesday the Thirteenth*, Orestis Laskos, 1963). In this film a provocatively dressed voluptuous middle-aged woman tries to buy an apartment from the protagonist Mr Kosmas, a particularly superstitious *polykatoikìa* builder-developer.

Architects' and Other Intellectuals' Views

In contrast to the optimistic, overwhelmingly positive perception of *polykatoikìa* life portrayed in popular culture and in documents such as magazines and films, there were many critics of the *polykatoikìa*, especially among architects and other intellectuals. Already in 1960 and 61 the important interdisciplinary magazine *Zygos* printed a series of texts entitled "Good and Bad Taste". I believe that this was the first time that the issue of "taste" was actually discussed in the Greek context by notable intellectuals. It is also interesting because it gives us an overall sense of interiors and how people reacted towards them.

Aiming to reveal research by various people from different professions about the state of the postwar Greek house, the way in which the topic was articulated by this journal was reminiscent of how laographers phrased their attempts to understand rural life in the 1940s and 50s. Even though not explicitly about the *polykatoikía*, the study focused on urban interiors. The results of this research were utterly pessimistic. The group of—primarily male—respondents reacted to their findings in strong negative terms where typically the blame fell to the ignorance of "the ladies" who had control over the interior.

Penny Sparke has mapped the debate on taste in the Anglo-Saxon context in terms of gender politics. For Sparke, male modernists from Charles Eastlake in the 1860s onwards felt threatened by feminine culture and particularly by women's power as consumers. Thus "masculine power attempted to redress the balance of gender power by condemning and devaluing the alliance between aesthetic, commercial and feminine culture. In its place they posited a high cultural model that aligned itself with universal values and the pure logic of function".[35]

Remarkably, some of these same issues appear in *Zygos*, as if this same debate was transposed and surfaced suddenly in the context of postwar Greece. For instance GP Savvidis, a respected literary critic in the world of high modernism, complained that "the people of [good] taste are self-appointed due to their social position; they have help from some artists, from many more tradesmen and from even more *women*. Or *Dictators*." To justify such an extreme characterization, Savvidis proceeded to bemoan the fact that Greece had such a short history ("in our case 'taste' was imported by Governor Kapodistrias [in the nineteenth century] alongside the potato") and no clear cultural identity of its own in matters of taste ("they brought taste here to us from the most kitsch capital of Europe, Munich, which also had imported it from somewhere else"). Yet Savvidis ultimately blamed women—"the ladies"—who,

> with a chance leafing through the magazines and confused memories from hurried trips 'to Europe', as well as with collaborations with merchants, have suddenly discovered that 'crystals' and 'the modern' are more profitable than [other things].[36]

Once again, the illusive idea of Europe was placed in quotation marks. Ultimately, we sense that Savvidis had tired of this discussion and ended up declaring that in Greece "taste simply does not exist". It was none other than the architect Aris Konstantinidis who agreed with Savvidis's verdict in *Zygos*. He too, was contemptuous of those who sought to be tasteful and ironic towards those who believed they possessed it: "the person with bad taste is clearly uncultivated. The one with good taste on the other hand, is superfluous and even harmful for society since he can only offer his personal vanity."[37]

Not surprisingly, for Konstantinidis taste is akin to fashion (associated with women); since by nature it is perpetually in transformation and change, it goes against the ideals of timelessness and "the eternal" that he sought along with many other European modernists.[38] Critical of those who sought "a cosmopolitan life" with "no [stable] beliefs" and "no roots", Konstantinidis wrote that "what we call taste clearly has no relation to [spiritual] cultivation and beauty".

A few months later the notable female journalist and critic Eleni Vlachou presented her own research in *Zygos*, agreeing with the overall conclusions of her male colleagues. In her article Vlachou wrote that "the Greek house [...] is the ugliest in Europe".[39] Bringing up a comparison with dress, Vlachou noted that whereas the inhabitants of a middle-class apartment might be able to dress well, they were completely "ignorant" as to how to put together their interiors. Whereas they would not venture to walk out in a "rose-colored nylon shirt nor a gold glittering dress first thing in the morning",

> [their house] wears a rose-colored nylon shirt and a gold glittering dress. It has no harmony. It is either totally bare or totally over-decorated with the worst, most confused items, the ugliest paintings, lamps, rugs, vases and furniture.[40]

Thus this round of research ended badly. Echoing European modernist architects and her colleagues, Vlachou, too, was dismissive of feminine attempts to "beautify" and "embellish" (*stolizw*) the urban interior, whereas she found no fault in similar attempts in the rural house.

None of these writers were able to see that there was perhaps something interesting happening here, despite the dubious aesthetics: on the one hand there was an attempt to construct a sense of comfort (perhaps initially based upon foreign prototypes). There are certainly interesting precedents for the desire to participate and to display a new middle-class quality of life. To that end, women were not just totally passive receivers of products offered to them by "merchants" or "tradesmen". Rather there was a much more complex and dynamic interaction between the marketplace and women's acts of consumption which they—like elsewhere in Europe and America—began to use in order to formulate their own modern identities.

Lastly, there was a literal transfer of certain values and ways of inhabiting the interior from rural into urban life. Just like the exterior of the *polykatoikìa* drew extensively from the builders' rural background, so did the interior, where decorative aspects, such as hand-embroidered tablecloths, blankets, linens and other such (dowry) items, remained as embellishments in the urban apartment. This was not necessarily "tasteless", but it was markedly different from professionally executed works. I will return to the issue of consumption in relation to women in a moment. For now I want to turn to one more architect and her criticism of the *polykatoikìa* interior.

About 20 years after the *Zygos* research, the well-known architect and critic Suzanna Antonakaki, part of the husband-and-wife team Atelier 66, put forward a similarly negative view of urban interiors, this time focusing specifically on the *polykatoikìa*. In her 1981 conference text "Dwelling and Quality of Life: The Dimension of Time in Design" ("*Katoikia kai Poiotita Zwis I Diastasi tou Chronou sto sxediasmo*"), Antonakaki discussed the repetition and "flatness" of the typical *polykatoikìa* apartment as being more than stifling. She condemned the fact that *polykatoikìa* apartments had by the early 1960s become no more than "a commercial product", a "piece of merchandise" that had to be as neutral as possible in terms of design so that they could be sold easily to the greatest number of people. Antonakaki's criticism was that apartments were not designed with individual owners in mind ("an unknown, average user-consumer") and they ended up being bland, impersonal.

She deplored the fact that the interior was "cut up" and "parceled according to the needs of the market", becoming "as readable and accessible as a blank page".[41] This was true. At the same time, as I have tried to show, it was not altogether a negative quality, since it allowed a greater number of people a share in postwar wealth, amenities and modern life. Antonakaki outlined the individual spaces of a typical *polykatoikìa* apartment and parodied the specific language in which it was "sold" to clients, and particularly to women, as we see in the use of her ironic analogy to fashion:

> the entrance lobby: a little marble, perhaps mirrors. A few Pelion stones, or a village look but if it's been worn too much, what would you say for a little textured look [*sagradaki*]? The Living Room/Guardaroba [coat closet]/WC/Veranda/Hall: all foreign terms, foreign words, foreign spaces... The kitchen: the housewife's kingdom, lit by a light shaft [...] hermetically sealed from the rest of the house [...].[42]

For her, dwelling in the post-Second World War *polykatoikìa* apartment meant merely "consuming [the house] like detergent".[43] Antonakaki did not leave architects without any blame for what she thought was a terrible predicament. She argued that the whole process of *polykatoikìa* construction became predictable, yet at the same time so full of potential mishaps, especially in terms of overcoming bureaucratic processes, that it resembled a "soap opera":

> Design time was minimized. The agreement for percentages [of the *antiparochè*] was judged in the schematic design. It was usually put together quickly since the commission was not secure at that point. If it was, then this quick sketch, usually drawn in such a way so as to be attractive to clients, could be decisive for the designers/engineers/owners/businessmen/and future inhabitants. The next major step was the planning permit—wherever used—since it was not always necessary. The planning permit [...] could give ample material for a soap opera with all the issues that arose from the interpretations of General Building Code, and all the other bureaucratic problems. They would then start construction, and then came the sale.[44]

She also convincingly outlined the difficulties that architects faced in trying to introduce any degree of innovation once this almost standard "model" was in place. From the point of view of architects working in the postwar city, there were endless government regulations that instituted restrictions rather than allowing, let alone encouraging, experimentation.

In addition, there was a limited range of new ideas typical clients were willing to accept. In her blame towards the "machine" of postwar *polykatoikìa* production, Antonakaki ended up scorning all *polykatoikìa* housing because it threatened "true" architecture, as well as for its endless repetition that precluded any possibility of developing more interesting, inventive and innovative alternatives.

Similarly, discussing the postwar city with Maria Zagorissiou, another notable female architect of the period—who had also worked as a "scout" for Doxiadis documenting rural architecture after the war (see chapter 4)—I was told that the *polykatoikìa* was not a "popular" way of building, that it would never be considered as such, because it was the work of "usurpers". Zagorissiou conveyed the anger and irritation of the educated, cultivated professional against those who—as she saw it— profited at the expense of the formal and aesthetic qualities of the postwar city. It was as if the wrong people had somehow "won" in the race or struggle for modernization.

Consumption and Traditional Life

> The question imposed itself: 'Does the process of civilization and the increased value of knowledge and labor destroy principles of taste?'[45]

Aside from an analysis of male versus female cultures in respect to the question of taste, there was yet another layer of complexity in Greek postwar life. Michael Herzfeld has shown that rather than talk about gender roles in postwar Greece, it is more useful to think about "a more general rhetoric of concealment and display".[46] As in other ethnographic contexts (Herzfeld cites Pierre Bourdieu's analysis of the Kabyle house), the condition of interiority and concealment is associated with women. He links this interiority with an interior side of Greek culture, the "Romeic", and which represents those aspects of everyday life, history and tradition that Greeks wish to keep concealed from a foreign gaze: "it represents the familiar self-image which Greeks entertain about themselves".[47] The Romeic is the opposite of the Hellenic, which stands for all those aspects of Greek culture—notably their ancient heritage—that Greeks wish to show to the world.

Herzfeld sees these two contrasting stereotypes as defining not only opposing sides of Greek culture, but also two conflicting models of Greek identity. He maps aspects of Greek culture—such as the demotic (Romeic) versus the *katharevousa* (Hellenic) onto this oppositional schema. In a fascinating way, this schematic opposition reminds us of the two ends of Karagiozis's stage, which we also saw in chapter 2 (see p 51): on the left the hut (Romeic/indigenous/"ours"), and on the right the palace (Hellenic/foreign/"other"). Herzfeld then disrupts this oppositional schema in a discussion of what he calls "code-switching": the idea that rather than keeping the opposing sides of their identity separate, Greeks have always negotiated between them.

To explain this point he uses the example of language and the constant "code-switching" between demotic and *katharevousa* routinely engaged in at least up to the 1980s if not later, and also, interestingly, architecture. He writes:

> The style of domestic architecture [he is referring to a neoclassical facade that might mask 'an extremely simple village-style interior'], like the extensive code-switching that takes place in language between *katharevousa* and demotic Greek, reproduces the fundamental historical and ideological experience of the Greek nation as an entity. The outside announces to the uninitiated that here lives a true Hellene. The inside, with its familiar intimacy, is an environment that every Greek recognizes characteristic of the culture as a whole, though not necessarily one that should be displayed to outsiders.[48]

In this chapter I have outlined how women represent or symbolize the interior, what could also be called the Romeic side of Greek culture. Not only have they more power and authority in the interior, but women are also associated with the interior side of Greek identity—an interiority that Greeks wish to keep hidden since it is associated with an older side of Greek culture, one that many continued to repress.

When women's magazines start to laud modernity as the utmost virtue in both a woman and home, and link this modernity with "cosmopolitanism", some of these long-standing dichotomies began to shift. Perhaps this might start to explain the bitterness of some of the comments about "taste" mentioned above, for the interior was no longer the place where these elusive—almost national—"secrets" were held. The postwar interior was not properly modern either. Seen in another way, the ability for these spaces to negotiate or even overcome the strict dichotomies in Greek culture was surely not a totally negative outcome. Like Karagiozis, who constantly crosses between the two extremes of the stage (hut and palace), the *polykatoikìa* interior, too, represents a similar conceptual negotiability between modern and traditional, male and female, urban and rural.

Wealthy Athenian
Atalanda Karella in
her interior, ca 1971.
From *Architektoniki kai
Diakosmisi* (*Architecture
and Decoration*), 1971.

At the same time, remnants of the culture of the East in traditional decoration and everyday life seemed somehow inferior to the culture of the West, to which Greece aspired. Reminiscing about the early postwar decades, one writer declared:

> Whatever bothered us in the decoration of the traditional house interior was 'eastern'; the small embroideries... the Persian carpet reproductions. We would eat *dolma*, bean soups and fried meatballs but when we had guests for dinner we offered cold risotto Milanese, a reminder that our heart belongs to Milan. And it was in truth a heart divided in two: one half belonged to our everyday lives and the other to what we hoped would change in our lives so as to civilize us, to make us more modern, more chic [...].[49]

Routinely teaching women how to set up their apartment and how to dress, magazines also taught them how to follow (alien) European habits in daily life such as "how to serve afternoon tea". Magazines also suggested to women how to reconcile past and present, modern and traditional, Greek and foreign. For instance, contemporary Scandinavian or reproduction Louis XIV furniture was shown to co-exist comfortably with objects from "traditional Greek art" such as carved wooden chests and hand-painted ceramic dishes, often creating intriguing visual oppositions. Most of all, to be cosmopolitan meant becoming *European* cosmopolitan. The fact that there was pressure on Greece to associate itself with the "West"—defined as anti-communist—added to this mix: the Cold War was a further impetus to identify with Europe, America and the "free world".

One particularly compelling example of a "cosmopolitan" inhabitant of a *polykatoikìa* apartment was Atalanda Karella, an upper-class Athenian featured in *Architektoniki kai Diakosmisi* (*Architecture and Decoration*) in 1971. Elegant, cosmopolitan, even otherworldly, she wore fashionable clothes, and the furniture and objects that surrounded her displayed both her independence and her knowledge of the world. Here Karella casually leans against a copy of *Vogue* magazine, while the caption reads "the

Angeliki Hatzimihali, interior sketches of a Skyros house, ca 1949. From *La Maison Greque*, Athens: Collection de 'L'Hellenisme Contemporaine', 1949.

plant pots are from Paris, the wallpaper from London, the ashtrays from Christian Dior, the vases Tao-Ki-Veng, the carpet 'Anatolia'".[50]

Yet, if we compare the image of worldly Atalanda to an image from the prewar rural house sketched by Angeliki Hatzimihali, we discover that despite all their obvious differences, there were also some important similarities. The drawing of a 1940s rural interior and the photograph of a wealthy Athenian from the 1970s both portray a woman surrounded by the objects that identify her with her surroundings. Her traditional responsibility and role of dressing the house remains much the same.[51] Whereas Hatzimihali's sketches show us spaces with handmade furniture and objects, clothes woven on the loom and walls with niches where things are put away, the photographs show us a spare, hybrid interior, but one that is still arranged, if not produced, by this lady of the house. The woman remains at the center of the space, indicating her power over it.

As in the rural interior, the idea of display remained central in the urban postwar period. However, women were now expected to provide modern consumer goods for the home. They could now even purchase "dowry items" in special stores for just that purpose. In these stores women could (and still can in some areas) buy white tablecloths, loom-woven sheets and bedding, and other such items that once made up a woman's handmade "dowry". Like in Kyriakidou-Nestoros's plastic cups explored in the previous chapter, this time the dowry items, once handmade, were now made by machines. But they did not change name or form in any significant way and remained similar in appearance, if not in quality, to handmade domestic clothing.

Despite this strange metamorphosis between items that were supposed to be very personal, woven with care by each young woman for her future home into products of small industry, the idea of machine-made dowry items was not considered particularly strange in the postwar city.[52] And whereas the interior once demonstrated a woman's skills as a producer of home goods, it now showed her skills as a consumer. Whereas it once showed her knowledge of domestic skills, the postwar *polykatoikìa* now displayed both her traditional items—or at least her knowledgeable purchases—and her modernity and cosmopolitanism.

Film stills, *O Thisauros tou Makariti*, (*The Dead Man's Treasure*), based on a play by Nikos Tziforos and Polivios Vasileiadis, 1959. The housewife and the builder come face to face. She cunningly tricks him into demolishing her old kitchen and as a result he provides her with a modern one. Notice the glee with which she looks upon the demolition of the old "traditional" fireplace and the way in which she has decorated her new sparkling white "modern" kitchen with pots in a "traditional" manner.

The wily housewife, played by actress Georgia Vassiliadou, lovingly wipes her new white *Izola* refrigerator having carefully maneuvered the developer, played by actor Vasilis Avlonitis, to purchase it for her. Izola was a legendary Greek company, founded in 1930; it produced the first refrigerator wholly made in Greece in 1952.

In addition, in terms of domestic culture, "consumption" did not mean the same things in Greece as elsewhere in Europe, where the house and household items continue to be a patrimonial good to this day. One senses that a great deal of the criticism voiced at this time by intellectuals was transposing some of these terms drawn from foreign sources into the Greek context without necessarily taking stock of their very different connotations. It would be much more fruitful for us here to adopt Michel de Certeau's idea of consumption as "ways of using" and "appropriating" material, by which users transform products and practices to suit their needs.[53]

Women were not simply manipulated by builders and advertisers; they too appropriated and manipulated the "language" that was given to them and created something new and unique to this context, using improvisation as well as their traditional skills. Thus the remnants from an older pre-modern rural life did not go away that easily; instead they remained alive in the *polykatoikìa* interior. Equally, the persistence of family values and rigid distinctions between gender roles in respect to things like housework and the dowry remained unchanged. The same is true with cultural politics: *mêtis* is still associated with women and the persistence of an older side of Greek culture, and, like in my family story, the term seeks to subvert authority with "cheeky subordination".[54]

To end this chapter, I will turn to a favorite popular comedy of 1959 that captures this idea of getting things done through one's *mêtis* or ruse (*ponirià*), connecting it to women and the *polykatoikìa*. *O Thisauros tou Makariti* (*The Dead Man's Treasure*), directed by Nikos Tziforos, features two protagonists, an urban housewife and a small builder-developer, Mr Neokosmos (Mr New World). He tries to trick her in order to buy her "worthless" old house and build a *polykatoikìa* on the site, while at the same time she tricks *him*—and other possible tenants—into updating her house by spreading rumors about a treasure hidden somewhere in the house by her late husband. Thinking the treasure may be located in the kitchen, the developer demolishes the old tiled fireplace and kitchen cabinets. She then demands a new, white kitchen which she lovingly shines every day. The movie culminates in the discovery of a hidden note that entitles her to a small fortune and even the possibility of a romantic affair with the developer. Like a modern-day Circe, this housewife succeeds in outsmarting the male developer through her (female) *ponirià*.

Once again we recognize that the world of the village in postwar Athens lived on in persistent tactics in everyday life, in women's worlds and work in the interior. It was the tension and negotiability between these processes and the always elusive notion of Europe and all that it stood for—progress, rationality, "scientific language", the world of men, the "exterior" sides of Greek culture—that was key in the production and transformation of postwar urban space. Most of all, the *polykatoikìa,* and specifically the *polykatoikìa* interior, began to reconcile these conflicting sides of Greek culture. This was a major part of its success from a cultural—if not an architectural—point of view.

1   Wigley, Mark, *White Walls, Designer Dresses: The Fashioning of Modern Architecture*, Cambridge, MA: MIT Press, 1995, p xv.

2   It is worth quoting Le Corbusier's passage about whitewashing and inner cleanliness a little more fully: "Imagine the results of the Law of Ripolin. Every citizen is required to replace his hangings, his damasks, his wallpapers, his stencils, with a plain coat of white ripolin. *His home* is made clean. [...] Once you have put ripolin on your walls you will be *master of yourself*. And you will want to be precise, to be accurate, to think clearly. You will rearrange your house..." Le Corbusier, *The Decorative Art of Today*, Cambridge, MA: MIT Press, 1987, first published as *L'art décoratif d'aujourd'hui*, 1925, p 188.

3   Herzfeld, Michael, "Within and Without: The Category of 'Female' in the Ethnography of Modern Greece", *Gender and Power in Rural Greece*, Jill Dubisch ed, New Jersey: Princeton University Press, 1986, p 220.

4   Heynen, Hilde, "Modernity and Domesticity: Tensions and Contradictions", *Negotiating Domesticity: Spatial Productions of Gender in Modern Architecture*, Hilde Heynen and Gülsüm Baydar eds, London: Routledge, 2005, p 9. A version of this chapter also appears in *Negotiating Domesticity*.

5   Heynen particularly refers to the collection of essays that presented the home "as the antipode to high art". *Not at Home: The Suppression of Domesticity in Modern Art and Architecture*, Christopher Reed ed, London: Thames and Hudson, 1996.

6   Rice, Charles, *The Emergence of the Interior: Architecture, Modernity, Domesticity*, London: Routledge, 2007.

7   Hatzimihali's work has not been given proper scholarly attention until very recently. Michael Herzfeld, who has written some remarkable studies of modern Greece and has studied the discipline of laography, does not mention Hatzimihali (see especially *Ours Once More: Folklore, Ideology and the Making of Modern Greece*, 1986). There is also evidence that her work was regarded with apprehension and even dismissal by some of her contemporaries, particularly by Aris Konstantinidis, who perhaps reacted negatively to her ideas of the value of the "decorative" and "decoration"—not unlike other European modernist architects before him.

8   The public activities of this association consisted of participation in international exhibitions during the 1930s (New York, Paris, Chicago, Leipzig and Alexandria) as well as a series of publications produced in 1948 and 1949. These publications documented buildings primarily from northern Greece as well as Athens and consisted of measured

drawings, photographs and, in Athens' case, paintings of domestic buildings. The large-format folios were almost forgotten until some of the original drawings were discovered again in an Athenian hotel in 1969 and donated to the National Historical and Ethnological Museum.

9   Hatzimihali's contribution to the "Circle of Technical Specialists" who assembled to discuss the state of Greek architecture and its postwar prospects (described in chapter 4) was based on her study of Skyros. A later version was published in 1949 and another more expanded version in 1955.

10   There were, however, footnotes in Konstantinidis's main text citing Dimitrios Kambouroglou discussing everyday life in the interior.

11   Aristotelis Zachos studied the noble houses of Eperus, a northeastern region of Greece. See *Epirwtika Chronika*, 1928. He was friendly with Hatzimihali and later designed a house for her in Athens. Anastasios Orlandos studied the urban houses of the last Byzantine years. He was a professor at the National Polytechnic University in Athens, and a teacher and colleague to Dimitris Pikionis.

12   Hatzimihali, Angeliki, *I Elliniki Laiki Techni* (*Hellenic Popular Art: Skyros*), Athens: PG Makris and Co, 1925, p 6.

13   Afterwards the women's work was also shown in the International Thessaloniki Exhibition of 1928, and in the Delphic celebrations of 1927 and 1930. According to one biography, during the war the workshops were kept in operation "due to Hatzimihali's female *mêtis*, craftiness [*polymihani*]".

14   Yet the *noikokyriò* always denotes a shared power, held equally by both husband and wife, each having separate responsibilities.

15   Dubisch, Jill, *Gender and Power in Rural Greece*, New Jersey: Princeton University Press, 1986, p 98. For more on the relationship between women and the house in contemporary rural Greece, see also a special thematic issue of the *Modern Greek Studies Yearbook*, "Constructed Meaning: Form and Process in Greek Architecture", Elephtherios Pavlidis and Susan Buck-Sutton eds, Minneapolis, MN: University of Minnesota Press, vols 10–11, 1994–1995.

16   Rushton, Lucy, "Cultural ABCs: Women," *GREECE, Insight Guides*, Karen Van Dyck ed, New York: APA Publications, 1991, p 308.

17   Sparke, Penny, *As Long As It's Pink: The Sexual Politics of Taste*, London: Pandora, 1995, p 5.

18   Directed by Yorgos Tzavellas. The title of the

film is taken from a biblical phrase from the Greek Orthodox Church. Here it is intended as an ironic reference, since in the end the wife's wishes prevail no matter how fearsome and stubborn the husband appears.

19   It seems that the book was sponsored at least in part by the German Siemens Corporation.

20   Very rarely they might say something like, "this image comes from Italy". In one instance I recognized an image I had seen in Thomas Hine's *Populuxe*, New York: MJF Books, 1986. Hine's image (p 7) is also undated and has no other information but it clearly belongs to a 1950s American suburb. The *Moderno Spiti* magazine does not mention the provenance of this image but adds a vague note: "Here too the space of the kitchen is divided by a series of closets that at the same time form the work area. The dining area is placed against the large wall of glass and leaves a lot of free space." *Moderno Spiti* (*Modern House*), June 1967, p 47, ELIA–MIET Archives.

21   Baudrillard, Jean, *The System of Objects*, 1968, London: Verso, 1996, p 173.

22   Sparke, *As Long As It's Pink*, p 229.

23   For the historical evolution of the meanings of this term in America, see the work of Gwendolyn Wright, especially *Moralism and the Model Home*, Chicago: University of Chicago Press, 1980, and *Building the Dream: A Social History of Housing in America*, Cambridge, MA: MIT Press, 1981.

24   Sparke, *As Long As It's Pink*, p 16.

25   *Moderno Spiti* (*Modern House*), August 1967, ELIA–MIET Archives.

26   There are echoes here of European modernists, such as Henry Van de Velde, whose dresses for his wife, Maria, were made to match the interior of the house and its furnishings, all of which he had designed (Bloemenwerf House near Brussels, 1895). Greek magazines seem to offer a pop version of this early *Gesamtkunstwerk*, albeit with no theoretical argument or references to elite architecture.

27   *Laòs kai Kolonaki* (*The People and Kolonaki*), directed by Yiannis Dalianidis, 1959. The title of the film implies the social contrast between the "people" (*laòs*) and the upper classes who live in Kolonaki, a wealthy central area of Athens.

28   Tsoukalas, Constantinos, *I Elliniki Tragodia: Apo tin apeleutherwsi ws tous syntagmatarxes* (*The Greek Tragedy: From Independence to the Colonels*), Athens: Nea Synora/Livani, 1981 (written in 1968), pp 115–116.

29   Delveroudi, Eliza, "*Ellinikos Kinimatografos*

1955–1965: Koinonikes allages tis metapolemikis epoxies stin othoni" ("Greek Cinema 1955–1965: Social Changes of the Postwar Era On the Screen"), in *Epistimoniko Symposio: 1949–1967 I Ekriktiki Eikosaetia* (*Scientific Symposium: 1949–1967 The Explosive Decades*), Athens: Eteria Spoudwn Neoellinikou Politismou kai Genikis Paidias/ Scholi Moraiti, 2000, p 163.

30 Delveroudi, "Greek Cinema 1955–1965", p 166.

31 In the 1930s and 40s the young maid was called *psychokòri* (a kind of "adopted daughter") to denote the protective relationship the family was obliged to have towards her. In the post-Second World War period, too, her masters had to watch out for the young maid's honor. Most films showed her to be flirtatious and easy prey to devious men lurking everywhere.

32 *Moderno Spiti* (*Modern House*), September 1967, ELIA–MIET Archives.

33 The title of the film *O Papatrehas* (from *papas*, "priest", and *trècho*, "to run") ironically refers to a not very educated, usually rural priest who hurries through the lengthy Greek Orthodox church service skipping parts or at least not reading all of them properly.

34 On *polykatoikìa* doormen see the very interesting article by Dimitris Philippidis in *Architektonika Themata/Architecture in Greece*, vol 12, 1978. See also a compilation of films about the *polykatoikìa* in Greek cinema co-written by Dimitris Philippidis and Giannis Skopeteas, *In Exchange for Five Apartments and One Shop, a Documentary Film About Architecture and Society in Athens as Shown in Greek Fiction Films (1924–2004)*, Athens: Benaki Museum, 2004.

35 Sparke, *As Long As It's Pink*, p 12.

36 Savvidis, GP, "Good and Bad Taste", *Zygos*, Athens, June 1960, pp 41–42.

37 Aris Konstantinidis, in *Zygos*, Athens, June 1960, pp 39–40.

38 On the complex relationship of modern architects to fashion and to dress as well as to the lineage of some of these ideas in earlier times, see Mary McLeod, "Undressing Architecture: Fashion, Gender and Modernity", *Architecture: In Fashion*, Deborah Fausch, Paulette Singley, Rodolhe El-Khoury and Zvi Erfat eds, New York: Princeton Architectural Press, 1994.

39 Eleni Vlachou, in *Zygos*, Athens, September 1960, pp 36–37.

40 Vlachou, in *Zygos*, p 36.

41 Suzanna Antonakaki, in *Zygos*, Athens, June 1960, p 17. On the minimal involvement of people in their dwellings Antonakaki also writes "unable to produce meaningful criticism... [the inhabitants] are left outside... [as] viewers [in the process of production]. Their involvement starts and ends with the negotiations of millimeters of property or price per square meter. Then comes the selection of finishing/cladding materials with a special interest in the bathroom areas.", p 18.

42 Antonakaki, in *Zygos*, pp 19–21.

43 Antonakaki, in *Zygos*, p 19.

44 Antonakaki, in *Zygos*, p 19.

45 Giedion, Sigfried, *Mechanization Takes Command: A Contribution to Anonymous History*, Oxford: Oxford University Press, 1948, p 361.

46 Herzfeld, "Within and Without", p 219.

47 Herzfeld, "Within and Without", p 217. These are long-standing and very important stereotypes even though they have since been criticized as being too oppositional (Tziovas, 1989). The word *Romeic* comes from the term Greeks were known as during the Ottoman occupation—its roots are in the word *Roman* and refer to the eastern part of the Roman Empire, ie Byzantium, which was—especially in its last period—mostly culturally Greek. Herzfeld updates the study of these stereotypes in interesting ways and puts them in the context of ethnographic scholarship.

48 Herzfeld, "Within and Without", p 218.

49 Mihalopoulou, Amanda, *Gynaika* magazine, Athens, March 2001, my translation. *Dolma* is the dish with vine leaves stuffed with rice that are considered a "traditional" Greek dish but which have a Turkish name, as do fried meatballs (*keftedes).*

50 "Anatolia" was the name of a local carpet manufacturer. This article is from *Architektoniki kai Diakosmisi* (*Architecture and Decoration*), no 84, 1971. This magazine succeeded *Architektoniki* founded by Kostas Kitsikis and was published by his son, architect Antonis Kitsikis. However it was short-lived, lasting from 1970–1971.

51 The interior sketches, made ca 1949 by Angeliki Hatzimihali, are from her *La maison Greque*, Athens: Collection de 'L'Hellenisme Contemporaine', 1949.

52 Long before such items started to be imported from abroad, such as from China, it was women trained in vocational schools who often furnished the new mass-produced dowry items through small-scale manufacturing. One notable exception was *Peiraiki-Patraiki*, which had a large modern factory producing fabrics of all kinds and which also employed primarily women workers.

53 Certeau, Michel de, *The Practice of Everyday Life*, Berkeley, CA: University of California Press, 1984.

54 Herzfeld, "Within and Without", p 230.

Polykatoikía registering
protest: the side wall
of a centrally located
polykatoikía in Athens,
near Syntagma Square,
was painted with the old
"No Signal" image from
the national channel ERT,
after it was forced to close
down, 2013.

Postscript

Cities, Crises and Innovation

Constantly made and re-made, cities are uniquely capable of improving people's quality of life, their health, housing and education. As Alejandro Aravena, 2016's Pritzker Prize winner and director of the Venice Biennale for Architecture noted in 2008, "cities are the most efficient vehicle for development that man has ever devised" and "a powerful means for generating wealth and improving residents' quality of life".[1] The *polykatoikìa* and the urban life it helped create is a compelling example of this claim. A resilient and easily adaptable building type, it enabled the transformation of countless rural migrants into citizens with what was then, in the early postwar decades, a largely equitable urban life. The processes that made it so successful, outlined in this book, helped bring about an increased sense of social and economic equity in a society that was still torn by civil war.

The work of uneducated builders and housewives was interesting and imaginative, no matter how unconscious or informally produced. It was their own interpretation of an idea of modern life that was formed collectively. It produced something new, and it represented something important about the context from which it grew, no matter how aesthetically displeasing it might still be for most observers and critics to this day. It also constitutes a very significant model of a collective response at a time of crisis that enriches our understanding of urbanism as a collective design activity by different agents: builder-developers, housewives—both truly informal groups—as well as architects, engineers, planners and bureaucrats, all of whom had their own design sensibilities.

The *polykatoikìa* is still very much alive today, both as concept and as architectural form, in large cities and small towns all over Greece, its characteristic small scale still largely discernible no matter what new programs might be introduced. During the military junta (1967–1974), there was an explosion of building, a lot of it informal, "legitimized" after the fact, which reflected the populist politics of the regime. Following the end of the junta there was a turn to a kind of postmodern vocabulary, with superfluous columns and other "quotations" of a style that came directly from a predominantly European and American architectural culture.

Since the end of the junta, as more affluent Greeks migrated to the suburbs in the north (the older suburbs of Psychiko and Kifissia) and the south (Glyfada, Neo Faliro, Voula, Vouliagmeni, all recently built), new migrants arriving from newly ex-Eastern Bloc Europe started taking over the humblest, smallest, least well-maintained *polykatoikìa* apartments in the center: the basements, the apartments with little or no direct sunlight. As Dimitris Philippidis put it: "[...] within the bowels of the earth, labyrinthine semi-basement and basement flats, next to Public Power Corporation meters, central heating facilities, inhabited by night-time shadows and the underprivileged or (if it still exists) the doorman's family, who have all sorts of inventive manners of ventilation, at times

Polykatoikía in Pagrati,
by Panos Dragonas and
Varvara Christopoulou,
1999–2002.

also of lighting, through holes, grilles, and gratings".[2] These same "dark" areas have
now been taken over by migrants from Southeast Asia, such as the Philippines, but also
Pakistan, Afghanistan and even more recently, from China. It would be fascinating to
see how they have adapted spaces, and particularly interiors, to suit their families
and ways of life—a topic for another book.

More recently, especially around the time of the 2004 Olympic Games that took
place in Athens, and just before the economic crisis and collapse (2008–2009), there
were a number of formally interesting and exciting new *polykatoikìa* buildings, such as
the examples shown here, explored it as an urban typology for the twenty-first century,

Dikatoikia on Kyprou
Avenue, Papagou, by
Nikos Ktenàs, 2000–2004.

Apartment building in
Nea Smyrnl by MPLUSM
Architects (Marita
Nikoloutsou and Memos
Filippidis), 2002-2007.

Dimosio Sima Community
Park, coordinated by the
office of doxiadis+, Athens,
2011.

creating remarkable new variations and updating its aging basic format. Among other places, this experimentation is amply illustrated in the well-designed and thorough exhibition catalog *Made in Athens*, for the 13th International Architectural Exhibition in Venice, 2012.[3]

Since the international financial collapse (2008–2009) and its aftermath, Greeks have had to confront new hardship to an extent not felt since the last war and occupation. The tough conditions of everyday life evident around Athens today, where pensioners rummage through trash, people sell any valuable belongings just to survive, and hundreds rely on soup kitchens for their food, are hard to miss. In an article published in the *Guardian* newspaper to coincide with the publication of the new poetry collection *Austerity Measures*, 2016, literary scholar and translator Karen Van Dyck noted parallels between the crisis today and Greece's period of dictatorship, commenting:

> When there is less to go around, people fight, grab, get tough. Lately, Greece and the Balkans have been living with more than their share of less. Hunger, unemployment, slashed pensions and ruined businesses are rife in Athens. Electricity and water shortages reach levels associated with countries at war. More than 27% of Greeks are unemployed.[4]

Compounding its own financial and social woes, because of its geographical position between Europe and Asia, Greece is also the arrival country of thousands of refugees fleeing the war zones of the Middle East. Any country would find it hard to accommodate such an influx of desperate people. Greece is especially challenged given its own

Gazi "pocket" DIY park by Atenistas, completed in one day. A team of fifteen people transformed an abandoned, trash-filled plot across from the city's "Technopolis" into a clean DIY park with signage made of empty plastic cups wedged on the wire fence, March 2016. Sadly, on a recent visit to this park the site was full of trash. The whole project seems to have died away.

precarious economic situation in the aftermath of the international financial crisis and its own involvement in this crisis. To make matters worse, for the last several months these refugees have been denied access to northern Europe by Greece's neighbor FYROM and find themselves in the middle of complicated negotiations between Greece, the other countries of the European Union and Turkey.

In the meantime the refugees, many of them families with young children, are stranded in northern Greece, in a makeshift muddy "camp" on Greece's side of a newly installed barbed wire fence that marks the borders with FYROM. With only basic accommodation, those who risked their lives to escape war and political aggression in their own countries face what one man told a reporter of *The New York Times* was "a high degree of miserable".[5] This terrible situation comes after more than a year of painful discussion about Greece's finances with the wealthier and more powerful countries of the north, who have been publicly humiliating Greece for not being adequately fiscally austere. It is as if once again the other, more powerful, more established Europeans view Greece's position in the European "family" with suspicion or doubt.

A New Civics: Urban Activism

Having left the government bankrupt, the most recent crisis has brought about a new popular movement to stand by those who are suffering most, and to offer mutual support, not charity. Despite their own limited resources, many ordinary Greeks have taken it upon themselves to help the refugees from the Middle East. This is especially the case in the islands closest to Turkey where those who survive the life-threatening journey over the Aegean wash up on the shores. For some older Greeks, the scenes of desperate people fleeing their own homes, often small children or entire families drowning in overcrowded makeshift boats, returns them to their own experience running for their lives in the Asia Minor Catastrophe of the 1920s. When photos of a group of older Greek women caring for a refugee baby while the exhausted mother took a break in Lesbos circulated on the Internet, the "grandmothers" protested that they were simply doing what is natural, helping other human beings. Plus, they said, their own mothers had arrived on Lesbos's beaches as refugees from Turkey in 1922; they were honoring the memory of their own mothers by helping out.

As noted in chapter 3, the government's response to the Asia Minor Catastrophe included a fine group of modernist apartments that offered a Greek version of *Existenzminimum*. Now on valuable land, across from the main football stadium, these apartments are threatened with demolition.[6] Since 2014, an energetic group of architects and artists, calling themselves Nomadic Architecture, took it upon themselves to serve the community of remaining inhabitants in the run-down buildings. At first prompted by the fight to prevent demolition, they formed a collective to help those they call "the city's displaced" (the refugees, the homeless, the unemployed). The group meet at the buildings weekly and facilitate "a social solidarity clinic", a collective kitchen, and maintenance services.[7] For this group, the so-called refugee buildings are a "center of self-organization and solidarity". They use the buildings, now far from looking perfectly clean and white as they were initially, but visibly falling apart, as a way to strengthen human ties and add a much-needed sense of community to the neighborhood.[8]

In a similar vein, since the worsening of the crisis and the arrival of refugees, ordinary Athenians have started to organize, sometimes in collaboration with municipal authorities, to use the generic *polykatoikìa* in new ways. Some have tried to create something they call "social *polykatoikìa*" (*koinoniki polykatoikìa*), by renovating old abandoned *polykatoikìa* buildings and organizing donations for everything that needs to be there for inhabitation, from furniture to children's toys, and provide it to families on a rotating basis. With this support, families tend to find work and be able to afford their own housing more quickly. They are then able to move on to make room for others who are more in need.[9] Compared to the response to the refugee crisis of the 1920s and 30s, today the demographics of the actors involved are different: today's informal acts are evidence of a movement toward self-organization for the greater social good.

We may consider this approach as an important effort toward a new "civics" that has gradually been emerging in Athens precisely during the last years of social and financial crisis. In fact we may argue that this crisis has contributed to a new mobilization of socially conscious citizens from all social classes. Proportionately, at this moment Greece and particularly Athens, has a huge number of highly educated, mostly unemployed people, a lot of them recent university graduates. Some have been organizing to improve their city's quality of life, sometimes working with the help or consent of city authorities and other times alone. One example is a group that calls itself Atenistas which has been self-organizing to create a multitude of activities, completely without involvement from any authorities or NGOs. On their website they explain that they are citizens who want to take action to improve their city and their own quality of life, with imagination and with only minimum means.[10]

Atenistas' teams have been spectacularly effective and successful: from cleaning abandoned lots to create "DIY" and "pocket" parks, to getting different organizations to donate plants and trees, improving pavements and bus stops, initiating cultural events, collecting food and household supplies and advocating for those in need. They are also trying to help Athenians see their city with new eyes, by organizing "tours" with emphasis on different historical epochs, buildings, streets, and so on. Theirs is an Athenian version of a "guerrilla urbanism" that is reminiscent of some of the best work by such groups in Europe and America.[11]

Others are organizing themselves to create provocative performance art as if to act out and lead a kind of mass catharsis. An article in *The New York Times* from April 2016 titled "Suffering for Art in Greece and Matching the National Mood" captured this idea. Rachel Donadio noted "the intensity of the performances and their explorations of time, fear, entrapment, discomfort and control [that] have tapped into the emotions of a country grappling with economic hardship and waves of migrants arriving via neighboring Turkey, factors that have caused a feeling of existential crisis".[12] Another article, also in *The New York Times*, reported on the use of Athenian streets and (*polykatoikìa*) buildings as a "canvas" for elaborate graffiti art, at times sanctioned by the State.

The strengthening of social solidarity through art and culture, whether by artists or by ordinary citizens, fulfills a crucial social function at a time when there is so much suffering, so visible and seemingly never-ending. Professionals such as architects are also organizing and collaborating with other citizen groups to contribute positively to the well-being of the city. One of these is doxiadis+, an office founded by Thomas Doxiadis, a great-nephew of Constantinos Doxiadis, in 2011. The project for a community park, the "Dimosio Sima", is an example of this kind of pro bono collaboration with volunteer groups such as Atenistas.

Completed in six days in a central Athenian neighborhood, this park offers a much-needed public community space over an area that had for years been out-of-limits to locals since it was designated an archaeological site, waiting for funds for excavation. The designers contributed a thoughtful approach that reimagines an abandoned city lot, endowing it with "a symbolic distillation of the Attic landscape" by using local materials and being respectful of the ruins underneath.[13] All the materials apart from the plantings were re-used from materials already on site, and much care was taken to elevate the level of the plantings on a podium, so that the ruins underneath will remain protected until excavation.

Alongside teams of ordinary Athenians and design professionals, new kinds of world-class, privately funded cultural institutions have added their support. Private sponsorship of public institutions and support for education is not new in the Greek context: in the nineteenth century, most important public institutions, especially those that had to do with education, were made possible almost entirely through donations by wealthy Greeks of the diaspora.[14] Today the long-established Deste Foundation for Contemporary Art (founded by the art collector Dakis Joannou in 1983) is joined by the Onassis Cultural Center, its well-designed building inaugurated in 2010. While very different in scope, both of these institutions have already established world-class contemporary art exhibitions (Deste Foundation) and public programing for music, the performing arts, as well as the visual arts and architecture (the Onassis Cultural Center).

More recently, a foundation called NEON aims to "activate" and revitalize the city and involve ordinary citizens more directly with the arts. It was founded by the collector and entrepreneur Dimitris Daskalopoulos. In an interview on the foundation's website,

Point Supreme,
"Legitimization of the
Undervalued", 2008. The
polykatoikìa as icon was
part of a project exhibited
during the Unbuilt events
organized by the School
of Architecture 4 All
(SARCHA). The team
was composed of Point
Supreme Architects, John
Karahalios, Mirto Kiourti
and Kostas Tsiambaos.

Daskalopoulos insists that the crisis Greece is experiencing is not merely financial, it is cultural. His organization was founded to respond and react to this crisis through culture. On a much grander scale, the highly anticipated Stavros Niarchos Foundation Cultural Center (SNFCC) opened in 2016. Designed by the Renzo Piano workshop, the SNFCC will potentially enhance the cultural life of the capital, and particularly of its immediate neighbor, the working-class neighborhood of Kalithea. The project, one part of the Stavros Niarchos Foundation, involves the construction and complete outfitting of facilities for large cultural events, a new National Library, a National Opera, as well as the design of an extensive and beautifully planted park by American landscape designer Deborah Nevins. These privately funded organizations are emphatically and successfully contending for the value of the arts and culture to support and relieve hardship. They also demonstrate a new active civic conscience emerging among certain cultivated wealthy elites that is commendable and encouraging.

A New Mêtis: The Incremental Polykatoikìa and Other Uses

The *polykatoikìa* has proven to be a resilient and adaptable building type able to meet needs for housing for different social classes, as well as a variety of other programs, from offices to commercial space. Especially in the outskirts of Athens and in the countryside, this quasi-informal, incremental building allowed for even greater flexibility and adaptability. One of the processes outlined in this book, the so-called "up-lifting" technique (*panosikoma*) was key to its persistence through today. Ordinary people created *polykatoikìa* buildings slowly by adding floors above simple one-story structures. They also often "finished" a *polykatoikìa* in stages, filling in a basic framework slowly, as funds became available or as another child was married and needed a dowry—phased out legally but still there, especially in rural communities—or a place to live.

In a fascinating sense, some of the most interesting professional designers today are looking at urban informality and coming up with processes to help communities do exactly that: to build incrementally. Alejandro Aravena and his group Elemental, who are based in Chile, have realized some extraordinary projects based on incremental construction. Their strategy came about as a way to economize on cost and at the same time create the maximum amount of social housing. In some instances, such as in the Quinta Monroy project in Iquique, Chile, the architects provided a reinforced concrete framework with only the necessary structures and services, such as load-bearing walls and stairs, bathrooms and kitchens: inhabitants then "fill" in the rest of the buildings themselves.

It is as if Aravena and Elemental are engaging a new *mêtis*: they have figured out a way to help the maximum number of people by seeing their role not as elite and detached professionals, but as an architectural practice that facilitates building processes that are culturally understood, and that already constitute the reality of cities in Latin America. There are similarities between this approach and the work of other current practices, such as that of Teddy Cruz, who also studies informal buildings primarily in Tijuana, on the border between the US and Mexico, and then facilitates his own innovative solutions.

Some Greek architects today are trying to engage with informal techniques and development and to recognize its successes, even it if it is still a tongue-in-cheek conversation. A group calling themselves Point Supreme Architects, founded by

Konstantinos Pantazis and Marianna Rentzou in 2007, have injected a great deal of humor to the discussion with their provocative projects and collages. As they seem to point out, paradoxically we may find some of the qualities that we now consider "sustainable" in Athens already: a building type that is culturally relevant and understood, made of easily found materials, in a small scale and without the involvement of large corporations; a relative ease of accessibility to public space (the space of the street, the space of terraces and balconies); potential for extensions (both legal and "illegal"); an ease of building processes; and a potential for income generation. All of these things are still applicable today and render the majority of the *polykatoikìa* buildings in Athens—possibly also in the countryside—potentially sustainable in today's terms.

The aging *polykatoikìa* infrastructure could benefit from careful and innovative re-use and remodeling, as in the approach of the French office of Lacaton & Vassal for the renovation of working-class housing on the periphery of Paris. Several Greek architects and critics are actively conducting research along the same lines. Others work with the *polykatoikìa* as a typology, updating its basic framework, and utilizing far more intelligent systems and techniques, more appropriate for the twenty-first century. Others have been making suggestions to do with improving the quality of public space, potentially both on top of *polykatoikìa* buildings and around it.

Thomas Doxiadis imagines a kind of "green paint" over the city, transforming the old infrastructure of *polykatoikìa* urbanism into solar-powered, green-roofed oases, with vegetable gardens, bike lanes and increased pedestrian streets. Doxiadis claims that his office's work is not so much about taking down huge swaths of the existing city and planting large parks, but about "peeling back the asphalt" to reveal the earth underneath so that it can thrive again. The office of Aristide Antonas also proposes the creation of gardens, their vision involving tools like "more flexible civic legislation to allow new urban practices to arise", an "alternative public democratic use of the web" as "an architectural tool for the emancipation of infrastructure", so as to develop what they call Athens' "fragmented interior garden".[15]

In conclusion, I would like to suggest that alongside the formal built environment, we need to look closer at the informal in world cities, whether illegal, semi-legal or totally self-made, and to try to construct more complex cultural and historical analyses. We could then use these insights to produce new, critical reconceptualizations of the ever-expanding cities of today, in terms of design, planning and sustainability. The relevance of the work of uneducated builders and housewives in the construction of Athens in the postwar may lie in the idea of innovation at a time of crisis, for it constitutes a very significant model, even though it might no longer look exciting or innovative.

If there are "lessons from Athens", they have to do with how to create a more humanistic or "soft", altogether more intelligent society, less reliant on big technologies, large corporations and expensive infrastructure. We must learn again an ancient sense of resourcefulness and wit, as well as an economy of means, so as to achieve Aravena's idea of a "city as a form of equity", for which we still have a long way to go.

1   Aravena, Alejandro, "The City as a Form of
     Equity", *VERB Crisis*, Mario Ballesteros ed,
     Barcelona: Actar, 2008, p 161.

2   Philippidis, Dimitris, "Polykatoikìas", *Made in
     Athens*, exh cat, 13th International Exhibition
     of Architecture, La Biennale di Venezia, Greek
     Pavilion, 2012, p 223.

3   *Made in Athens* was curated by Panos
     Dragonas and Anna Skiada and produced by
     the Hellenic Ministry of Environment, Energy
     and Climatic Change and the Consulate
     of Greece in Venice. See especially "New
     Architectural Narratives for Athens", pp
     138–208, and "The Athenian Polykatoikìa and
     the modern tradition", pp 218–306.

4   Van Dyck, Karen, "The new Greek poetry",
     The Guardian, 25 March 2016, https://www.
     theguardian.com/books/2016/mar/25/new-
     greek-poetry-karen-van-dyck.

5   Yardley, Jim, "A 'High Degree of Miserable'
     in a Refugee-Swollen Greece", *The New York
     Times*, 17 March 2016, http://www.nytimes.
     com/2016/03/18/world/europe/greece-
     idomeni-refugees.html. The article claimed
     that "more than 44,000 people are already
     trapped in the country, a number ticking
     upward each day, as aid groups warn of a
     potential humanitarian crisis by summer."

6   For recent material on these buildings see
     the National Research Foundation, http://
     www.eie.gr/archaeologia/gr/arxeio_more.
     aspx?id=1.

7   See http://nomadikiarxitektoniki.net/en/
     projects/utopia-meeting/the-refugee-
     housing-complex-at-alexandras-avenue.

8   For more examples of such bottom-up
     activism see Letty Reimerink, "How Greece's
     Economic Crisis Produced an Emerging Civil
     Society in Athens", *Citiscope*, 8 January
     2015, http://citiscope.org/story/2015/how-
     greeces-economic-crisis-produced-emerging-
     civil-society-athens.

9   For an update on these efforts, see Marialena
     Perpiraki reporting in the *Huffington Post*
     in January 2016 (in Greek): http://www.
     huffingtonpost.gr/2016/02/29/koinonia-
     koinoniki-polykatoikia_n_9342276.html#.

10   There is no credit given to any particular
     individuals in the group. Rather, credit is
     given to teams that are organized around
     different interests and activities, such as
     "culture", "act", "plus" and "polis": https://
     atenistas.org/poioi/.

11   For an overview of this kind of "guerrilla
     urbanism" see an exhibition organized by the
     Canadian Centre for Architecture "Actions: What
     You Can Do With the City", November 2008.

12   Donadio, Rachel, "Suffering for Art in Greece
     and Matching the National Mood", *The New

York Times, 8 April 2016, https://www.
     nytimes.com/2016/04/09/arts/design/
     suffering-for-art-in-greece-and-matching-the-
     national-mood.html?_r=0.

13   doxiadis+ ,"Junk to Park Over Ancient
     Athens", http://doxiadisplus.com/
     community-created-public-space/.

14   Some of the institutions supported by
     wealthy individuals included the University,
     the Academy, the National Library, the
     Observatory, the Technical University, the
     Arsakeio School for Girls, the Varvakeion
     School for Boys, the Archaeological Museum,
     the Zappeion Exhibition Hall and Gardens,
     the Stadium, both the Municipal and Royal
     Theater, the Marasleio School, and most
     hospitals prior to the First World War. Many
     wealthy Greeks who lived in Greece at that
     time had spent their fortunes supporting
     the War for Independence against the
     Ottomans; the diaspora Greeks stepped in
     to play a hugely important role in early post-
     Independence cultural life.

15   Antonas, Aristide, "Back to the Garden.
     Athens and Opportunities for New Urban
     Strategies", *Uncube*, no 43: "Athens", p
     31, http://www.uncubemagazine.com/
     magazine-43-16565819.html#!/page31.

Woman cleaning her white
walls in what appears to
be a neoclassical interior.
Photograph by Dimitrios
Harissiadis, 1946.

Index

Image credits

Unless otherwise listed, the images in this book are copyright of the author. All reasonable efforts have been made to obtain permission from the appropriate copyright holders wherever possible. In the case that none could be reached, information about the image source is provided.

Afoi Roussopoulloi Production Company: 158
Aikaterini Laskaridis Foundation: 48
American School of Classical Studies at Athens, Gennadius Library: 23 (above)
Angeliki Hatzimihali, *La maison Greque*, Athens: Collection de 'L'Hellenisme
      Contemporaine', 1949: 167; *Hellenic Popular Art: Skyros*, Athens: PG Makris
      and Co, 1925: 150
Architektoniki kai Diakosmisi (*Architecture and Decoration*): 166
Architektoniki magazine: 128
Archives of the Greek Ministry of Public Works: 114
Archives Patroklos Karantinos: 70 (above)
Aristides Romanos: 70 (below)
Art Resource/bpk, Berlin, NY: 42; bpk Bildagentur: 13
Artists Rights Society (ARS), New York/Bildrecht, Vienna: 10
Astiko Elliniko Spiti Thessalonikis 1880–1912 (*The Urban Greek House in Thessaloniki
      1880–1912*), Laographiko-Ethnologiko Mouseio Makedonias (Folk-Ethnological
      Museum of Macedonia), Thessaloniki, 1985: 30
Atenistas: 177
Athens National Polytechnic School: 54
Benaki Museum: Documentation Center for Neohellenic Architecture: 69;
      Chatzipanagiotis Archive: 138
Benaki Museum Photographic Archives: Voula Papaioannou Archives: 92; Dimitrios
      Harissiadis Archives: 66, 117, 184; Costas Megalokonomou Archives: 2, 16, 74,
      76, 110, 116, 120, 122, 132, 137, 141, 153
Carnegie Library of Pittsburgh: 24
Constantinos A Doxiadis Archives/Constantinos and Emma Doxiadis Foundation: 86,
      97, 100, 101, 104, 106
Dimitri Konstantinidis. Courtesy of gta Archiv/ETH Zurich (bequest library of Albert
      Heinrich Steiner): 40; Courtesy of the University of Virginia Libraries: 44
doxiadis+: 176
Dragonas Christopoulou Architects: 174
Eikones Magazine: 135
Electric Home: 157 (right)
Eli Papadimitriou, *Palies Fwtografies, Athina-Peiraia-Kaisariani*, Athens: Ermis, 1979:
      34 (below)
Ersi-Alexia Hatzimihali, *A Walk With Aggeliki*, Kaktos Publications, Athens, 1999: 149
Finos Films and Dionysos, Greek Performers Royalties Collecting Society: 168
George C Marshall Foundation, Lexington, Virginia: 107
Georgios Megas, *Thessalikai oikiseis* (*Houses in Thessaly*), Athens: Ypourgion
      Anoikodomiseos, 1949: 90
German Federal Archive/Bundesarchiv: 84

Gynaika kai Spiti: 154 (left)

Hellenic Literary and Historical Archive-Cultural Foundation of the National Bank of Greece (ELIA-MIET): 38, 155; Kannelopoulos Archive: 11; Papadimou Archive: 27

Irini-Kalistheni Avdelidii, redrawn and translated by Ilana Curtis: 22, 67, 136

Karagiannis-Karatzopoulos: 34 (above)

Kathimerini newspaper: 112, 146

Kimon Laskaris and Dimitrios Kyriakos: 64

Kostas Biris, *Ai Athinai apo ton 190–200 aiona* (*Athens: From the 19th to the 20th Centuries*), Athens: Melissa Publications, 1966: 25 (below), 26, 72 (above left), 113

Kostas Kitsikis, *Leukoma Peninta Chronon* (*Compilation of Fifty Years of Work*), Athens, 1965: 72 (above right)

Kostas Mitropoulos: 15

Library of Congress: 20; American National Red Cross Photograph Collection: 58, 65

Manolis Marmaràs, *I astiki polykatoikìa tis mesopolemikis Athinas* (The Urban *Polykatoikìa* In Interwar Athens), Athens: Politistiko Technologiko Idryma ETBA, 1991: 72 (below)

Manos Vernardos: 25 (above)

Maria Zagorissiou, *Folk Architecture in Crete,* Athens: Benaki Museum, 1995: 93

Moderno Spiti: 154 (right)

MPLUSM Architects, Photo: Erieta Atali: 175 (below)

Museum of Greek Folk Art: 50

National Academy of Drawing, Munich: 23 (below)

Nikos Ktenàs, Photo: Erieta Atali: 175 (above)

Ohio State University Libraries: 51

O Papatrehas (1966): 159

Panos Kokkinias: 8

Point Supreme Architects: 180

Stelios Skopelitis, *Neoclassical Houses in Athens and Pireus*, Athens: Dodoni Publications, 1975: 33

Sygxronos Oikodomiki, Kornarou Group Publication, Athens, 1961: 119, 125, 126, 127

TEE Archives: 68

Women's Almanak: 157 (left)

Yannis Tsarouchis Foundation: 45

Acknowledgments

This book is based on the doctoral thesis I defended in 2007. As such it owes a huge debt to the rigorous scholarly community of the PhD program in architecture at the Graduate School of Architecture, Planning and Preservation at Columbia University in New York. I was fortunate to study with some of the most intellectually generous and engaging figures at Columbia: Kenneth Frampton, director of the PhD program at the time, who I thank for writing such a thoughtful foreword to this book, Gwendolyn Wright, who was my primary advisor, Mary McLeod, Robin Middleton, Mark Wigley and Karen Van Dyck. I developed this material with their inspiring input and encouragement, as well as with that of my peers and fellow explorers in some of the most intense years of my life.

The dissertation benefited from strict deadlines and ongoing conversations at academic conferences, some of which were followed by invitations to contribute chapters to books. I wish to thank the scholars I have worked with over this time for their thoughtful editorial comments and questions: Hilde Heynen and Gülsüm Baydar, editors of Negotiating Domesticity: Spatial Constructions of Gender in Modern Architecture; Michelangelo Sabatini and Jean-Francois Lejeune, editors of Modern Architecture and the Mediterranean: Vernacular Dialogues and Contested Identities; Panayiota Pyla, editor of Landscapes of Development: The Impact of Modernization Discourses on the Physical Environment of the Eastern Mediterranean; and more recently Gaia Caramelino and Federico Zanfi, editors of Post-War Middle-Class Housing: Models, Construction and Change.

I am grateful to Jean-Louis Cohen who kindly agreed to review the book and offer his erudite comments at very short notice, and to Victoria Newhouse for her support and encouragement. I am also grateful to Saskia Sassen, with whom I had the honor of collaborating on several conferences when I was at Columbia, who encouraged me to keep searching for the right publisher for this material. An invitation from Panos Dragonas and Thomas Maloutas to participate in the recent "Re-think Athens" conference at the Onassis Cultural Center in Athens provided the final impetus to start work on the book.

I am indebted to Giota Pavlidou, archivist at the Constantinos A Doxiadis Archives in Athens, for offering her extraordinary guidance during all stages of my research. Panagis Psomopoulos, a friend and colleague of my late father, Emmanuel, shared fascinating stories with me about the intellectual atmosphere of the Doxiadis office, and helped me become one of the first scholars to access the archives. I also wish to extend a great deal of thanks to the staff at various institutions who have contributed to the research of this book, including the Hellenic Literary and Historical Archives (ELIA-MIET); the Museum of the City of Athens; Philippos Mazarakis-Ainian at the Historical and Ethnological Society of Greece; the staff at the Hellenic National Library; the Benaki Photographic Archives; the Costas Megalokonomou Archives; the Technical Chamber of Greece's Archives; the Museum of Folk Art and Tradition (the Angeliki Hatzimihali House Museum); Kaktos Publications; Hermes Publications; the Library of Congress; and the Avery Library at Columbia University.

An early grant from the Council on Library and Information Resources (CLIR), funded by the Andrew W Mellon Foundation for Dissertation Research in the Humanities in Original Sources, was an enormous vote of confidence for a fragile doctoral candidate. This project was made possible by the fiscal sponsorship of the Storefront for Art and Architecture and funding from the New York State Council on the Arts, with the support of Governor Andrew Cuomo and the New York State Legislature, with additional support generously provided by Parsons School of Design, The New School and the Architectural History Foundation.

The transformation of the dissertation into this book was guided by the brilliant Sarah Rafson, the dynamic founder of the editorial agency Point Line Projects. Sarah and her team, Ilana Curtis and Adam Kor, helped with all aspects of preparing the book for publication with intelligence, a sense of humor and outstanding organizational skills. Working closely with the team at Artifice books on architecture to develop the book further, especially Kate Trant, Hannah Newell, Simon Arthur, Lydia Cooper and particularly the designers Emma Kalkhoven, Albino Tavares and Joseph Atkinson, was both a pleasure and a valuable learning experience.

I would like to extend my thanks to Christian Hubert for the intellectual sustenance he has given me over the years. This book was realized with the love and support of my family, to whom it is gratefully dedicated.

Thanks to the attention of filmmakers Tassos Langis and Yiannis Gaitanidis, a new partnership was formed that will hopefully bring this story to life. It has been an honor to work with Afroditi Panagiotakou and Pasqua Vorgia of the Onassis Foundation in Athens, whose leadership in promoting engaged discourse around Greek culture has made this edition possible.

This edition has been commissioned by the Onassis Foundation.

Designed by Emma Kalkhoven and Joseph Atkinson
Edited by Sarah Rafson

All opinions expressed within this publication are those of the authors and not necessarily of the publisher.

ISBN 978-618-83618-1-2

Cover: Athens, ca 2016. Photograph by Panos Kokkinias.

NEW YORK STATE OF OPPORTUNITY. | Council on the Arts

ONASSIS
FOUNDATION